5.00
1/81

THE

LAST

SAIL

DOWN

EAST

THE
LAST SAIL
DOWN EAST

Giles M. S. Tod

BARRE PUBLISHERS, BARRE, MASSACHUSETTS

DEDICATED

TO MY FAMILY

ACKNOWLEDGEMENTS

Here below I would like to offer a word of thanks to at least some of the very many who helped to make this book possible.

Firstly, I owe a debt of gratitude to Charles F. Chapman, long time editor of *Motor Boating* magazine, and to John Herbert, editor of *The Patriot-Ledger* of Quincy, who both encouraged me to write and burrow for ship histories. Then there are Kenneth Barnes of the Boston Public Library and Ebenezer Gay of the Boston Athenaeum who, with their respective staffs, were so helpful in locating material. Also, there are many friends who added notes and paragraphs — Charles Morgan, Andrew Nesdall, Lewis Parker, Frank Kelly, Robert H. I. Goddard, Dana Story to mention only just a few of the very many, and sea-going friends like Biff Bowker, Louis Kenedy, Harold Foss, Hanna Whicker, and on and on, all so very helpful.

I would also like to acknowledge two publications. One is *"Sea Breezes"*, a small British magazine which, in the years before World War II, was a bible of windship lore, and the other, *"Log Chips"*, a mimeographed paper produced by John Lyman, which was in itself a miniature encyclopedia of Yankee sailing ship history.

Grateful thanks go to each of the following who made possible the photographs for this book: Francis E. Bowker, E. S. Clarke, Capt. A. J. Currie, R. S. Douglas, Frank F. Ford, Robert H. I. Goddard, Frederick B. Guild, Arthur Hanson, Nancy Hellier, Frank Kelly Collection, L. W. Lewis, H. MacKillop, H. R. McGregor, Charles Morgan Collection, Andrew Nesdall Collection, L. Parker Collection, Peabody Museum of Salem, Captain James L. Publicover, Smith and Ruhland, William B. Taylor, Times Wide World Photo, U. S. Coast Guard, U. S. Navy, Universal Pictures Company, Johanna Loesche Whicker, Ann White, Andrew Willis Collection, Frank E. Wilson, Woods Hole Oceanographic Institution.

CONTENTS

DEDICATION   v

ACKNOWLEDGEMENTS   vi

CONTENTS   vii

INTRODUCTION   viii

    I. OF SHIPS AND MEN   1

   II. SCHOONERS: A 5- AND 4-MASTERS   10

  III. MORE 4-MAST SCHOONERS   34

  IV. LAST OF THE THREE-MAST SCHOONERS   60

   V. MORE TERNS   87
  VI. AND STILL MORE TERNS   116

 VII. TWO-MAST SCHOONERS   134

VIII. THE FISHERMEN   159

  IX. THE SQUARE RIGGERS   178

   X. MORE SQUARE RIGGERS   203

  XI. THE CAPE VERDE PACKETS   232

 XII. HULKS AND BARGES   249

       APPENDIX   266

       INDEX   276

       ILLUSTRATIONS   *following pages* 68, 148, 212

Introduction

~~~~~~

TWENTY-FIVE years ago this month, the author of this book turned up in my office at the Peabody Museum of Salem, bearing a letter of introduction from Lincoln Colcord of Searsport, Maine, which read:

> This will introduce Mr. Giles M. S. Tod, who has the most interesting moving pictures of schooners and ship operations I have ever seen. He ought at once to be a Marine Associate and show his pictures at a meeting next winter. You will see at once that in addition to his having gone a trip around the Horn in the *Herzogin Cecilie,* he is in the way of being a first class schooner historian. In fact he's one of our crowd but up till now has been operating apart from us. He will be keenly interested in the *Neptune* and may well have material for it.

The Peabody Museum Marine Associates, founded the previous year, met one Monday evening a month in the Work Room of the Peabody Museum of Salem. The only qualification for membership was knowing something (seriously) about some aspect of maritime history. The organization operated on principles that can best be described as Tory-Anarchist. There were no dues, no officers, no by-laws. Qualified people somehow got on a mailing list; the Museum rounded up a speaker, sent out post card notices, unlocked the doors at the appointed time, turned on the lights, and let nature take its course. Those Associates who wished to dine together beforehand did so. Those who did not, or lacked the price came straight to the Museum at eight o'clock. The company was extraordinarily varied. A Swedish watchmaker who had gone sealing in his youth, an eminent naval architect, an Italian stone mason who was a skillful builder of ship models, the principal of Exeter, a Boston admiralty lawyer, a newspaper editor, a Harvard professor, a brass-founder who knew a great deal about eighteenth century naval architecture, might all turn up the same evening. It was the kind of company where the owner of a steamship line and a liberally tattooed stoker from one of his ships might meet congenially and exchange useful information.

Lincoln Colcord was a long-distance but greatly valued member of the Marine Associates. Born at sea in 1883, he had grown up on board his father's ship. After some years of journalism, and idealistic dabbling in Wilsonian politics through friendship with Colonel E. M. House, he had returned to Searsport, where he sat on his back porch, overlooking Penobscot Bay, and commented on the foolishness of mankind. With affectionate teasing, his friend Samuel Eliot Morison referred to Linc as 'the Sage of Searsport.' Linc's ideas on many subjects were volatile and unique, but in anything to do with maritime history he was first-rate. He knew the sea at first hand, and in Searsport he lived in close proximity to retired shipmasters who were more familiar with Hong Kong and Calcutta than with Bangor, Maine. Venerating the standards of the old-time merchant marine, he had unconcealed contempt for what passed as sea-going "adventure" in the best sellers and magazines of the thirties.

In October 1939 Lincoln Colcord came to Salem to address the Marine Associates on "The Last Forty Years of American Sail." In the course of a good dinner beforehand, abetted by some Caldwell's Newburyport rum, he developed the idea that what the United States needed was, not so much a good five-cent cigar as Vice-President Marshall had once alleged, but a good quarterly journal of maritime history. The inspiration took hold of him. By the time he reached the Museum work room he had jettisoned all thought of his subject, and delivered a plea so eloquent that plans were there and then concerted for the creation of *The American Neptune* — a labor of love that, since the appearance of the first number in January, 1941, has somehow, without subsidy, kept its nose above water for a quarter of a century.

The members of the Peabody Museum Marine Associates, some of whom were also on the editorial board of *The American Neptune,* were what Linc Colcord called "our crowd." And a good crowd it was, and is too, with a liberal mingling of sailors and scholars. Any man whose pictures of ship operations were the most interesting that Lincoln Colcord had ever seen was obviously worth having in camp. And a "first class schooner historian" was more than welcome, for if the research material of the Peabody Museum was shy of anything at that moment it was information about coasting schooners.

John Robinson, treasurer and trustee of the Peabody Museum for the half century from 1875 until his death in 1925, had done marvels in assembling pictures and information about square-riggers, but the schooners that were in and out of Salem harbor, bringing coal, wood, and other commodities, had seemed to him no more worthy of record than the ice wagons, hacks, and grocer's pungs that moved through the Salem streets on useful but humble missions. They were just part of everyday transportation. But by 1936, when I turned up, it was clear that, with square-riggers over the horizon, schooners were worth recording, particularly as it was even then apparent that they were not going to be long with us. Thus I was grateful to John R. Herbert, Editor of the *Quincy Patriot-Ledger,* for his kindness in sending a photographer to record any that came within decent reach of Quincy, and passing negatives on to the Museum, as well as to members of the Marine Associates, like Charles S. Morgan, W. J. Lewis Parker, Robert H. I. Goddard, Andrew F. Willis and others, who were seriously at work on schooners. Thus the prospect of a man who was "in the way of being a first class schooner historian" was more than welcome.

When Giles Tod turned up at Salem, he fulfilled the expectations raised by Linc Colcord's letter. He was then in his mid-twenties — a tall, slim, handsome young man, quiet and modest, but clearly an experienced sailor, and literate into the bargain. For several years he had seized every occasion to go to sea, for he was keenly aware that opportunities to do so in sail were steadily diminishing. He was the kind of man who could ship before the mast, make his way successfully, and then slip back into life ashore without being obtrusive about his experiences. When he showed his moving pictures of *Herzogin Cecilie* at the Marine Associates meeting on 23 November 1940, I fully understood Linc Colcord's enthusiasm, for among them was a remarkable storm sequence, the like of which none of us had seen before. Coming up the English Channel, *Herzogin Cecilie* ran into a squall, which promptly carried away a certain amount of her sails and rigging. On his way to the post of duty, Giles Tod had the forethought to thrust his movie camera into the hands of a disoccupied passenger, with hasty admonition to aim it in any appropriate direction. Thus a sight long familiar to those who had sailed in square-riggers, but probably never before photographed, was caught at one of the last possible moments. Eleven months later, on 27 October 1941, Giles showed the Marine Associates moving pictures of a cruise in the four-mast schooner *Theoline,* taken the previous summer.

Thereafter I saw less of Giles Tod than I would have liked,

for we were both in the process of disappearing into uniform. But I had some idea of his wartime service at sea in the United States Coast Guard, for every now and then while stowing away the thousands of ships' war diaries that arrived in the Office of Naval Records at the Navy Department, I would see the neat signature "Giles M. S. Tod" at the foot of a day's entry in one of them.

After the war the opportunities for his particular kind of roving under sail were greatly diminished. Moreover, having acquired a family, he settled in Hingham and embraced a profession in Boston. But although he had personally swallowed the anchor, his historical concern with the last days of sail increased, if anything, for he felt the need of rescuing all possible facts about the few commercial vessels in New England waters. For a number of years, I have frequently encountered him in the Boston Athenaeum at the end of the day, and have thus known something of the progress of his work.

This book is based on wide experience and diligent research. It is not an autobiography or an adventure story, but a wholly unassuming assembly of the histories of the last sailing vessels to be seen in New England waters. The kind of information that it contains is not readily to be found in libraries, for what is in print is buried in newspaper files, or scattered through the pages of the British magazine *Sea Breezes* or John Lyman's little periodical *Log Chips*. The rest has to come from men who have known the vessels at first hand, or have sought out those who did. From my recollection of Giles Tod's talk at Salem in 1941, I deduce that he was a witness of the dramatic meeting of two four-mast schooners in a Gulf of Maine fog, that is described in the early paragraphs of the first chapter, but characteristically he does not say so. Unlike the late Fleet Admiral William D. Leahy, who called his memoirs *I Was There* — a title that an unsympathetic reviewer in *The Times Literary Supplement,* under the heading "Cream Vichyssoise", likened to the "Kilroy Was Here" that soldiers scrawled on every available wall, Giles Tod minimizes his personal involvement in his subject.

Although the book is cast in the form of an orderly inventory by types, the reader will find dramatic incidents like the rescue of the crew of the *George E. Klinck* by the carrier *Wasp,* and fine bits of language like the seaman's description of the new master of the *Helen Barnet Gring* — "a large moon-faced man with an enormous belly, a moustache that would have made a good swab brush, a voice like a foghorn, and enough bull to have saved the owners sending us to Venezuela for the load of goat manure we later lost, except that I am afraid it was too strong."

The Barre Publishers have already served maritime history well by making available Gershom Bradford's two volumes of sea stories, the late Frederick P. Harlow's recollections of the sea chanties of eighty years ago, and M. V. Brewington's account of figurehead and ship carvers. I am grateful to them for launching Giles Tod's *The Last Sail Down East,* and to him for constructing it.

WALTER MUIR WHITEHILL

Boston Athenaeum
27 August 1965

CHAPTER I

Of Ships and Men

~~~~~~

A S THE Four-mast schooner *Theoline* slowly slipped across the Gulf of Maine towards Cape Ann, a thick wet fog silently dropped over the water, a blanket of mist that made the windship the orb of its own narrow white world. The ocean gurgled about her stem with the passing swells, dripping from her chain bobstays, splashing off her anchors, and aft hissing around her rudder before angrily dropping astern in little swirling circles until it was lost from sight in the blur. Aloft the rigging creaked, sheets strained and gently heaved, with sails wing and wing gaffs quietly spoke against the masts, and the canvas rippled in the light, damp breeze.

Captain Edward Long stood aft by the helmsman, staring out into the fog. The crew lounged atop the lumber cargo, passing the time in chatter. Forward the cook baked pies in his oven while he hummed a doleful tune to himself. On the forecastle the lookout sometimes cranked the weary foghorn which gave forth a mournful moan that hardly carried aft to the wheel.

Captain Long stirred. "Hey you fellahs, get up forward and see if you can pick up the Gloucester buoy. It should not be far off."

The hands joined the lad on the bow, all peering out into the white wall on all sides. The cook, with time to spare, stepped from his galley and climbed the steps to the head. The long jibboom with its sails seemed to cut a path for the ship to follow through the fog. For many minutes there was nothing to break the monotony of the mists until one of the boys pointed: "There!" A needle-like object off to starboard ahead seemed to dangle in space before slowly taking shape, the whistle buoy. And then, as if sighting the schooner, it gave a low groan of warning.

Aft the Captain nodded as he got his fix; all was well. But now the cook cried out: "Look to port!"

Out of the fog appeared a huge dark shadow, looming like a mountain on the move. Quickly it took shape, another schooner bound for the same buoy, close hauled and moving fast. A three-master, she was quickly recognized as the *Albert Willis*. She seemed to rapidly slide over the crests, gathering speed as she rolled downward, then slowing as she pointed her nose to meet the next swell. The *Willis* by rules of the road had the right of way but as the *Theoline*, with her booms and gaffs on either side, could not swing off, the helmsman on the three-master put his wheel up, pinching her into the wind as she slid across the stern of the *Theoline*. For a second or two the captains exchanged a wave of their hands. Then the distance between the schooners grew greater; a moment later the fog had cut them apart again. While the *Willis* eased in for Gloucester, the *Theoline* rolled on for Boston.

This chance meeting off Cape Ann of two Yankee-built wind-ships had taken place in the late summer of 1941. Such a meeting fifty years before would have been an usual occurence; this one was a rarity, and only three years later it would have been an impossibility for by then the four-masters had gone, and the few remaining three-masters had moved to other waters. Sail had passed on.

The first World War brought the last boom for the canvas-driven ships, and many three-, four-, and even five-mast schooners were built in 'down east' yards. For a short time while profits were high, the owners rode the crest of the wave. In 1916 the four-mast schooner *Jacob M. Haskell* was chartered to take a cargo to the West Coast of Africa for $120,000, and she could make another $90,000 on her return passage. Her total earnings for one voyage were more than she had originally cost to build. In November, 1918, another four-master was able to load close to 2000 tons of coal at Norfolk for Para, Brazil, at $25.00 a ton. In 1919 tern schooners were getting $25.00 for each thousand feet of lumber that they could carry from Mobile to Cuba, while others were getting $50 and $60 to cross the Atlantic to the Canary Islands.

However, within two years it was all over. In 1920 schooners were getting $3.00 a ton for coal from Norfolk to Boston; in 1921 they were lucky to receive $1.00 a ton. After that, the coal trade gradually was taken over by the steam colliers. A few schooners still managed an occasional coal charter in later years, but it was not frequent. Some of the smaller terns were able to load coal for out-of-the-way ports in Maine, and a few Canadian schooners carried coal to Nova Scotia during the 1930's.

Lumber was the last principal cargo of the windjammers in New England waters. A few of them managed to get charters to load salt in the West Indies, and one or two of the larger schooners continued to bring fertilizer north from South America. In 1925 the Miami boom brought together the last large group of active sailing ships along the East Coast. When that was over, the decline began and never ended. In 1927 many of the larger four- and five-masters were able to carry creosoted railroad ties from New Orleans, Savannah, and Brunswick to Boston and New York, and at one time there were no less than 25 schooners in this trade. However, within four years the New England Maritime Company, owners of one of the largest remaining fleets was bankrupt. A sale of nine of their vessels brought a total of $13,425, a sum far less than any single one of them had cost to build a decade before. The four-mast schooner *Charles D. Stanford* had cost $100,000 in 1918; eleven years later she was sold at Providence for $5000, one twentieth of her original cost. There was no demand for windships by then.

There were several reasons for the decline of sail during the 1920's. Steamers with their regular schedules were getting the majority of the coastwise charters; windship owners were unable to sufficiently under-bid them. The upkeep of the sailers was not inexpensive, and a long passage could completely wipe out any profit. Long waits in ports while steamers used docking facilities did not help. And lastly, there was the crew problem. Few of the younger men turned to sail as the reward was too low, and working conditions did not compare with those in power driven craft. So it was that many of the larger sailing ships were laid up or sold to the Canadians who were content to sail for normal fees, not asking the high modern rates which made it prohibitive for some American owners to keep active.

The men who sailed the last windjammers off the New England coast were not 'wharf rats', but real sailors. Although many of their vessels were old and run down, they managed to keep them on the move. When storms threatened, they would poke into the nearest port if one was available, or do their best to ride it out offshore. Many times they worked their ships badly undermanned, standing extra watches, doing extra work, two men doing the job

[3]

of three or four. There were cases of three men taking three-masted schooners across many miles of ocean simply because they could get no one else to join them; rather than stay in port, they had put to sea shorthanded. They were men who got little praise for their work because they did it quietly and unobtrusively. Their goings and comings were scarcely noticed yet they carried on a tradition which had been founded before the days of the clipper ships.

It would be impossible to give a list of these last real sailors without slighting many. The men who owned the ships, the captains and their officers, and the men before the mast should all deserve mention for it was they who brought an era to a close in 'down east' waters. However, a few names must suffice.

Captain James L. Publicover

The patriarch of the last windships in these local waters was Nova Scotian-born Captain J. L. Publicover, owner and operator of sailing vessels. Born in 1877 and at sea when he was twelve, he had been master of his own vessel since 1902 when he had the schooner *Virginia* built at Lunenburg. During a very heavy southerly gale and blizzard, he piled her up at four in the morning in January, 1911, on Rosehead at the mouth of Lunenburg. In May he bought the brigantine *Leo,* changing her over to schooner-rig. He sold her to Prince Edward Island a year later. His next vessel was the three-mast schooner *Ladysmith,* formerly a barkentine. In June, 1912, he got the schooner *W. N. Zwicker* which he sold in Buenos Aires in July, 1916, although he later sailed her up to New York with a cargo of linseed. While in this vessel in December, 1912, he was 41 miles off Cape Cod during a howling north easter when he sighted the American schooner *Henry R. Tilton* in a foundering condition, only her lumber cargo keeping her afloat, her crew lashed to the rigging as her decks were awash. Although terrific seas were running, Captain Publicover put over his long boat, and in three trips was able to save all hands from the sinking schooner. Later, President Wilson presented the Captain with a watch, chain and compass fob for his daring deed.

In the fall of 1916 he took over the tern *James Slater,* rebuilding her and making her into a four-master. In December, 1919, bound from Liverpool, Nova Scotia, to New York in her, he ran into a terrific snow-laden gale. Before long ice had covered the rigging, making the schooner unmanageable. At two a.m. on the 21st she struck a bar 250 feet off the Cape Cod beach, promptly starting to break up. The Coast Guard sighted her flares through the flying snow, but they were unable to launch their surf boats owing to the rolling combers. They fired a breeches buoy line to the schooner. This was useless as the masts had gone from the schooner, and there was nowhere to make it fast. Just after dawn they were able to make contact with a heavier line, and with the help of this and a dory, all the crew were taken ashore. Fifteen minutes after Captain Publicover had left the schooner, she turned to wreckage under the pounding seas.

His next vessel was the *W. H. Eastwood* which had been built as a steam dragger; he made a four-master out of her. He did not stay with her long, leaving her in Halifax in 1920. He now bought the U.S. four-mast schooner *Joan Kielberg*, sailing her until January, 1926. He then put another man in her for a couple of trips. She caught fire outside of Shelbourne, and was so badly damaged that he condemned her. In 1924 he had bought the tern *Jean F. Anderson,* selling her ten years later. In 1923 he had launched the tern *Village Queen* which his son William lost off Cape St. Mary's in 1938. In February, 1925, he purchased the four-mast schooner *George W. Elzey,* selling her to New York in 1930. He built the two-mast schooner *Sesame* in July, 1924, selling her to Stamford, Connecticut, also in 1930. For a time she had been the Publicover family yacht. On November 2nd, 1927, he launched the tern *Elfreda E. Publicover,* selling her in April, 1930, to Newfoundland interests.

He bought the four-mast schooner *Laura Annie Barnes* at Providence, Rhode Island, in March, 1930, losing her on Tuckernuck Shoal in January, 1939. The passing of the *Barnes* was a great blow to Captain Publicover as she was more than just a means of earning a living; she was a home as well. His family sailed with him. His son William went as first mate, another son Bruce was second mate, and a third son, Charles, was cook. In the summer months his wife Elfreda joined him, as well as his married daughter, Mrs. Richard, with her two children, and the 'baby' of the family, 'Dolly'. Sometimes his son-in-law went as mate.

Captain Publicover also had several other vessels. He built the tern *Maid of La Harve* in 1919. She was lost at sea on her maiden voyage from Newfoundland to Brazil with a cargo of fish. He bought the three-mast schooner *Lillian E. Kerr* in 1938, making her over into a four-master. She was run down and sunk by a steamer in convoy during the war. His last vessel was the two-mast

[5]

Burgers George which he had from 1939 until he condemned her in 1945. In all the years that he was master, he never lost a man, an outstanding record for such a long period of service.

The Captain had a family of seven, four boys and three girls. His eldest, a girl, was killed in the Halifax explosion in the first World War. His second daughter, Virginia, was named after the schooner which had been lost shortly before she was born. Her husband, John Richard, as well as her elder brother William, were both lost when the *Kerr* was sunk. Captain Publicover was one of the 'sea dogs' of an era nigh past. He spent most of his life in windships, and knew them well. In 1948, at the age of 71, he retired from the sea to run a store in Lunenburg.

His brother Archibald Publicover was another member of the sea-going family. Early in the war he bought the old tern *Maid of France* which had sunk at her anchorage on the flats in Lunenburg harbor. At high water her decks disappeared from view. After pumping her out, he took her around to La Have for repairs. Rebuilding her, he made her a whole deck deeper which gave her about double her original capacity. He put engines in her as well. When she departed south with lumber, she was a fine craft. However, on her return north with salt from Ragged Island, Turks, she struck something in the water, and foundered in short order.

Captain Louis Kenedy

Captain Louis Kenedy, vessel operator of Conquerall Bank, Nova Scotia, certainly should be mentioned as his tern *City of New York* was the last three-mast schooner without an engine in the Maritime Provinces. Perhaps his best known tern was the *Abundance,* a very fast vessel which put up some fine records. Originally the *Richard B. Silver,* she once went from Shelburne to Barbados in nine days; Captain Kenedy took her fully loaded over the same course in 12½ days in 1932. That same year he pushed her from Halifax to Funchal, Madeira, in 14 days 19 hours. He once wrote of her: "The *Abundance* was the fastest thing I was ever shipmates with. She could go up to ten knots as soon as there was any breeze, and several times she did 14. She was very handy and a lucky vessel as far as not getting headwinds went." She was lost in a hurricane at Jamaica in 1932.

Captain Kenedy also had the tern *Adams,* last of the Yankee-built three-masters. Although her keel had been layed at Essex in August, 1920, she was not launched until April, 1929. The *Adams*

[6]

carried the rigging of the tern *Lincoln* which had been rammed off Cape Cod not long before. After a short active career, the *Adams* was layed up until January, 1933, when Captain Kenedy bought her for the West Indies trade. However, he did not have much luck with her. In April she took a bad pounding in the Bay of Fundy when inbound from New York. Severely strained, she was hardly able to make Yarmouth without foundering. In July, while in ballast awaiting a salt cargo, she dragged her anchors and was blown to sea during a hurricane over Turks Island. And finally, in December she was hit by a gale not far from Bermuda. When her gasoline supply for her pumps gave out, the tern rapidly took on water, and the crew abandoned the sinking vessel as the freighter *Blairesk* came on the scene. The *Adam's* first mate Johnson of Nova Scotia lost his life while attempting to launch the lifeboat.

During the war years, Captain Kenedy had a small steel three-mast schooner, the *Wawaloam,* until a German submarine caught up with him. He also had the iron schooner *Sea Fox* from 1934 to 1939, and again in 1943 and 1944. Although she had been built as a yacht in 1888, she was in very fine shape, retaining her two topmasts and all her rigging. She was not a small vessel, being 101 gross tons and 96 feet long, but on one occasion Captain Kenedy and one other man sailed her in the month of January from Connecticut to Barbados in sixteen days. In order to get away from the wharf, he had been forced to kick a sheriff ashore after she had been seized.

Captain Kenedy later got the bark *City of New York* which he converted into a tern, and when he sold her he purchased in 1953 the lovely three-mast schooner-yacht *Vema,* eventually selling her to Columbia University's Lamont Geological Observatory.

Captain Edward Long

Captain Edward Long was active up to the end of sail in New England waters. He took the *Theoline* into Quincy in 1941, the last of her type to visit that old port. One winter when the *Theoline* was laid up at Jonesport, Captain Long and his wife together overhauled the four-master's stern which had taken a decided sag. Putting in two huge turnbuckles, they were able to pull her back into position, correcting the weakening timbers. He had had the *J. O. Webster* when she had piled ashore on Connecticut in 1931. He used to tell of another accident that he had had in deep water in the Bay of Fundy during a heavy fog. Without warning, his schooner suddenly struck her bowsprit and headgear into a forest growing on a point. Although his fore canvas fouled the trees and shrubs, he was able to back off, the only damage being to the jib-boom which snapped. The hull of the schooner never touched the shore.

Captain Harold G. Foss

Captain Harold Foss was probably the only man in the world who ever owned outright and wholly alone two five-mast schooners. They were the *Edna Hoyt* and the *Dunham Wheeler*. And he also had the four-mast *Harold G. Foss*, ex-*Thomas N. Barnsdale*. Later he was a member of Foss & Crabtree, a firm in Boston that managed the last five-master and the four-mast *Edward L. Swan*. In the late 1930's Captain Foss finally gave up sail, turning to steam.

Captain Robert W. Rickson

Captain Rickson commanded several of the larger schooners in their last days 'down east'. For some years he had the *Edna Hoyt*, giving her up to take over the four-mast *Herbert L. Rawding*. On his honeymoon in November, 1910, Captain Rickson and his bride were aboard the three-mast schooner *Cox & Green* when it foundered in a gale, leaving the sinking vessel in a small boat. A year later he was aboard another windship which was considered lost following a bad gale, and it was not until many days later that the schooner staggered into a Floridian port.

Captain William F. Plummer

Captain Plummer had the *Edna Hoyt* for a short time after Captain Rickson gave her up. His first command had been the schooner *Ben Hur* which he had at the time of the Portland Storm in 1898. In the years that followed he was master of nearly twenty sailing vessels, including such well-known schooners as the *Josephine A. McQuesten* and the *Doris F. Hamlin,* both fine four-masters. In 1940 he took the four-master *Helen Barnet Gring* from the scrap heap, putting her back to sea again after a re-fit in Boston.

There were many others. The Ogilvies, W., N. Hilton, and Ralph M. who sailed the smaller terns out of Nova Scotia. There was Captain Burton E. Merriam, who had the *Victory Chimes* while his son Joseph had the *Nova Queen* and another son George, the *Mina Nadeau*. A third son, Calvin, was also a schooner captain. Captain Wallace H. Smith was in charge of the *Minas Prince* from the time she was built in 1919 until his death in 1937. Captain Burtis M. Wasson and his sons Alvin, Harold, James, and Paul were well known in Maine ports, and they might be credited with commanding the last true-Yankee three-masters, the *Rebecca R. Douglas* and the *Lucy Evelyn* before they were sold away from Maine in the recent war years.

The names go on and on, Baird, Torrey, Trynor, Coleman, the Wilkies, Taylor, Decker, Antle, and the rest. But there is no room for all. They made their niche in the history of sail, the captains who closed a chapter of an era.

CHAPTER II

Schooners: A 5- and 4- Masters

~~~~~~

T HE FIRST five-mast schooner was the *Governor Ames* which was built at Waldoboro, Maine, in 1888; the last five-mast schooner was the *Edna Hoyt* which came from Thomaston in 1920: The first four-mast schooner was the *William L. White,* built in Bath in 1880, and the last four-master was the *Josiah Chase,* launched at Boothbay in 1921. The *Hoyt* ended her days as a barge in Portugal, and the *Chase* became the *Mihkel* in 1934 under the Esthonian flag. These large schooners together with their sisters and a few six-masters were sails' last challenge to steam.

When the square-rigger was failing, the fore-and-afters made their bid to keep canvas on the seas. They were not beautiful beside the full-rigged ships, and were hardly more than boxes when compared with the clippers. However, when they became the sole survivors of an age, they took on a charm of their own. A four-master becalmed off Mount Desert made a lovely picture, and a tern bowling into Boston Harbor with a brisk breeze was a grand sight. Although they lacked yards and braces, their rigging still appeared like a spider's web against the evening sky.

The majority of the schooners were built for carrying large loads so their lines were not fine. Nonetheless, these vessels on occasion showed that they could step along if conditions were right. Captain Foss once said that he had had the *Harold G. Foss* averaging 16 knots for several hours, and when he was master of the *Sallie C. Marvil* he saw her average 12 knots for four days. On one occasion the big six-mast *George W. Wells,* deeply loaded with coal, averaged 16 knots from Cape Henry to Montauk Point. If the winds had always been favorable, sail would have held its own, but there were calms, and the delays of days waiting for a change in the weather, the hours and miles lost in beating and tacking, the uncertainty of arrival dates — these defeated sail.

A small group of the larger schooners survived to sail in New England waters after 1935; one was a five-master.

Edna Hoyt

The last active five-mast schooner was the well-known *Edna Hoyt,* one of the smallest of her type being only 1512 gross tons, and 224 feet long. Built by Dunn & Eliot, she cost about $280,000, somewhat more than a similar vessel built a year or two previously. She was well put together, lasting through the years in amazingly good condition, and only hogging slightly with time.

Her earlier years saw her owned by the Superior Trading and Transportation Company of Boston who kept her in steady operation along the coast in general trade. In late August, 1924, she had a trying trip from Brunswick, Georgia, to Boston with a cargo of resin. After a terrific storm had swept her far off course, she was not sighted for many days. The owners sent out a tug to look for her without success. However, she finally sailed in from over the horizon on September 5th, 23 days out. She reported poor weather luck, and for her first nine days at sea had been becalmed, covering only 200 miles, less than 23 miles a day. In November, with 7000 barrels of rosin from Norfolk, she was kept out of Boston for two days by a heavy northwest gale.

January, 1929, found her in distress off No Man's Land with a cargo of 1,100,000 feet of hard pine, valued at $60,000, from Beaumont, Texas, for Boston. A Coast Guard boat towed her into Vineyard Haven. Three or four days later she arrived at her destination, 47 days out. In October she made a long 40 day voyage from Venezuela to Boston. She arrived with the four-mast schooner *Catherine G. Scott* which had come from the same port in 18 days. In May, 1930, she was in the newspapers again when she was on her way from Eastport to Baltimore with fish fertilizer. She was the first of her type to pass through the Lubec Narrows, causing something of a sensation as she was the first five-master many had seen.

About this time she was purchased by Foss & Crabtree, also of Boston, for the fertilizer trade between Venezuela and New England ports, to replace their *Harold G. Foss* which had been wrecked. With Captain Rickson in command she was never without work, and kept reasonably clear of trouble.

In December, 1931, she came into Boston a month out from

Las Piedras loaded down to her marks with 2000 tons of guano. Most of the voyage had been uneventful, but she had had to stop in Nantucket Sound for three days to await a slant of wind to take her around Cape Cod. A year later she had to be towed into port when the Coast Guard picked her up off Cape Hatteras in a leaking condition, taking six inches of water an hour. At the time she was bound for Baltimore, 30 days out of Venezuela with guano. In July, 1935, she put into Vineyard Haven with a cracked rudder post, but after repairs, she went on to Portland, Maine, to load barrel shooks for Barbados. On January 9th, 1936, she swept into Mobile, 19 days from Barbados. In August of that year the Coast Guard along the Atlantic seaboard were asked to keep a lookout for her when she was unreported on a passage from La Vela de Cero, but she turned up off Nantucket all well, arriving at Boston 30 days out. She had been becalmed a week off Haiti while a hurricane was blowing to the north of the island.

After discharging her 900 tons of goat manure, she took 12 days to reach New York. She then went to Norfolk to load coal for Maine. Sailing from Hampton Roads on October 26th, she passed Highland Light on November 4th, and on the 6th entered Provincetown to shelter from the weather for two days. She arrived at Searsport some days later. On her return to Norfolk the winds were with her, and she did the run in a week. Again she set a course to the north, coming into Boston four days out on Christmas Day with 2500 tons of coal. She next went to Charleston in 19 days, and three days from there to Norfolk. Her next run was with coal to Guadeloupe.

In the summer of 1937, the *Edna Hoyt* loaded 1,000,000 feet of lumber at Halifax, departing from there on September 1st for Belfast, Ireland. Now under the command of Captain George Hopkins, she had a fair weather passage for the most part, doing the trip in twenty-two days; her owners had expected her to take at least a month. After discharging, she was a week going down the Irish Sea to the Bristol Channel where she picked up Welsh coal for Venezuela. Putting to sea on November 2nd, the five-master ran into late fall weather in the Bay of Biscay where a sharp gale gave her a terrific beating. The running seas threw her about, wrenched her aging hull, bent and twisted her all along her length. With the heavy cargo she fought to keep afloat, her pumps going to keep out the water that now leaked in through the many loose seams. The gale did not last long but the damage was done. In

November 25th she was towed into Lisbon. A survey showed that the schooner was beyond repair, and she was condemned as unseaworthy. In January, 1938, she was sold to Portuguese interests who planned to use her as a coal supply barge which would move at the end of a tow line.

For seventeen years the *Edna Hoyt* had given good service. She had never been laid up during that period excepting for overhauls; she had always been good to her owners. She was a comfortable vessel for her crews, not heavy to handle, and her after quarters were almost yacht-like. When Captain Hopkins had her, his wife generally sailed with him, adding the female touch to their cabins and saloon. The five-master was always a mecca for sightseers who were attracted by her towering masts that generally rose high above the surrounding port sheds. Although there were many larger schooners built, the *Hoyt* appeared huge as one walked her spacious decks, and only those who climbed aloft in her rigging realized how tall she really was. Never again will her like be seen in New England waters.

There were a number of four-mast schooners.

Albert F. Paul

One of the busiest of this class on the East Coast was the *Albert F. Paul* of 735 gross tons. Built in 1917 by the W. G. Abbott Shipbuilding Company of Milford, Delaware, for the C. C. Paul & Company of Baltimore, she spent her entire life in the coastal trade, chiefly with coal and lumber, although on occasion she did work offshore as far as Bermuda or down into the West Indies. Having built up a good name for herself, she was often able to locate freights when other windships were forced to lay up on account of shipping slumps.

Much of the *Paul*'s success was due to Captain Robert O. Jones, her commander from 1924 to 1941. Born near Portmadoc, Wales, Captain Jones came from a section that developed great seamen and fine ships, and although their vessels seldom exceeded 300 tons, they were found in all parts of the world, always outward bound with Festiniog slates. Many of the Jones family commanded Portmadoc vessels; Robert O. Jones followed in their footsteps with the *Paul*.

For the most part, the *Paul* was a lucky vessel, seldom in trouble. In the fall of 1933, deep with some 525,000 feet of southern pine lumber for cargo, she rode out a hurricane while at anchor near Georgetown. A few days later she found herself in a heavy gale off Cape Henry. After anchoring, she was towed to a better, safer berth in Hampton Roads to await the end of the storm. In January, 1938, she was again in danger, this time springing a leak 350 miles south east of Cape Henry. Floating on her lumber load, she was towed to Baltimore. In November, 1939, she was caught by a hurricane when bound light to Jacksonville from Bermuda. Although Captain Jones attempted to dodge the storm, the center suddenly veered, hitting the schooner with all its force. A sail or two ripped to shreds with a roar as the four-master lay before the blast, but with the exception of lost canvas, she weathered the blow without further damage.

As far as New England was concerned, the *Paul* was occasionally seen at both Providence, Rhode Island, and Portland, Maine, in recent years, having come north with lumber, returning south light. Not a consistently fast vessel, the *Paul* did have some good passages to her record, as well as some lengthy ones. Some of her passages are as follows:

1935—arrived Hampton Roads October 31st; 12 days from Georgetown, S.C.

arrived New York December 22nd; 8 days from Georgetown.

1936—arrived New York May 18th; 23 days from Georgetown.

1937—arrived Portland May 3rd; 21 days from Jacksonville.

1938—arrived Portland June 3rd; 16 days from Jacksonville.

arrived New York October 3rd; 8 days from Sheet Harbor.

1939—arrived Providence May 5th; 15 days from Jacksonville.

arrived Providence August 9th; 10 days from Sapelo Sound, Georgia.

arrived Newport News October 13th; 5 days from Providence.

arrived Providence December 9th; 10 days from Jacksonville.

1940—arrived Portland June 27th; 11 days from Jacksonville.

arrived Cape Haitien, August 11th; 29 days from Portland.

arrived Portland November 6th; 13 days from Jacksonville.

arrived Norfolk December 3rd; 8 days from Portland.

This latter trip was the last time the *Albert Paul* was in New England waters. During the next year the schooner remained in the south, running coal to Bermuda, and logwood from Cape Haitien to Baltimore. One of her best passages at this time was one of four days two hours from Newport News to Bermuda. When she was dry-docked at Baltimore in April, 1941, she was found to be in "A-1" condition by the American Bureau of Shipping, an indication of how well she had been built a quarter century before.

When the *Paul* arrived at Baltimore on October 10th, 1941, twelve days out from Cape Haitien with logwood, her original owners decided to sell her as war restrictions were making it ever more difficult to operate their vessel. A month later she was purchased by the Albert Shipping Company of New York. With Captain Martino in command, she took a load of coal to Bermuda, and then went south light to Turks Island. In the latter part of February, 1942, the *Paul* headed north laden deep with salt. A severe storm swept her course about this time. As she never made port, it was thought ashore that she had been overwhelmed by the ugly seas. Long later word came out that she had been overtaken by a German submarine on March 2nd. It had not taken long to send her to the bottom. Thus passed a fine schooner.

Alvena

The *Alvena* was one of the large type of West Coast four-mast schooners, heavily constructed and strong. Built by H. D. Bendixen in 1901 at Eureka, California, she was 772 gross tons and 186 feet long. In more recent years, she operated on the East Coast with her homeport Jacksonville. She generally carried lumber north to New York or New England ports, with occasional jaunts to Bermuda and the West Indies. When the wind was just forward of her beam, she was very fast, and could leave most fore-and-afters in her wake.

In 1932 she was slow when she took 17 days from Bermuda to Jacksonville. In December she was in trouble off Cape Cod while bound from Jacksonville to Portland with lumber. Caught in a very bad winter gale, she had been practically given up as lost when the Coast Guard sighted her without sails seventy miles off shore. After a tow line had snapped, the large 'schooner anchored. However, upon trying to get under way later, the crew found that they were not able to get the anchor all the way up, so had to tow it in the water below them all the way to Provincetown.

On June 6th, 1934, she appeared off Savannah 49 days out from Boston with her supplies nearly gone. She was bound for Jacksonville at the time, and had to be towed to her destination, arriving on the 8th, 51 days en route. On January 24th, 1936, the *Alvena*, after discharging a cargo of lumber at Portland, was on her way light for Jacksonville when a sudden gust of wind carried her into the Portland Lightship. Scraping along the bow of the moored vessel, the *Alvena* tried to work clear, but not succeeding before the lightship's spare anchor had crashed down on her quarter deck, followed by 15 fathoms of chain. Railings and planking were torn on the wooden schooner, and she had to return to port for repairs to damage which was estimated at close to $4000.

The captain and owner of the *Alvena* at this time was Thomas Bram whom the newspapers recalled as being one of the central figures in a very strange murder case before the turn of the century. The barkentine *Herbert Fuller,* in command of Captain Charles I. Nash, had loaded lumber in Boston, sailing for Buenos Aires on July 3rd, 1896. The captain had his wife Laura aboard with him. The first mate was Thomas Bram who had already been on quite a few vessels by this time, and who was known to have attended sailors' missions, and to have led religious services. The second mate was a Russian Finn named August Blomberg, and there was a passenger, L. H. Monks. The crew of seven were made up of French, Dutch, Germans and Swedes.

Bram had the midnight watch on July 14th, and Charles Brown, a seaman, was at the wheel. In the early morning hours the passenger was awakened by strange noises in the after cabin. Loading his revolver, Monks went aft, and was horrified to find the captain lying on the cabin deck in a pool of blood. After he had told Bram what he had seen, the two men kept the deck until daylight, wondering who the murderer was. When they found a bloody axe on deck, they heaved it overboard so the crew would not use it against them. At dawn they discovered that the second mate and the captain's wife were also butchered. Bram became master of the vessel, and he had Charles Brown put in irons as the murderer since he could have entered the captain's cabin to commit the crime without being seen by anyone. Later, however, when Brown said that he had peeked through the cabin port, and seen Bram with an axe, the crew jumped their new captain, putting him in irons while the *Herbert Fuller* was turned towards Halifax. The three bodies, placed in the long boat, were towed astern.

When the case finally came up in court in Boston, there were several conflicting stories, but Bram was found guilty, and sentenced to hang. In a second trial, he was again guilty, but got life imprisonment this time. He served at Atlanta until 1913 when, through the efforts of Mary Roberts Rinehart, the novelist, he was paroled by President Taft; President Wilson pardoned him.

After Bram left jail, he opened a bar in Atlanta, in time earning enough money to purchase several schooners, one of which was the *Alvena* which he himself commanded. Not long after the accident with the lightship, Bram sold the schooner although she continued to work along the New England coast.

With Captain Winsor Torrey in command, the four-master made some fast runs. In April one year he took her out of Boston at 6:30 in the morning on a Saturday; he was at St. John, New Brunswick, by 10 p.m. on Sunday. Without her topsails set, she had plowed north at an average speed of twelve knots for her forty hours underway. In August, 1936, she arrived at New York 18 days from Parrsboro with lumber. She went back north to St. John in 13 days, and back to New York in 11 days. In March, 1937, she took five days for the trip from Boston to St. John. In August that year she limped into Boston short of provisions and leaking while on a run from Chatham, N.B., to New York. A month later she showed that she could still sail when she romped from New York to St. John in four days. She needed twelve days to get back to New York.

On November 14th she began her last passage under sail. As she raced over the Shoals, she passed four schooners bound west, an unusual meeting as late as 1937 when even by then windships were becoming a scarcity in the New England waters. On the 18th she put into Boston for shelter from the heavy fall gales. After picking up another mainsail and a couple of coils of line, she pushed on down east. Another storm sent her into Northeast Harbor. Captain Torrey wired her owners that she desperately needed overhauling but the only replies that he got were to proceed to Sheet Harbor. After some weeks he set out although the schooner was in very poor shape; he told the crew he would pay them off if they did not wish to take the chance.

Weather was bad off Nova Scotia, and somehow the four-master missed Sheet Harbor in the mists. The schooner was leaking badly when she at last limped into Canso. Captain Torrey had a Halifax tug come to tow her down there for repairs. Weather forced them into Sheet Harbor where the lumber company wanted her to load as she was, but the captain would have none of it, proceeding to Halifax when they got the chance.

Captain Torrey left the schooner in Halifax, being replaced

by a Canadian who took her around to Meteghan for repairs. However, it was found that she was too far gone to rebuild, and she was sold to become a dance hall at Point du Chene Pier in northern New Brunswick. The main deck was roofed over, the ceiling being held up by the main and speaker booms. The orchestra played from the top of a hatch. Swords and cutlasses adorned the old bulkheads to add atmosphere.

The *Alvena's* work days were not yet over, though. In June, 1941, she was towed around to Halifax where she was cut down to a towing barge named *Cape Forchu*. She survived the recent war, but was later taken outside the harbor to be sunk as a naval target.

Anna R. Heidritter

The oldest Maine-built four-mast schooner that was still sailing when the second World War broke out was the *Anna R. Heidritter*. Launched in 1903 at Bath, from the yards of Kelly, Spear & Company, she was first named the *Cohasset,* spending the earlier years of her life in the trans-Atlantic trade between the States and South Africa. She was about six years old when she caught fire while at sea, being badly burnt out. The charred hulk was towed to port to be later rebuilt by the Shartown Marine Railway Company in Maryland. When she was re-launched she came out as the *Anna R. Heidritter,* almost a new vessel from her waterline up. She was a small four-master, only 694 gross tons and 185 feet long, but she proved to be an excellent little vessel, standing up well through the years.

The first World War found her busy. However, before peace came, she was caught by a German submarine which badly pounded the schooner although not sinking her. A British warship, sighting the wreck, towed her into Gibraltar where she was repaired. On her return to the States, a group headed by Captain Bennett D. Coleman purchased the vessel. Captain Coleman took command in 1925.

The *Heidritter* spent the next years in the coastwise trade, generally coal south from Perth Amboy or Newport News for southern ports, returning north with lumber from Jacksonville, Charleston, or Georgetown for New York or New England ports. In her later years she was a lucky vessel, seldom without charters, and not often in trouble. Once in August, 1928, she was in distress off the Georgia coast when bound from Brunswick to New York as seas had destroyed her food and small boats. A passing steamer called the Coast Guard to her aid. About the only serious accident that she had took place in November, 1937, when she crashed with the liner *S.S. Pennland*. The steamer carried away most of the windship's headgear, but little other damage was done. After her cargo had been discharged at Norwich, Connecticut, repairs were made so she could return to sea.

The following are a few of her passages:

1934—arrived Providence January 4th; 31 days from Georgetown.
1936—arrived Charleston August 2nd; 29 days from New York.
1937—arrived Charleston March 27th; 11 days from New York.
1938—arrived Jacksonville April 24th; 14 days from New York.
    arrived Providence May 18th; 7 days from Jacksonville.
    arrived New York August 12th; 7 days from Charleston.
1939—arrived New Bedford May 6th; 13 days from Jacksonville.
    arrived Norfolk November 16th; 14 days from Bermuda.
    arrived Barbados January 15th; 21 days from Norfolk.
1940—arrived Charleston March 31st; 28 days from Barbados.
    arrived Jacksonville September 14th; 10 days from New York.

The war years found the aging schooner going further afield with trips to the West Indies, out with coal and back with logwood or fertilizer. In December, 1940, the *Heidritter* sailed from Newport News with a cargo of coal for Guadeloupe, the *Herbert L. Rawding* following close astern. The *Rawding* made her destination in 18 days, but there was no sign of the *Heidritter*. Captain Coleman had worked too far to leeward, taking an extra week to beat back. After quickly unloading, the *Heidritter* departed for Las Piedras to take on 'goat', the *Rawding* following her by six days this time. When the latter schooner arrived at the Venezuelan port, she found that Captain Coleman was having trouble with the authorities as he refused to allow them to take his ship's papers ashore, and they, in turn, refused to load him, or even allow him to go ashore. However, Captain Decker of the *Rawding*, being well-known in those parts, was able to smooth over the problems so both vessels were able to load.

The run northward was a hard one for the two schooners, the *Heidritter* arriving at Charleston on March 13th, 1941, 21 days out, with several of her sails in rags. Shortly after this trip, Captain Coleman, now 72 years old, retired from the sea to undergo a serious operation. After several more passages to the West Indies, the four-master went to Haiti in early 1942 for a cargo of logwood.

On her northward run, her new captain was taken ill, the schooner putting into Charleston to land him. Once again Captain Coleman took over. On February 25th the schooner set forth to deliver her load to Chester, Pennsylvania. Hugging the shoreline to keep clear of submarines which were now a menace to coastwise shipping, she pushed her way northward, a rare picture with her white sails drawing strongly, the sturdy old hull shoving the white-capped seas aside in a smother of foam.

The schooner was nearing the dreaded Cape Hatteras when the wind began hauling ahead, gaining strength all the time. Before long, Captain Coleman found himself facing a lee shore with a raising gale. Soon it became apparent that the ship was not holding her own, and the Captain ordered both anchors let go. All night the anchors held, but not long after light, the schooner began dragging. One of the chains parted. Somehow the crew managed to get over a third anchor, but it was to no avail. Shortly after noon on March 3rd, the remaining two chains snapped, and the *Heidritter* rapidly backed onto the beach, breaking her back as she struck the outer bar. For an entire day the crew clung to the rigging as seas swept over their doomed vessel, hanging on through a dreadful night of wind and spray. For many hours it was too rough for a rescue party on the beach to shoot out a line, but on the 4th the Coast Guard got a breeches buoy across to them, saving all hands.

Much of the cargo on the schooner was salvaged, but the four-master herself joined the long list of vessels to have been wrecked along that treacherous stretch of sand. In normal times she would never have ventured so close to shore; the German submarines had driven her in, so were indirectly responsible for her loss.

A final word must be written about Captain Coleman. One of the last of the New England windjammer captains, his career had been spent under canvas, twenty-two years in the *Heidritter* alone. He had been shipwrecked twice before, once in a winter storm off the Delaware Capes, and another time he and his crew had been forced to spend eight days in an open boat between Bermuda and Nova Scotia after their vessel had burnt at sea. Although he was an elderly man in years, he was amazingly active for his age, and it appeared that he still had many years before him. However, only a week after the loss of the *Heidritter,* Captain Coleman was killed when a taxicab in which he was riding collided with an auto in Newark, New Jersey.

Annie C. Ross

The last surviving four-mast schooner on the East Coast was the handsome *Annie C. Ross* which was built at Bath, Maine, in 1917. Named after the wife of Captain Alex Ross who had her for many years, she was not a particularly large vessel, being only 791 gross tons and 175 feet long. However, she was a good carrier, and a most successful vessel through the years.

One of the few times she was in trouble was in February, 1926, when she went ashore near Pensacola after her captain had sighted the Maine schooner *Robert E. Dean,* and thinking her in the channel, had followed her in. The *Dean,* however, was hard ashore; the *Ross* followed her up onto the beach. For several days it appeared that the *Ross* would be a total loss, but early in March she was safely refloated, not too seriously damaged from her experience.

Her maiden trip had taken her from Newport News to Demerara with coal. In the years to follow she was constantly in the coasting trade. Well kept up, she was classed "A-1" for fifteen years in the Records of American and Foreign Shipping by the American Bureau of Shipping. During the 1930's she was employed chiefly in the lumber trade between Georgetown or Savannah and New York. With a deck load, she could carry close to 700,000 feet of wood. Although she was by no means a clipper, she did put up several good runs. On December 29th, 1936, she arrived at New York 9 days from Georgetown, not exceptional in itself, but she had made the round trip, including time to take on a full cargo, in twenty days.

For a time after the war broke out in 1939, the *Ross* continued to keep to the seas. In March, 1940, she made a good run south from New York to Jacksonville, 7 days 23 hours from her Bay Ridge anchorage to her anchorage at the river mouth where she had to wait 36 more hours for a fog to lift before entering port. She went north from there to Searsport, Maine, in fifteen days, anchoring during the only bad weather of the trip in Vineyard Sound. It was not an easy passage as her spanker gaff broke twice, making plenty of work for her crew.

Captain Joseph Zuljevic was in command of the *Ross* during these last years, and he was very proud of his vessel. Although he was noted as a 'driver' amongst crews, he still had a happy ship for the most part. That the schooner was not involved in accidents or other mishaps was greatly due to his seamanship and handling; he was a real sailor.

In the latter part of 1940, the *Ross* was laid up in Newtown Creek at Maspeth, Queens, New York. There was talk of her going back to sea in 1947. She was given new booms, her masts were scraped down, hatches refitted, and painted over. A new owner, Captain John Rosario, planned to enter her in the Cape Verde trade. Her topmasts were lowered for her to pass out under a new bridge. But nothing more happened. The *Ross* gathered soot on her decks and rigging, her mooring lines creaked, and she occasionally heaved to the wash of a passing tug. A watchman kept an eye on her. Then, in 1954, she was purchased by the Catholic Sea Scouts of America. Towed around to an anchorage off Hempstead, Long Island, she was to be re-fitted by the cadets, but in September, 1955, she sank at her moorings. It was her end.

A few typical passages:

1935—arrived Hampton Roads February 12th; 9 days from Georgetown.
  arrived New York December 20th; 21 days from Georgetown.
1936—arrived New York May 24th; 7 days from Georgetown.
  arrived New York November 20th; 20 days from Brunswick.
1938—arrived New York July 21st; 5 days from Savannah.

Avon Queen

Originally launched as the *Jessie Louise Fauquier* from the yards of Fauquier & Porter at Hantsport, Nova Scotia, in 1918, the *Avon Queen* was a medium sized four-master of 1035 gross tons and 201 feet long. At one time she was fitted with auxiliary power to help her along through calms, but in her later life, she was a pure sailing ship.

Although there is only one record of the *Avon Queen* entering a New England port in recent years, she was frequently in New England waters during her travels; she came into Boston on August 23rd, 1935, eight days out from Sheet Harbor with lumber. She made several trips between Nova Scotia and New York, very likely using the Nantucket Sound route. The majority of her runs were to the West Indies, especially in her last years when she was regis-

[22]

tered in Bridgetown, Barbados, making her home there to avoid rising Canadian taxes.

For the most part, the four-master steered clear of troubles although, there are one or two mishaps alongside her name. On November 18th, 1931, she arrived at New York with a load of lumber. Two weeks later, when she was being towed under Brooklyn Bridge, her main and mizzen topmasts fouled the span, the wood snapping off and falling in a tangle of wreckage. She was again in trouble in New York waters in April, 1935, as she was leaving her anchorage at City Island, bound for Halifax in ballast. A sudden gust of wind sent her ashore, but she was hauled off in short order. Five days later, on May 2nd, she arrived off the Nova Scotian port leaking quite badly from the strains that she had received during her grounding. Later she was given a thorough overhaul.

Her end came in 1937. Off San Salvador Island in the Bahamas, she developed a severe leak. As the pumps were broken, there was nothing that the crew could do. When the U.S. destroyer *Fairfax* came upon her, the entire starboard side of the main deck was under water, and the schooner had a twenty degree list. After the eight crew members were taken off, the schooner was set on fire and sunk to prevent her from becoming a menace to navigation. The last owner of the *Avon Queen* was her captain, Robert Alexander McLean.

Helen Barnet Gring

One of the best looking four-mast schooners to sail in New England waters was the handsome *Helen Barnet Gring* which was built by R. L. Bean at Camden, Maine, in 1919 at a cost close to $200,000. A flushed decked vessel, she carried a balustrade rail in place of bulwarks, giving her a smart appearance. She was a good sized schooner, 1226 gross tons and 202 feet long. When she was launched in July, she went down the ways fully rigged, topmasts and spars in place. She was christened with clear spring water. Her first charter was to coal for Lisbon, Portugal.

Part of the great Boston fleet of windjammers owned by Crowell & Thurlow, the *Gring* was kept fairly busy during her earlier years, plodding up and down the Atlantic coast with lumber and coal and any other cargos she could find, just another of the many windships still active in the days directly following the first

World War. She first visited Boston, her home port, in April, 1921, when she brought in 1500 tons of coal from Norfolk.

She was very nearly lost in 1928. Early in April she had sailed from Norfolk with coal for Calais, Maine. On the 26th, at one in the morning, some three and a half miles south east of Chatham on the Cape, the *Gring* suddenly plowed into the three-mast schooner *William Booth* of Rockland which was deep laden with a cargo of granite paving blocks for New York City. The *Booth*, a vessel of 435 tons and 176 feet long, had been laid up at Vinal Haven during the winter; this was her first trip of the season. With her planks ripped open, the tern went to the bottom within five minutes. All her hands were picked up by the *Gring*. As neither vessel had wireless, the first the Coast Guard knew of the accident was when they sighted the masts of the *Booth* jutting out of the ocean. The *Gring* with her stem damaged and bowsprit smashed was towed into Boston for repairs.

Not long after this, the *Gring* was laid up at Eastport for lack of work. Steam colliers had killed the coal trade for the schooners, there was not enough lumber to keep all the windships on the move, the Florida boom was over, and a depression was setting in. Some time later she joined the silent fleet of big schooners at Boothbay Harbor; it seemed that she would never sail again. However, in 1937 she was purchased by Captain William F. Plummer who, although in his sixties, was one of the outstanding windjammer skippers along the coast. As he felt that a windship could make a profit if run properly, he found the best vessel available, the *Gring,* and had her reconditioned at Port Greville, Nova Scotia, where prices were lower than in American ports. The Portland, Maine, firm of Bernstein & Jacobson were co-owners of the *Gring* with Captain Plummer, but they relied on his judgement in most matters.

After taking aboard a large lumber load, her hold filled and more piled six feet high on deck the *Gring* sailed from Parrsboro on September 17th, bound for England. She put into Eastport for final supplies, and was on her way again on October 15th, heading out into the Atlantic. On the 25th she was sighted at 45 degrees 20' North, 45 degrees 14' West, all in good order. After that she seemed to disappear; a month passed and there was no word from her. A howling fall gale had swept the Atlantic, causing fears that it might have torn the schooner apart. Her owners had expected her to take 25 days for the crossing; now she was long overdue.

Hope had just about been given up when the liner *Washington* sighted her, still all well. A few days later, on December 4th, she arrived at Birkenhead, 50 days out from Eastport.

Captain Plummer had hoped to get a return cargo at fourteen shillings a ton, but as none was forthcoming, he was forced to sail empty, leaving Liverpool on December 29th bound out into the winter storms on the North Atlantic. However, she did not do too badly against the Westerlies for she made Charleston on February 16th, 49 days out. She remained there at anchor until May when she made a 12 day run up the coast to Providence, and then on to the Cape Cod Canal.

A tug, the *Plymouth,* had been sunk in a crash off the Eastern entrance to the Canal. Bernstein & Jacobson, who had contracted to remove the wreck, planned on using the *Gring* and a sister four-master, the *Harry G. Deering,* as pontoons to float the hulk. With the two schooners lashed together over the *Plymouth,* chains were run between the ships and the tug. At low water the four-masters were partially filled with water, and the chains drawn tight. The idea was that as the tide rose, the schooners would be pumped dry, lifting the tug clear of the bottom so it could be moved to shallower water. However, the stunt backfired. The tug did not budge, and the two schooners rolled against one another, locking their rigging. In the end, the tug had to be removed with dynamite, and the remains dragged to sea and sunk.

The *Gring* was towed to Boston where she was attached by the backers of the salvage attempt for the bills which had mounted up. After being idle for many months while the case went through the courts, the *Gring* was again put into sailing condition by Captain Plummer at Chelsea in May, 1940. A New York group, who had bought a large share of the schooner, hoped to gain from some of the war profits that were now to be had. After a thorough overhaul, she was once more in good shape. Early in June she left Boston, proceeding to Newport News to load coal for St. George, Bermuda. She had a most contented crew this trip as the captain had laid in an exceptionally fine supply of stores, much better than usually found aboard windships. However, they did have a poor cook who, it was said, 'even found ways of spoiling rotten meat'; as soon as the schooner returned to the States, Captain Plummer gave the so-called cook just a half hour to get off the ship.

The *Gring* had taken about a week from Boston to Newport News, eight days from Cape Henry to Bermuda, and some fourteen days returning to Newport News. Now Captain Plummer decided at this time to stay ashore for a spell to take care of his personal affairs. The new captain arrived with his own mate and bo'sun — an almost unheard of thing.

The rest of the *Gring's* story is best described in a letter from Francis E. Bowker who was serving before the mast:

"The new skipper came aboard first, a medium-sized half bald, little man, carrying a battered papier-mache suitcase, and wearing a baggy blue suit, dirty shirt, and, as I remember, no tie. He soon informed us that on his last ship he had carried the same crew for four years (they were so happy) and that he was a lawyer by profession.

"The mate came later, a large moon-faced man with an enormous belly, a mustache that would have made a good swab brush, a voice like a foghorn, and enough bull to have saved the owners sending us to Venezuela for the load of goat manure we later lost, except that I am afraid it was too strong. We had too much as it was for it was that that laid the poor old *Gring* in her last resting place.

"Poor old bo'sun (as near as we could learn) had picked up all his schooner lore in an insane asylum from a former skipper of the schooner *M. Vivian Pierce,* who went insane. Bos'un admitted to us that he had been in an asylum, and the only ship and skipper he ever talked about was the *Pierce* and her skipper. He was a harmless little creature, and the first night aboard, under the pretext of having been too long ashore, he asked me to explain the topsail gear, and how it was handled.

"One morning after we had loaded, and were lying off the coal dock waiting to sail (ten days), Norman, one of the crew woke up in a silent mood. When Bill, another of the crew, and I inquired what the trouble was, he was at first a little embarrassed. Then he told us he was leaving the ship. We wanted to know why, but at first he wouldn't say. Then he begged us to come with him. Finally he said that he knew that the vessel was not going to come back from this trip. He couldn't tell us how he knew it, but he couldn't be budged.

"Bill and I wouldn't be budged, either, and wild horses couldn't have dragged us off the vessel then. Neither of us were superstitious ,and we were bound to discredit Norman if we had to die in the attempt. I believe I would do the same thing again in spite of what later transpired. When it comes to some things, I am a stubborn cuss to convince.

"After Norman had left, and also our old 'chief', we shipped a colored cook named Luther Kirby, a kid named Bill Greenman, who wanted a summer trip, and a chief from Baltimore named Hack Coggins. Hack had only been aboard a couple of days when one morning while the skipper was ashore he packed his bags, and said he was leaving when the 'old man' got back. We asked him what was the matter, and he said: 'Three times in my life I have gone aboard vessels, and before they sailed I had a feeling that I shouldn't go in them. Not one of those vessels ever returned!' I remember one of those vessels was the schooner *Doris Hamlin;* I believe the bark *Matanzas* was another, but I don't remember the third. We had plenty of cause to think back on his words later.

"He didn't get a chance to leave us as the skipper came out on the tug, bringing our fourth sailor, a fellow called Joe Bush. Joe was more of a steamboat man than a sailor, and was violently 'union'. However, he did well in his work, and I think under Captain Plummer would have gotten along.

"I can't detail all the queer things that occurred on this trip. Many of them seem unbelievable but they are true. First, the skipper called us together on the forecastle head one night, and told Bill and me that we were fortunate that we hadn't left. His confidential advisers in Washington had told him that all sailors leaving their ships, unemployed men ashore, negroes and bums were to be drafted, given six weeks training, and shipped to England. Then they would be transported to the French coast as shock troops in an invasion. They would immediately be killed off by the Germans who would tire themselves out in the effort. Then the trained English soldiers would land and clean up the exhausted Germans.

"By this time it was too late to quit; we were lying off Lynnhaven Roads, waiting for a slant.

"Next the mate came forward, made his way out along the jibboom, and on his way in remarked: 'When I was the master of the *Horatio G. Foss,* I carried away the jibboom five times and the bowsprit twice. I wouldn't be surprised to see this jibboom alongside before we got very far!' Nice words, for an already jittery crew. The next thing, the mate removed all the bars from the compass, and adjusted it himself; this may have been a factor in later events. Another bright idea of his was to send up a new fly with the vessel rolling a good twenty degrees in the ground swell. I got the job.

"After we got to sea, all signs of discipline vanished. The mate took Bill and Joe in his watch. Bill was fairly quiet but when Joe was at the wheel it was a treat to hear him and the mate yelling insults at each other. I was in the skipper's watch with young Bill Greenman who was altogether green, and the bo'sun who was useless. The first night out I was at the wheel. The air was light, and the skipper was turned in. Suddenly the breeze shifted, coming fairly fresh from dead ahead. The sails all came aback. The bo'sun, leaning against the corner of the house with a dreamy expression enjoying the soft summer night, remained entirely unaware of the change. Finally, I summoned up courage to speak to him. 'Bo'sun, she's going off her course,' I remarked. 'Is she?' 'Yes, she's all aback.' The bo'sun looked around in surprise, and then resumed his position. It seemed as though the breeze was going to stay, so after a while I said: 'Don't you think we ought to get the sails over?' 'Yes, I believe we should, but I hate to call the captain.' I decided to take the bull by the horns then, and said: 'I think you better either call him, or get them over yourself.' In the end he called the skipper who came on deck and took the wheel, telling the bo'sun to take me forward and get them over. It was then that I found the bos'un didn't know one damn thing about a schooner. From then on I was unofficial bo'sun with two absolutely green hands to show what to do each time we handled a sail. Especially at night, I had to tell them what to do, and then check to make sure they had the right line before doing anything. It was a great job.

"A few days out, Bill heard over his little portable radio that there was a hurricane making up the coast. There was a strong south east breeze, and a great, heavy south east swell. The sky was murkey overhead but the mate, who showed up as the actual skipper, kept the vessels close hauled on the port tack with all four topsails and the headsails on. The *Gring* drove and strained and smashed and pounded, meanwhile getting nowhere and working towards the center if the hurricane decided to veer our way. Finally, the mate went into the engine room to tell the chief how to run his pumps, and Hack backed him into a corner with a stilson wrench, and told him if he didn't get the topsails off he would kill him. About fifteen minutes later he got them in and tied them up. All the lower sail was kept on, however, and the course kept the same. Shortly after supper that night our starboard jumper stay carried away, and upon examination it was found that the turnbuckle had been sawn almost through with a hacksaw, then screwed in one turn. The Captain said that Captain Plummer had probably done it, and that he was going to have him investigated when he got back. Bill and I were beginning to have other ideas as to who was going to be investigated when we got back.

"I think we were thirty-three days from Cape Henry to Barbados. The whole trip was a series of similar goings-on. The boiler tubes gave out, and the mate refused to have the vessel pumped. Joe Bush got appendicitis, and the mate logged him, charging him with mutiny for refusing a cathartic and turning-in to his bunk. When we finally arrived at Barbados, he brought the health doctor up to expose Joe for a fraud. The doctor took one look at him, and rushed him to the hospital where the appendix burst before it could be removed.

"The mate shot at the bumboat man who hung around on the ladder, and wanted to come aboard. Hack got heat prostration running his engine unloading, and joined Joe in the hospital. Bill Greenman got fed up, and had his father send enough money to get home on, leaving by steamer. The skipper went ashore, and bragged that he had not had a bath in six weeks. Then he tried to hire a couple of niggers to go in the forecastle with us upon which I went down to the cabin to tell him that I knew of a couple of white men the *Wawaloam* who could come instead. He got me so mad I threatened to kill him, and he ran up on deck calling for harbor police.

"As I left myself, I found the colored cook standing in the cabin door with a carving knife. 'Mist Bowka,' he said, 'ah was just waitin' fo' you to knock him down. He wouldn't nevah bothr'd no one no mo'!' Thank God, I didn't knock him down.

"We finally went to the American Consul to ask him to investigate the officers, but the skipper had been there first, and on his desk was a large box with the Captain's return address in large letters in the corner. The Consul told us we would have to wait until we got back to the States before we could press any charges, or call an investigation. We told him the only reason we were there was that we didn't think we would ever reach the States. That did us no good, either, so we had to stay with the ship. We got the two fellows from *Wawaloam*, however, Donald Gould, a young fellow from New Jersey, and another young fellow named Rockwell.

"On September 25th, we left Bridgetown, and made Las Piedras,

Venezuela, in a few days. We loaded about 1200 tons of goat there, and at Las Tacas, a little up the coast. While there, the mate did two great things. He ruined the yawl boat engine, and he rigged flying backstays to the fore topmast, saying that he would make Jacksonville in twelve days or take the sticks out of her — he did neither!

"I haven't got the dates for the rest of the trip, but we got off from Las Tacas with a fine breeze which lasted, as usual, until we were under Cape Dame Marie (S.W. Haiti). Then we got calms and squalls, and had a slow beat up through the Windward Passage where we got a good slant for Old Bahama Passage.

"At midnight of the night of October 22-23, I took the wheel from 12:00 to 1:00. The orders were to look for a light showing four quick flashes on the starboard bow. Shortly after 1:00 while I was on lookout, the bos'un being on the forecastle head with me, we picked up a light dead ahead flashing one flash. The mate claimed that there was no such light, but after seeing it himself, had to admit that it was there. Finally, he decided that the flash must have been altered since the chart was put out. He ordered a course just south of it as he said it was Lobos Cay. At 3:00 I again took the wheel, and it was only about five minutes later that Hack, my watchmate (he hadn't been allowed to resume his job as chief after his prostration) sung out: 'Breakers to leeward.'

"The mate said it was moonlight on the water, but soon we could hear it as well as see it. Then he said the current must have set us down, and so hauled our course up two points for a little while. By that time, our light was only about four miles off. We were making about seven or eight knots with the wind on the starboard quarter, and all sail set. We pulled away from the breakers, and the mate ordered me to the old course to the south of the light. Then saying that he was going down to look at the chart again, he went below. He stayed there about a minute, and was half way up the steps, when I felt the bow lift. There were three distinct shocks through the vessel, and the wheel flew out of my hands.

" 'Put your wheel hard up! the mate shouted. I pulled for all I was worth, waited a moment, and said: 'She's jammed hard and fast.'

"The mate walked to the rail to look over the side. There in the clear moonlit water the bottom was plainly visible. We slacked off the sheets, but there she was. By now it was 3:45 a.m. Bill and Red Gould were sleeping on top of the forward house, and so easy had been her grounding that they slept right through it. I walked up to them, gave them each a shake, and said: 'One bell — and hard and fast aground!'

"The two boys opened their eyes, looked up at the full sails over their heads, felt the easy roll of the ship as the swell rocked her back and forth, and started to laugh 'Look over the side, boys,' I said.

"One look was enough. 'Well, I've been expecting something like this,' Bill said.

"I went back to the wheel, and watched and listened while the skipper and the mate discussed the situation. Finally, I went to the spanker crosstrees, and there, far off on the starboard bow I could make out the loom of four quick flashes. It now transpired that the mate had been going by a small scale chart of the Channel which had been aboard since 1921. At that time Lobos Cay was the only lighted island in the vicinity. The flash hadn't been changed, but a new island had had a light placed on it, Verdi Cay. There was no excuse for losing the vessel as on the run out to Barbados I had borrowed a larger scale chart from the captain. This chart was new when we left Newport News, and the Verdi Cay light was on it. The smaller scale chart of course gave more detail but that was absolutely no excuse for not checking with the new one, especially when there was such doubt about it from the start.

"Shortly after daybreak, a small fishing boat came down from Verdi Cay, and after breakfast the skipper took it to Neuvitas, about 40 miles to the south east, which is the nearest port. That was the last we saw or heard of him until we ourselves got a fishermen to bring us there three days later. We learnt then that he had got himself a good hotel room, and wired the owners 'VESSEL LIGHTLY ASHORE. NO DAMAGE DONE. SEND TUG.'

"That morning it breezed up strongly from the north east, and the vessel soon showed signs of breaking up. The seas smashed at her broadside on, and sent spray flying across the decks which lay over at a thirty degree angle. With each sea, the vessel rolled on the coral bed. Large chunks of her bottom soon began to tear off and drift to leeward. The water began to discolor with goat manure which seeped through her sides. The deck seams opened up, and the masts criss-crossed dangerously.

"The mate and bo'sun disappeared below, and began to top some bottles of rum they had been bringing home. Several native fishermen wandered about the ship, their boats lying easily in our lee. The rest of us hung around the forecastle. About noon we were startled to hear a loud 'bang' followed by a whoop. We jumped to the forecastle door to see what was going on. There was another 'bang'. A splinter flew from the door join, and one of the two remaining chickens we had from a few we had picked up in Venezuela for extra food, flew squawking by the corner of the house. The mate and bo'sun were staggering in drunken abandon up the deck, the mate with a revolver in his hand, and the bo'sun following after. We dove for shelter, but Luther proved himself a hero. The chicken poised for a moment on the waterway near the fore rigging. Luther, with a flying tackle, landed fully on it, and with a quick twist of its neck, removed that source of sport.

"The other chicken, however, flew onto the forecastle head, and after a couple more futile shots, disappeared down the hatch to the paint locker and toilet which were located under the deck there. The bo'sun went to the bell, solemnly striking it 'bong-bong-bong'; I suppose he was tolling the death knell. The mate disappeared after the chicken, but after a few more shots ran out of ammunition. Bill then went down himself, caught the frightened bird, and dispatched it in the manner Luther had his. That game over, our two heroes chased off the fishermen with the empty gun before going aft to continue their libations. After dark, the two passed out so we proceeded to the lazarette. It was half under water but we salvaged a lot of canned stuff. We put half of it in the yawl boat which we made ready for lowering if the situation became desperate, and the balance we brought forward.

"That evening the mate came forward with his gun, accused us of stealing all his food, and told us to carry it all back to the cabin. We did take a few armloads, but by that time he was drinking again, and wasn't interested.

"That night it breezed up real heavy, and late in the evening the ship lifted several times, swinging head to sea. In this position her motion was easier with the seas breaking their strength directly on the bow, and then rolling along her sides. By this time the vessel was so strained and broken that as the seas rolled by, the whole deck rippled and lifted with their passing. We spent the night in the forecastle dozing and talking. One man was detached for a deck watch in case things took a change for the worse. However, when day broke, the wind eased up a little. By this time the *Gring* was a hopeless wreck. Her masts still stood, but we feared at any moment one might go.

"That morning no fisherman showed up, evidently frightened by the mate's gun. We decided that we might as well leave for there was no hope for the vessel, and the next night might bring anything. Consquently, when that afternoon a boat sailed down, we called him in. Then we informed the mate that we were leaving the ship. He was still drunk and full of bravado. He and the bo'-sun would stay and take care of the schooner.

"Our bags were all packed; we soon got them over the side. Half an hour later we were ashore on Cayo Verdi which is a tiny island about 100 yards across. There were two palm thatched huts and a steel frame light. That night it blew hard again. We expected to see the vessel gone when dawn came, but she was still there. After breakfast, two of the boys sailed down to see how the others had fared.

"The *Gring* had fallen over broadside to the sea, getting a good washing down during the night. The cabin had flooded. Both the mate and the bo'sun were more than glad to leave. We started about noon to sail down to Neuvitas, going inside the reef and through the narrow, swamp channels. We finally arrived about 1:00, bedding down on the dock while one man went up to the consulate.

"It was two weeks before we could leave Neuvitas, during which time we spent making out affidavits, and trying to get a little money for drinks. We were sent back north on two molasses tankers, and our pleasant voyage was finished."

And so deck hand Francis Bowker wrote of the end of the *Helen Barnet Gring*.

CHAPTER III

More 4-Mast Schooners

~~~~~~~~~~~~~~~~~~~~~~~~~~~~~~~~~~~~~~~

ONE OF THE better known schooners along the New England coast was the four-mast *Herbert L. Rawding* which was named after Herbert L. Rawding, formerly Master of Steamers of the Crowell & Thurlow Steamship Company's fleet, and one of a family of five brothers, four of whom were sea captains. He had come from the land that bred windjammer men, Annapolis County, Nova Scotia.

Built by the Atlantic Coast Company of Stockton Springs, Maine, and launched in 1919, the *Rawding* was 1219 gross tons and 201 feet long. Owned by Crowell & Thurlow for the first part of her life, she was employed in the West Indies and coastwise trade, carrying many cargoes of coal from Hampton Roads to Calais, as well as railroad ties, lumber, and the like from southern United States ports to Boston and other New England harbors. She made an occasional deep-water run, and in October, 1920, arrived in Boston 42 days from Lisbon, Portugal, with salt. She also loaded coal from the U.S. to the West Indies, returning with salt or molasses.

In January, 1925, loaded with 1500 tons of salt for Boston, she sprang a leak 100 miles off Cape Henry. A Coast Guard cutter went in search of her, but the four-master was able to work her own way into an anchorage. She received temporary repairs at Norfolk before proceeding. At the end of the year she was one of the schooners to profit from the Miami boom. In late 1927, after she had delivered a cargo of salt from Cabo Rojo, Puerto Rico, at Portland, she caught fire while her crew were trying to thaw out some frozen pipes; damage was slight. March, 1928, found her in Boston with rudder trouble on a passage from Norfolk to Portland.

During the shipping slump which came in the late 1920's, the *Rawding,* which had cost $190,000 to build, was auctioned off in January, 1929, for the paltry sum of $1600. In December she arrived at Boston 35 days from Turks. Three months later she loaded 4500 empty barrels which she took to Puerto Rico, waiting there while they were filled with molasses. Her return from Mayaguez took 19 days.

Not long ago after this she was laid up with the fleet of schooners at Boothbay Harbor, staying there until 1937 when she was purchased by Captain Foss who had her completely done over before sending her back to sea. Although she had been in the mud for several years, she was still in good condition, having only hogged nine inches since she was launched. While dry-docked at Portland, many years growth of barnacles were scraped off her bottom. The *Rawding* was finishing her repairs at Brown's Wharf when it was discovered that her spanker mast was badly rotted. A new spar was made from the fender floating between her and the wharf; it had once been a mast in the five-mast *Oakley C. Curtis.* Much of her rigging had to be renewed, and a full suit of sails were made for her in New York. She was given an auxiliary dynamo to furnish electric light. When she was at last ready for sea, she was probably the finest commercial four-mast schooner in service, almost a new vessel.

Her first run from Portland, sailing on June 9th, took her to Miramichi, New Brunswick, to load lumber for New York. She was now under the command of Captain Rickson, sailing for the Kiraco Transportation Company of New York. The captain's wife and a crew of ten sailed with him. After loading, the *Rawding* headed south, working her way through fogs that blanketed the area. For several days she was 'lost', being two weeks overdue at New York when the fishing trawler *Foam,* out of Boston, sighted her 150 miles off Boston lightship with a distress signal in the rigging as her rudder was disabled. Captain Rickson had been trying to work his way toward Cape Cod through the light airs, but he had not been having much success. The *Foam* called for the Coast Guard, and the cutter *Algonquin* came out to her rescue, supplying the men with food and water which were now almost gone, before towing her into Vineyard Haven.

The end of the year found her arriving at Miami after a trip from Portland. She went on to Mobile. In January, 1938, she sailed to Santiago, Cuba, and some months later to San Juan. In the spring of 1939, Captain Rickson purchased the schooner, planning to use her in the general freighting business, picking up cargoes where they were offered. In May she arrived at Hampton Roads to get coal for Bermuda, but she came too late as a strike broke out, causing her to lose her charter. However, she did take on coal for the island, and took ten days to cross the Stream. Next she went to Haiti, returning to Baltimore on August 7th.

War in Europe brought her several charter offers. In the summer of 1940 she took coal from Norfolk to Martinique, and from there took goat manure to Baltimore. Of late, Captain Winsor Torrey had sailed the *Rawding,* but now Captain Mitchell C. Decker took over. In November she took 2200 tons of coal to Guadeloupe. As she departed from Hampton Roads, the four-mast *Anna R. Heidritter* was in company with her, the first time in ten years that two schooners had left that port on the same day.

The *Rawding* then went on to Las Piedras for fertilizer. Deep laden with 1700 tons in her hold, the four-master headed north for Massachusetts. While rolling heavily in a swell off the Bahamas, she snapped her mizzen topmast which smashed a hatch and part of the railing in its fall. Entering New England waters, she ran into heavy weather, and before the gale had passed she had lost an anchor off Cross Rip Lightship. However, there was no other damage, and she came into Boston on March 22nd, 37 days out.

When discharging was completed, repairs were made to the rigging before departing for Norfolk to take another coal load to Martinique. Now she was chartering at a rate of $8.00 a ton; before the war she would have been lucky if she could have secured $2.25 a ton. Her next charter was salt from Turks to Boston, and then lumber from Sheet Harbor to New York. Against the advice of the mate who had been with the schooner some time, the captain took on a large deck load with the result the schooner had a thirty degree list on either tack, practically drifting to Cape Cod before getting a tow over the Shoals.

For the first time in many years her owners were able to pick and choose their freights, with offers as far distant as South Africa. Thanksgiving Day found her on the road again for Martinique with coal. While she was off the Bahamas, war was declared. The big schooner was creeping through calms, sometimes just rolling under bare poles to save chafing her canvas. On December 21st the windship was approached by an aircraft carrier with her escorts. A crew from the destroyer *U.S.S Stack* boarded the *Rawding* for inspection, to make certain that she was not out there to supply enemy submarines with supplies. Hardly a day went by when aircraft did not come over to take a look at the old windjammer as she slowly worked southward. She arrived at her destination the day after Christmas.

The best part of the winter was spent unloading at the island, and proceeding to Cape Haitien to take on logwood. In February and March of 1942 she beat her way north against the usual heavy northwesters, through the Nazi submarine belt, to Baltimore, taking about five weeks for the run. In September, the *Rawding* again changed hands, now being owned by the Inter-Continental Steamship Company of New York, Captain Decker remaining in command.

Some time before Christmas, she put out from Norfolk heavy with scrap iron in her hold, but when she started leaking badly, she put back to port. Later she was attached by the sheriff on account of unpaid bills; the war boom for windjammers was at an end. For a time it seemed that the *Rawding* would never go to sea again, but a Nova Scotia buyer saw a use for her, and the aging schooner went down east once more.

In the fall of 1946 she was taken to Pictou for a reconversion. Not only was she cut down to a three-mast schooner without topmasts, but heavy diesels were put in below decks, turning her into a motor ship with auxiliary sails. On March 1st, 1947, she chugged out of Halifax for Alexandria and Cyprus with a million feet of lumber. On her maiden voyage she had crossed the Atlantic to France when under Captain Charles Gleason (who was lost when the six-mast *Wyoming* went missing in 1921), but this time she was not to return. After discharging her wood, she loaded salt for Nova Scotia. It was too much for her wooden hull. The engines had shaken her on the voyage over; now the heavy load strained her when she hit the head seas of the Atlantic. Her seams opened up in a gale, and soon water was beyond the control of the pumps.

When the American steamship *Robert Hart* appeared on the scene, the *Rawding's* crew of twelve abandoned her to sink 250 miles west of Cadiz. This was in early June, 1947.

Although the *Rawding* outlived many of her contemporaries, she was never considered a good sailer, and the general opinion of the men who served before her mast was that she had two feet too little beam for her length, so that when she was light or carried a deck load, she was 'the crankiest thing that ever put to sea'. One of her sailors once wrote: 'The *Herbert L. Rawding* has her virtues but speed is definitely not one of them'. Perhaps it is remarkable that she lasted so long.

James E. Newsom

A fine example of the Maine shipbuilder's art was the four-mast *James E. Newsom* which was built in 1919 at Boothbay Harbor by the East Coast Ship Company. Not a large vessel, she was 671 gross tons and 178 feet long, being considered one of the best of her class. Part of the Crowell & Thurlow fleet for many years, she was named after a Boston fruit and produce merchant.

Even before she was launched, she was chartered to carry 700,-000 feet of lumber from Boston to Buenos Aires at $50 per 1000 feet. She first hit the water on August 23rd, fully rigged and ready for sea; she arrived in Boston two days later. She sailed south on September 19th, arriving at her South American destination in 67 days.

Her earlier years were spent in tramping up and down the East Coast. Some of her runs were good, others poor. In January, 1923, she was listed as overdue on a passage from Paramaribo, Dutch Guiana, to Mobile, but she finally turned up after fighting head winds all the way. The Florida real estate boom made work for her although it very nearly ended her as well. Early in 1926, the *Newsom,* arriving off Miami deeply loaded with 710,000 feet of lumber, found that a harbor blockade was on, forcing her to anchor outside for several weeks. On February 10th, she started up the Government Channel, but she had not gone far when she suddenly grounded on the bottom, blocking at least half the channel with her hull, and threatening to swing around and completely shut the channel to all shipping. With help of tugs and the Coast Guard, she was pulled free, but her rudder post was so strained she started leaking faster than the pumps could work. She grounded again in nineteen feet of water.

After some of the cargo had been removed, she was towed back to the waiting anchorage where still more lumber was taken off by lighters. On the 16th, squally weather struck the badly water-logged craft, sending seas over her low bows, the swell sweeping across her decks. Bits of bulwark were smashed away as she slowly dragged into the surf, pounding on the bottom. When it did not seem possible for the schooner to survive, the crew of eight were taken off by the local pilot boat, leaving the vessel to her fate.

However, her strong construction saw her through the ordeal; she was eventually towed clear to be repaired.

Crowell & Thurlow sold the *Newsom* in October, 1928, and she went under the British flag, being owned in Nova Scotia. In later years, to dodge Canadian taxes, her port of registry became Bridgetown, Barbados, although she continued to operate in the Nova Scotian trade, generally lumber south to U.S. ports or to the British West Indies, returning north with salt or coal, and sometimes in ballast.

On occasion she had minor troubles, but she always weathered the crises successfully. In April, 1935, she grounded when bound from Halifax to New York, coming off undamaged. Later, when on her way north with coal for Prince Edward Island, she was damaged in a collision; after repairs at Port Hawksbury, she was able to continue her passage. Another time, she got too close to shoal water off the East Chop near Vineyard Haven, having to anchor until the Coast Guard could tow her back to the the channel. Once she lost her rudder in wintery seas off Cape Sable when bound from Turks to Liverpool, Nova Scotia, drifting helplessly until a Canadian Government steamer could come to her rescue.

In 1934, the *Newsom* took a cargo of lumber from Port Williams, N.S., to Preston, England, crossing the Atlantic in the early fall in 38 days. From England she went to Turks for salt, and took 26 days from there to Lunenburg. Her whole voyage had taken four months and four days. Three years later she made another Atlantic crossing. Sailing from Halifax on July 4th, 1937, she arrived at Preston on August 3rd, 30 days out. After discharging, she went to Swansea for coal. She took 49 days to sail back against the Westerlies to Charlottetown.

A few other passages of the *Newsom* were as below:

1936—arrived St. John October 15th; 5 days from New York.

arrived St. John December 1st; 7 days from New York.

1937—arrived St. John May 12th; 8 days from New York.

1938—arrived Turks Island April 16th; 12 days from Lunenburg.

arrived Lunenburg May 14th; 17 days from Turks Island.

arrived New York September 18th; 19 days from Lunenburg.

arrived Halifax October 28th; 7 days from New York.

1939—arrived Barbados February 14th; 18 days from Lunenburg.

arrived Lunenburg July 5th; 19 days from Turks Island.

The *Newsom* kept to her usual runs when the war broke out,

finding no lack of cargoes. However, early in 1942, when loaded with salt from Turks for Nova Scotia, she was caught by a German submarine. After the four-master's crew had taken to their lifeboat, the Nazis hit the schooner several times with gun fire. Then the Germans discovered that the windship men in the boat had no oars, sails, water nor food, and that in their haste to abandon ship, they had even forgotten the battery for the boat engine. The sub towed them back to the sinking schooner so they could get some supplies, but as the cabins were already flooded, they were unable to get food or the battery. The Germans gave them a case of rations.

Sometime later, the castaways were picked up near Bermuda.

Josephine A. McQuesten

The big four-mast schooner *Josephine A. McQuesten* was the last sailing ship built by the Cobb yards at Rockland, Maine. She was 1607 gross tons and 230 feet long, a good deal larger than quite a few of the five-mast schooners of her period. She was an excellent carrier with good capacity. In January, 1930, she arrived in Boston from Jacksonville with a million switch railroad ties.

The *McQuesten* spent the greater part of her active life in the coastal trade. She was a lucky vessel, seldom in trouble. However, in May, 1924, she dragged her anchor while in Boston Harbor, fouling the five-masted *Edward B. Winslow*. Damage was slight, though, as she only carried away part of her railing and a stay.

Crowell & Thurlow layed up the four-master at Eastport in the early 1930's. In 1936 she was sold to Esthonian interests who renamed her *Viktor*. After refitting, she departed from Eastport for her new home. However, she did not last long. When 31 days out, she was wrecked on Shillay Island in the Sound of Harris, becoming a total loss.

J. W. Clise

The *J. W. Clise* was one of the smaller West Coast schooners, being 845 gross tons and 185 feet long. Built by the Globe Navigation Company at Ballard, Washington, in 1904, she was operated by them for several years in the coastwise trade. Later she was owned by the Port Blakeley Mill Company of San Francisco who used her in their lumber trade.

Towards the end of World War I, the *Clise* went under the

Norwegian flag, her port of registry becoming **Porsgrund, Nor-**
way. However, she was under the American flag again in 1922,
now registered at Mobile, Alabama. A year or two later, she was
taken over by the Putnam Lumber Company of Jacksonville, who
put her in the East Coast lumber trade. Although the *Clise* made
many runs to New England waters in the years following, the
majority of her passages were south to the West Indies, Barbados,
Puerto Rico, Martinique, and the like.

For the most part she kept well clear of trouble. In the spring
of 1924 she caused concern when she was four weeks and more between Portland and Jacksonville, but she came in eventually after
fighting head winds and bad weather much of the way.

The *Clise* came to her end in August, 1940, when she was
struck by a terrific gale in the Gulf of Mexico. She was so terribly
battered by the seas and the wind, so badly strained, that she was
not worth saving. Not long after her crew of seven were taken off,
she foundered. According to the U.S. Printing Office, she went
down in Latitude 26° 50' North, Longitude 88° 10' West.
West.

Some average passages follow:
1936—arrived Bermuda September 12th; 18 days from Jacksonville.
1937—arrived Portland October 26th; 13 days from Jacksonville.
arrived Jacksonville December 21st; 9 days from Bermuda.

Laura Annie Barnes

The four-mast schooner *Laura Annie Barnes* was constructed
in Phippsburg, Maine, in 1921, by Frank S. Bowker & Sons. A
medium sized vessel of 642 gross tons and 181 feet long, she was
built to the order of Captain Charles H. Barnes, of Salem, who
operated her successfully for many years along the Atlantic seaboard in general trade. There were a few occasions when she found
herself in trouble. In October, 1925, she was picked up by the
Coast Guard in a badly leaking condition. Towed into the Brandy-
wine Shoals, she was turned over to a tug that brought her into
port. She was busy during that Florida land boom, and managed
to keep going in the years that followed.

In March, 1930, Captain Barnes sold her to Captain Publicover to replace the *Joan Keilburg* which had been destroyed by
fire some time earlier. The *Barnes* sailed north with a cargo of
anthracite coal for Bridgewater. In November, 1931, she was given

a considerable overhaul aloft, the mizzen mast being spliced, and a new masthead installed. Captain Publicover put his schooner in trade between Nova Scotia and New Haven, taking baled pulp south and returning north with coal from New York, or light; only occasionally did she vary this run; below are a few of her typical passages:

1934—arrived Halifax June 5th; 11 days from City Island.

1936—arrived New Haven April 27th; 22 days from Bridgewater, N.S.

arrived Boston August 5th; 9 days from Bridgewater.

1937—arrived La Have November 20th; 10 days from New York.

1938—arrived New Haven February 7th; 4 days from La Have.

The last voyage of the *Barnes* began in January, 1939, when she sailed from Lunenburg for New Haven with $10,000 worth of wood pulp. From the start, the winds were against her, bitterly cold and biting, causing her to beat her way down the coast. Shortly after daybreak on January 17th, Captain Publicover was trying to pick his way over the Nantucket Shoals, searching for the buoys in the thick, cold mists that covered the water. Without warning, the schooner suddenly shuddered all over and stopped; she was aground in nine feet of water, and she drew fourteen. She was fast on Tuckernuck Shoal, four miles S.S.E. of the Cross Rip Lightship in Nantucket Sound.

The weather was calm, and at first there was no cause for alarm. In the late afternoon, the Coast Guard patrol boat *Thetis* came out from Woods Hole, and at high water attempted to pull the schooner free, but without success. On the following morning, Wednesday, a strong easterly breeze sprang up, bringing thick snow and rising seas that began pounding the schooner as she lay completely exposed to the elements. The cutter *General Green* joined the *Thetis,* the two straining in the rising gale to move the wooden schooner on an exceptionally high tide. A line fouled the *Thetis's* propeller, putting her out of action for a short time, but the *Green* kept right at work, even budging the four-master some 16 feet; it was not enough. Late Wednesday afternoon, the seams of the *Barnes* began to open up, letting water into her hold. As it was not considered safe to remain on the schooner during the night, the Captain and his six men were moved to the *Thetis*. Shortly after dark the large Coast Guard cutter *Tahoe* came on the scene, but she was too late for the winter gale was already smashing the wreck. By Thursday morning, the decks of the *Barnes* were awash, and it was impossible to board her. Waves were crashing their might against her sides, crushing in her deck house, wrenching free the bulwarks of the beautiful vessel. The 40 mile-an-hour gale soon reduced her to a worthless hulk, a total loss. She was insured for $5000, only a part of her value.

The *Barnes* had been a fine vessel, and well suited for the trade that Captain Publicover employed her in. She was a handy schooner, needing only six men in her crew. She was the last commercial schooner on the Atlantic coast to set a "queen staysail", one of her original sails which says much to the credit of those sail makers of another day.

The *Barnes* did not remain in sight long after stranding. Another gale on January 30th finished her off, smashing her to bits. Some weeks later the Coast Guard destroyed the floating section of a wooden vessel found twenty miles off Nauset Beach, Cape Cod; it was believed to have been the end of the *Barnes*.

Lillian E. Kerr

One of the finest three-mast schooners ever built on the East Coast was the *Lillian E. Kerr,* which was launched from the yards of E. James Tull at Pocomoke City, Maryland, in 1920. She was very strongly constructed, there being only a few of her type which could compare with her in strength. However, she was not a fast vessel, and one of her crew claimed that it took a gale to move her; in a half gale she would go sideways, he added. She was a large three-master, being 458 gross tons and 160 feet long.

She was built to the order of J. W. Somerville who had a small fleet of three- and four-mast schooners which he operated in World War I. Later the Kerr changed hands, going to C.A. & B.F. Small Corporation of New York in the 1920's, working coastwise and anywhere else she could find cargos. In 1937 she was sold to Captain J. L. Publicover, changing to Canadian registry when her home port became Dublin Shore, Nova Scotia. When the Canadians put her into the West Indies trade, they felt that she was too heavy to be a three-master, so re-rigged her as a four-mast schooner; it improved her speed, and made her an easier vessel for her crews.

The *Kerr* had numerous adventures through the years, but perhaps the strangest one took place when she was still new, in November, 1921. During a voyage north from Jacksonville with lumber, Captain George W. Pope, her skipper, was challenged to a duel by one of the crew, a West Indian. While Mrs. Pope took the wheel, her husband managed to wound the native. When the vessel arrived at the Boston anchorage, the Captain and mate hurried ashore to report to authorities, leaving the brave Mrs. Pope on board in charge with a gun. The wounded man was later taken ashore to the hospital.

In recent years the *Kerr* was kept fairly busy. Although she was laid up much of 1933, she was on the move again a year later, running lumber from North Carolina to New York. In 1935, when filled with wood, she was caught in a November gale off Cape Henry. At first her captain thought he could weather the blow at sea, but high waves crashing across her rails pounded her deck cargo from its lashings, tearing at the rigging. In the end, the schooner had to be towed into port. In 1936 the *Kerr* gave up the southern lumber trade, going to Nova Scotian ports instead. In June of that year, she was 14 days from Halifax to New York, an average run for the *Kerr*. On August 18th, 1937, she departed from Portland, Maine, bound for Dublin Shores. After crawling across the Gulf of Maine, she ran into a fierce autumn storm that drove her ashore at East La Have; she was twenty days out at the time. Damage was slight, the *Kerr*'s strong hull absorbing the pounding. After this, she took a load of lumber to Turks Island, returning with salt.

In April, 1938, the *Kerr* had her rig altered at Robar's Shipyard at Dayspring. Her first run as a four-master took her to Barbados with lumber; she was about 36 days on passage from Weymouth. Then she sailed to Turks to load salt for Nova Scotia. She was somewhere off Cape Hatteras on September 21st, 1938, when the infamous hurricane of that year came sweeping up the Atlantic with all its fury and might. There was no shelter for the schooner; all she could do was ride it out. The terrific wind tore at her furled sails, ripping some to shreds. Mountainous seas towered on all sides, and it never seemed possible that the schooner could survive, but once again her strong hull saw her safely through the ordeal, the only damage being to her canvas. After repairs, she was layed up for the winter at La Have

Although Captain Publicover had intended to run the *Kerr* in the West Indies trade, he had to change these plans when he lost his *Laura Annie Barnes* which had built up a lucrative business between Nova Scotia and New Haven. The Captain replaced her with the *Kerr*, and from then on she came south with lumber to the Connecticut port, returning sometimes via New York with coal.

Few of her runs were outstanding although in January, 1942, she made a round trip in 14 days, including her discharge time. For a windship, she was generally clear of trouble. Once in January, 1940, when awaiting a wind in Nantucket Sound, she was very nearly set ashore by drifting ice; a Coast Guard cutter took her into the safety of Vineyard Haven harbor. A year later she had another close call when she was hit by a heavy mid-winter northwester off Cape Ann. Loaded with wood pulp, she was driven offshore by the gale. At the height of the storm, the Captain found that they were not too far from the dangerous Georges Bank, a lee shoal for the schooner. As she began to crawl away from the shallows, her headstay let go, leaving her in a very bad spot, especially as the weather had not let up. The crew fought their way forward over the icy decks, and somehow they managed to make repairs in the face of the bitter gale. With sail on again, the *Kerr* edged away from the danger. Before she made New Haven, a second storm caught her, forcing her to shelter at Vineyard Haven. She was nine days out from Lunenburg by this time with her provisions gone. However, once the weather cleared, it was a quick run down the Sounds.

In November, 1942, the *Kerr* loaded coal at New York, and after a few days in port, she sailed for Halifax. Although most vessels travelled in convoy at this time, the *Kerr*, using only the wind to move her, sailed on her own. The weather was good, the winds right, and it seemed as if she would make a fair passage home.

It was approaching midnight on November 12th when the lookout on the *Kerr* sighted a convoy bearing down on them. Her lights were lit so there would be no doubt about her being sighted; even blacked-out, her white sails could have been seen as visibility was perfect. In the convoy was the steamer *Alcoa Pilot*. Her lookout sighted the sailing ship far ahead at ten minutes to twelve, reporting her to the bridge. At midnight, when the watches changed, the new lookout was shown the windjammer, and to be on the safe side, he, too, reported her. Still the *Alcoa Pilot* kept her course. The Commodore of the convoy was aboard the *Cyrus Field,* a cable ship. When he sighted the *Kerr,* he shifted his course so the *Alcoa Pilot* could swing away from the schooner. But she never did; with a sickening crash she plowed into the *Kerr* by the foremast, cutting her very nearly in two. Her coal cargo took the windship down like a stone.

The *Alcoa Pilot* steamed on while the *Cyrus Field* was ordered to put back to pick up survivors. One man, John P. Richard, Captain Publicover's son-in-law, was found still afloat; he had been in the cold water for 55 minutes. He died soon after he was taken aboard the steamer. Not one man of the crew of seven were saved. They had gone down on Friday, November 13th.

By a strange coincidence, the *Alcoa Pilot* was owned at one time by J. W. Somerville, the same man who had had the *Kerr* built.

Mabel A. Frye

The *Mabel A. Frye* was the last of the large schooners which the Frye, Flynn Company of Harrington, Maine, built. Launched on Thanskgiving Day, 1920, she was a fine four-master of 1151 gross tons and 193 feet long. After some finishing touches in Boston, she set off on her maiden voyage on December 18th, bound for Hampton Roads to load coal, less than a month after hitting the water.

During the next few years she was employed in the coastal trade, taking charters when and where her owners, Crowell & Thurlow, could find them. At the end of February, 1925, she sailed from Searsport for a coal cargo at Norfolk. A week out put her no further than Boston; she just could not get around the Cape owing to the weather. When her captain became sick, her managers became disgusted, so gave up the coal charter, and had the schooner towed to Portsmouth to load fertilizer for Charleston, South Carolina. The four-master continued active until the end of the 1920's when she was laid up at Boothbay Harbor.

Still in good condition in April, 1936, she was put up for sale at a Marshall's auction to cover her expenses. She was purchased by Captain Alexander Rodway of Newfoundland who planned to use her in the general trade, perhaps salt fish to Europe, returning with salt from Spain or Portugal, lumber to the West Indies, and salt or coal returning. In July she made a run to Turks Island before going north to Newfoundland.

Her end came in October of that same year. Loaded with coal, the *Frye* was bound from Sydney for Bay Roberts, Newfoundland. She had not been out long when she ran into a severe gale, one of those early winter storms that occasionally sweep the area. The shrieking wind whipped the sails to shreds; the huge, angry seas caused such rolling that her masts could not stand the strain so they went by the board in a tangle of wreckage. After five days of beating, the seams gradually opened, letting in the ocean. The crew manned her pumps but these were soon choked, clogged with coal dust. By now the crew were desperate as it was obvious that their vessel with seven feet of water sloshing in her hold would not stay afloat much longer. Then, out of the stormy dusk, came the *S.S. American Banker* in response to the sinking schooner's flares. As the *Frye's* own small boats had been smashed by the seas, the steamer dropped a lifeboat in command of Chief Officer Theodore Christensen. They worked their way over the curling waters to the four-master, picked off the entire crew safely, and returned to their ship.

The *Frye* was left at 44° 44' North, 45° 35' West on October 3rd, 1936. She must have gone down very shortly afterwards.

M. Vivian Peirce

Named after the daughter of Edward Peirce of Boston, the four-mast schooner *M. Vivian Peirce* was launched in July, 1919, from the yard of the Atlantic Coast Company in Thomaston, Maine. A sturdy vessel of 1511 gross tons and 224 feet long, she was chartered to make her maiden voyage from Baltimore to Genoa with coal. In December she got an order to take 750,000 feet of lumber at $45 per thousand feet from a Gulf port to Buenos Aires.

In March 1921, the *Peirce* caused her owners much concern when she departed from Norfolk on the 15th, bound for Portland, and was then unsighted during the next ten days. However, early in April she arrived after being blown offshore for a spell. She was not always slow. In January, 1924, she sailed from Perth Amboy to Jacksonville in six days from port to port. Under Captain Ernest J. Peirce, who was temporarily relieving Captain A. B. Chaney, she drove southward at her top speed. In 29½ hours, from 6:30 a.m. New Year's Day to noon on the second, she covered 330 miles, averaging better than 11 knots.

After sailing from Baltimore for Tampa with a cargo of bricks on October 10th, 1926, the *Peirce* was struck by a hurricane on the 21st. Hove to, she was driven far off her course, but in spite of the terrific winds and mountainous seas, she was little damaged. She put into the Bahamas on the 27th for supplies and minor repairs before proceeding.

[47]

She made another slow passage in early 1927 when she arrived at Boston on February 8th, nearly a month out from New Orleans with 33,700 creosoted railroad ties. A sister schooner, the *William H. Harriman,* had left New Orleans ten days after the Peirce, and had arrived a day ahead of her.

The *Peirce* was sold at auction for $2400 to the Superior Trading and Transportation Company of Boston in January, 1931. They renamed her *Edward L. Swan,* keeping her in the same coastal runs. In 1932 she was sent to La Vela de Coro, Venezuela, to take on 2100 tons of fertilizer to replace a cargo which was lost when the *Charles D. Stanford* went missing. On her way north, she put into Key West for coal, water, and repairs to her pumps. She arrived at Boston on August 19th, 45 days out from Venezuela.

As the *Swan,* she continued to work until late 1936. Then the end came very suddenly. She was in dry-dock at Perth Amboy, New Jersey, for scraping and painting when she rolled over. She was so damaged, she was not worth repairing. Her hulk was later made into a breakwater at Astoria, Long Island.

Passages:
1934—arrived Le Vela de Coro May 17th; 38 days from New York.
1935—arrived New York October 29th; 10 days from Georgetown.
    arrived Eastport, Maine, December 18th; 20 days from Philadelphia.

Reine Marie Stewart

The *Reine Marie Stewart* was launched in 1919 as a four-mast barkentine of 1307 gross tons and 218 feet long. Her builders, who were also her owners for many years, were Dunn & Eliot Company of Thomaston, Maine. She was a well constructed vessel with good material throughout, her original cost being around $210,000. Her earlier years were spent mostly in coastwise trade, although it is said that she also made a run to Greece with coal. However, her square-rig requiring more of a crew than a plain fore-and-after, probably caused her to be laid up before her time, and for many years she was moored in Thomaston harbor, a mecca for camera fans and artists.

In 1932 plans were made to send her to sea for the West African Trading Company, but reconditioning probably proved too expensive, and she remained at the wharf. When it seemed likely that she would stay there the rest of her days, she was purchased by Captain R. S. MacLean of Chatham, Nova Scotia, in July, 1937.

She left her birth port on August 2nd in charge of two small tugs that took her down the river for the first time in ten years, towing her across to Yarmouth for a complete overhaul. After she had been put on the marine railway, five truck loads of weeds and barnacles were scraped off her bottom before caulking and painting. She was re-rigged as a four-mast schooner to make her easier to handle. Her new fore-mast was one of the masts from the five-mast *Mary H. Diebold* which was being broken up at Eastport then. Most of her standing rigging was renewed as the old had aged during the years of wind, sun, and rain without care. When she was ready for sea at Halifax, where the last of the work was completed, she was in fine condition, as good as when launched.

She began her new lease of life on February 22nd, 1938, when she departed from Halifax for Turks Island. She took twenty days for the passage. There she loaded 1900 tons of salt before sailing for Boston on March 23rd. All went well over the first miles of the course, but as the schooner approached Vineyard Sound she ran into a severe gale and blinding snow storm, the worst weather that Captain MacLean had ever experienced. As she was working in for an anchorage off Vineyard Haven on April 8th, her mainsail split with a roar as the canvas went to ribbons, causing her to fall off. Shortly after dark, just as she was reaching calmer waters, the big schooner touched bottom, sliding to a halt. Winds of more than fifty miles-an-hour screamed through her rigging, and the seas, whipped to fury, beat against her hull, sending sheets of spray sweeping across her decks. The Coast Guard cutter *Faunce* stood out to the *Stewart's* rescue, but as it was too rough to go alongside, she could only heave to while awaiting better weather.

Fortunately, the schooner had struck sand; there were no rocks to chew her bottom to bits. On the 9th, at high water, the *Faunce* got a line aboard the wrecked vessel, towing her off shortly afterwards with little effort, and leaving her safely anchored to wait out a fog that had settled over the Sound. Monday, April 11th, broke clear and fresh, giving the schooner a chance to make up for lost time as she sped before a strong south westerly breeze at twelve knots, white foam breaking around her dark bows while she plowed through the blue waters off Cape Cod. As she swept by Highland Light, another sail was carried away by an extra strong squall; this was real sailing. She came into Boston Harbor on April 12th, 20 days out.

After discharging, she proceeded to Hampton Roads to load

coal, sailing from there on May 20th for Guadaloupe. This run took 21 days. Her next port was Turks. On June 27th she grounded on Man of War Shallows on the eastern end of Anegada, but with the help of a fishing boat, she got clear without damage. The voyage north was uneventful although as she approached Nova Scotia in thick fog, she went aground once more, this time near Yarmouth. She got free only to ground again. When she finally made port and had her cargo taken out, her underbody was examined to find the extent of the damage. It was found that repair costs would be as high as $10,000, so the four-master was left on the mud flats off Yarmouth with the tides running in and out of her holed bottom. Later she was towed up the Bay to be beached beyond Metaghan. An unexpected gale drove her still higher up the beach, and now once more it seemed certain that she had arrived at the end of her active span. She was well ashore in poor condition. The war, however, called her back again to sea. Repairs were made, a refit completed.

Her new owners, the Shepard Steamship Company, loaded her in New York for East Africa. Setting out in the early summer of 1942, she was well on her way when she became becalmed south of the Line. For some reason, her captain decided to turn back. For three weeks the *Stewart* drifted off Dakar, waiting for a breeze. One day a British man-of-war came alongside to suggest that they get to other waters where there was less submarine activity. But without wind, the *Stewart* was helpless. A few days later a German submarine popped up, and that was the end. After the crew had left the *Stewart* in her long boat, the Nazis shelled the beautiful schooner to the bottom.

Sally Persis Noyes

Built by Frye Flynn Company of Harrington in 1918, the *Sally Persis Noyes* was a fine four-mast schooner of 1034 gross tons and 187 feet long. One of the Crowell & Thurlow fleet, she spent her first years chiefly in coastal trade carrying lumber and coal.

She was an able vessel which was well proved in January, 1922, when she arrived at Boston, 24 days out from Cockburn Harbor, Turks Island, with 43,528 bushels of salt. Although she had had to fight gales, high seas and strong winds the entire way, her cargo was bone dry in spite of the pounding that she had taken. She had a good turn of speed, too. One Friday in November, 1925, she left Norfolk with 1600 tons of coal. She passed out by Cape

Henry the same day, and Monday afternoon was beating her way up the Penobscot River to Fort Point, near Bangor, 3½ days out, having come up the coast in steamboat time. When the shipping slump came, she was one of the group of lonely schooners that found their way to Boothbay Harbor to lay up.

The *Noyes,* however, was not to be left alone for long. In 1932 she was purchased by Robert L. Royall who planned to turn her into a New England nautical school, renaming her *Constellation.* According to advertisements that appeared at the time, she was completely rebuilt and equipped as a training ship during 1932 and 1933, being 'especially planned for health, comfort and safety at sea'. She was given 'modern sanitary plumbing, steam heat, electricity, mechanical refrigeration, modern galley, spacious dining saloon, lounge, library, large staterooms with wide upper and lower berths, closets, hot and cold running water, and electric lights, ventilated storage rooms for luggage; spacious awning deck . . . . steam power for handling heavy sails, pumps, boats, anchors, etc.' She was given a new suit of sails. Captain Armstead Rust, U.S.N. (retired), former Superintendent of the Massachusetts Nautical School, and Captain of the schoolship *Nantucket,* was to be her commander. Cadets were to pay $125 to $175 per month, and a cruise was laid out to take the vessel through the West Indies.

In spite of the best laid plans, nothing seems to have come of them for less than a year later the four-master was up for sale. She was in excellent condition at this time. The noted marine writer Mark Hennessey wrote that she 'must be recognized as the queen in her class under American registry'. It was unfortunate that such a fine vessel could not have been made to pay for her upkeep. A great deal of money was spent in overhauling her. Her thirty large staterooms had ample accomodations for fifty passengers. She would have been an ideal cruise-ship, but there was just no interest.

She left Boothbay Harbor in 1936, proceeding to New York. August 20th saw her putting out to sea on a treasure hunt, taking divers who were to attempt to recover the gold lost on the sunken Ward liner *Merida* off Cape Charles. However, it was not a successful trip. Storms drove her away from the wreck, and nitroglycerine stored in her forward hold began to give her crew anxious moments. During her run back to New York before a storm, she touched 16 knots, passing one coastwise passenger liner en route. She made port on September 3rd. There she stayed as the years passed; it appeared that she would never put to sea again. Then came World War II.

With the demand for ships at its peak, the *Constellation* was reconverted back into a cargo vessel. Her expensive interior, hardly used as intended, was ripped out to make more carrying space. Her new owners, the American Intercontinental Steamship Company, had her ready for sea in the late spring of 1943. With 2000 tons of cargo, she set out on what was to be her last voyage. She had not been out long when her steam pumping gear broke down; her captain decided to make Bermuda for repairs. They were off the island on July 30th. During a flat calm, while awaiting a breeze and a pilot, the schooner was swept onto a hidden reef by the current, becoming a total loss. The U.S. Navy was able to salvage a considerable amount of the cargo, including 700 cases of whiskey, but they could do nothing for the ill-fated four-master.

Snetind.

Probably the last commercial four-mast schooner to ever be in Boston Harbor was the *Snetind,* a large schooner built by the J. H. Price Shipbuilding Corporation of Seattle, Washington in 1919. Like so many of the West Coast vessels, she was not particularly good looking, being rather on the heavy side. Her poop was much higher than those of East Coast vessels, making a steep walk-up from the main deck to the wheel aft. She was 1470 gross tons and 234 feet long.

First owned by the Mykrona Navigation Corporation, she came around to the East Coast not long after launching, and by the early 1920's had changed hands, her new owners being J. W. Gorman of Boston who employed her in the lumber and coal trades. A New England building boom brought her north from Mobile with a million feet of wood in May, 1922. In early January, 1923, when bound for Boston from Norfolk with 2300 tons of coal for the 'Boston & Maine', she was caught off Cape Cod in a heavy midwinter gale. After his schooner's headsails had been ripped away by the shrieking wind, Captain John Gilchrist was forced to anchor his vessel by the Peaked Hill bars near the tip of the Cape, a badly exposed position. However, a short time later the Coast Guard cutter *Tampa,* arriving on the scene, took the *Snetind* in tow, first to shelter in Provincetown, and later on to Boston.

The schooner's sailing days came to an end in 1928. In November, 1927, she had departed from Norfolk with Bangor, Maine, her destination; 2209 tons of coal were in her hold. She was hardly off the Virginia Capes when she met exceptionally heavy weather which ripped her canvas, and brought part of her rigging down. She got a tow back to her port of departure. After six weeks of repairs, she again started north. When she was ten days out, it was found that her coal, which had been in her hold for three months, had overheated, and was blazing in the after sections. Captain Gray, who was now in command, took his schooner into Province-town where two tugs, one a naval vessel, managed to bring the fire under control, but not before considerable damage had been done. The foot of the mainmast was completely burnt away, only the deck and the stays holding up the spar. Much of the interior of the hull was destroyed. A tug took the schooner into Boston. After her cargo was discharged, a cement block was placed under the mainmast. The schooner was laid up.

As the years passed, the *Snetind* sat by a wharf in East Boston, but she was not quite alone as the owners had permitted a woman and her son to live aboard. In January, 1936, when the owners decided to scuttle the schooner at sea as they felt she was of no fur-ther use, merely running up wharfage bills, the couple on board refused to leave their home. A legal battle began which filled the local newspapers. To save money, the owners towed the four-master into the harbor where they anchored her, and then turned over all rights to the woman on board. A month later, a howling westerly gale drove the old *Snetind* across the anchorage in the dark of night. Morning found her hard aground on Spectacle Island where she remained fast.

The couple stayed with the schooner until the war came along. By that time the vessel was in a poor state with the tides rising and falling through her seams. Her masts stayed erect until late 1947 when someone began to salvage them. In 1948 a fire did still fur-her damage, but it did not matter. In July, 1951, the rotting hulk was towed to sea to be scuttled in deep water off Boston Light.

Theoline

Probably the last active four-mast schooner to carry 'Boston' on her stern was the fine *Theoline*, a vessel of 594 gross tons and 172 feet long. Built in 1917 by F. Cobb at Rockland, Maine, for Crowell & Thurlow, she should not be confused with two earlier vessels of the same name. The first was launched in 1900 at Belfast, and was 587 tons; the second took to the water in 1905, also at Belfast, and was the largest of the three, being 981 tons. The first two did not remain long in the registry.

The maiden voyage of the third *Theoline* took her from Rockland to New York where she loaded coal for Calais, Maine. She then crossed the Atlantic to England with a lumber cargo. At the end of the first World War, the *Theoline* carried on in the coastal trade, from Florida and Georgia to Boston at first, and later to New England ports from the British provinces.

In 1928 she was sold to F. B. McQueston who had also owned the first *Theoline*. However, he did not keep her long for less than a year later she was taken over by C.A.&B.F. Small of Machias; they operated her for eleven years. With Captain Latty in command, she ran around from St. John to Halifax where she took on laths for Philadelphia. From there she proceeded to Norfolk, loading coal for Jonesport. Next she entered the Bay of Fundy to pick up pile wood at Apple River, taking it to New York City. Thus she tramped up and down the coast, loading when and where she could find cargoes. When she had the right wind, she showed that she had a good turn of speed, but more times than not, she fought head winds or calms, adding days to her passages.

She was a fairly lucky ship, but now and then she found herself in trouble. In October, 1930, when she was leaving Norfolk with 1001 tons of fertilizer, she struck a shoal, opening up so fast her pumps were unable to cope with the inflow of water. She finally settled on the bottom with her decks just awash at high tide. After 300 tons of her cargo had been dug out, extra pumps helped to refloat her, and she was put into dry-dock for re-caulking before discharging the remainder of her load. Up until this accident, the *Theoline* had had a slight list to starboard, but so much fertilizer had been forced between the port layers, she took on a perpetual list that she never lost.

In October, 1934, the *S.S. Empire State* of the New York Merchant Marine Academy found the four-master drifting helplessly at sea with her steering gear damaged. The schoolship took the *Theoline* in tow, turning her over to the Coast Guard cutter *Mendota* who took her into Norfolk for repairs. In 1937, when she was in tow down the James River near Newport News at night, her tug took her beneath the bridge without stopping to check heights. With a splintering roar, her four topmasts were snapped off. The two men on deck on watch dove under the wheel for protection as the upper rigging came tumbling down about them.

[54]

Captain Crynor, who now had the vessel, came racing on deck to find out what the trouble was. One look was enough; he turned and went below, and as he turned in for the rest of the night, he calmly called across to his cook: 'Cleaned the topmasts out of her, Jim!' A few days later, after the mess had been cleaned up, but without topmasts, the *Theoline* romped from Newport News to Eastport in 114 hours, fast stepping indeed for the four-master.

That same year the *Theoline* took a cargo of pulp paper from St. George, New Brunswick, to Albany. The schooner was towed up the Hudson from New York City, doing the short trip in forty hours. She was undoubtedly one of the last windjammers to visit that river port. After being towed back down the river, she loaded coal for Deer Island.

Captain Crynor was one of the outstanding coasting skippers, a fine sailor himself, a gentleman, and well liked by his crews. Sometimes when in port, he would wander forward to the forecastle to join the boys in a hand of cards, and if the forecastle was too crowded or cold, he would invite the hands aft to his own quarters. He was a man who got the best out of his vessel, but who knew when his ship was taking too much. As one of his crew once said, Captain Crynor would not tack and tack against a head wind, but he would sneak in close to shore behind a rock, anchoring until he could make his course again. A forecastle hand wrote: 'Crynor took us over the Nantucket Shoals without bothering to look at the compass in the wettest, thickest fog yet. Just gave me each course as we passed the buoys. Shortly after I turned in, I heard him let the anchor go — couldn't think why he had anchored in the middle of the shoals. When the fog lifted, there was the Vineyard breakwater two hundred yards away.'

In 1940 Captain Edward Long took over the *Theoline.* By now she was badly run-down; there had been no money for repairs. Steamers had taken over most of her trades, and she had been lucky to get an occasional coal charter, remaining at anchor at Jonesport the rest of the time. Captain Long did what he could for the ship. Not only did he work on her hull, but when he noticed a rotten bit in the mainmast, he dug it out, put in new wood, and bound the patch with a steel sleeve. He de-loused the ship so she was perfectly clean; that, in itself was a big undertaking.

Then the schooner was sent south for another trip of coal. When she left Jonesport, there was no wind, and she just drifted. Later, after a breeze came, she could not sail because her bottom was so foul with grass and marine growth. With their schooner unreported after three weeks at sea, the owners became worried, asking the Coast Guard to keep an eye out for her. However, she was perfectly safe, eventually crawling into Norfolk 28 days out from Maine.

Back at Jonesport, the *Theoline* was again laid up in the harbor. The general impression along the waterfront was that she had made her last passage under sail; she was finished, they thought. Nevertheless, with war times making an ever increasing call for ship bottoms, a Boston group felt the schooner was worth repairing. The four-master now made one of the slowest passages of her career. She was ordered from Jonesport to Meteghan, Nova Scotia, forty miles away, where she could have her bottom scraped before loading lumber for New York. She was to be completely overhauled in New York upon arrival there. She sailed from Jonesport on April 16th, at one in the afternoon. There was very little breeze, and the schooner would hardly steer as there was so much weed clinging to her hull below the waterline. When the zephyrs came ahead early on the 17th, she was forced to anchor as she was uselessly beating. At noon on the 18th the breeze swung again, and the schooner got underway, passing Grand Manan. On the 19th she had to anchor once more, now near Briar Island. In time she came to the Meteghan buoy. A small ferry boat tried to tow her into her wharf, but was unable to do so, both vessels losing ground. Finally, a fishing boat took hold of the *Theoline,* docking her on April 23rd. She had taken a week to cover forty miles.

The schooner was forced to wait a month before she could go on the marine railway which was most primitive, being worked by teams of oxen and horses walking around a giant capstan. Once clear of the water, she was given a thorough overhaul, scraped, caulked, and painted. She was jacked up amidships so a new shoe could be put onto her keel, at the same time filling her hog. Now she had a keel three feet deep beneath her main and mizzen masts. A government inspector insisted that a ton of metal fastenings be driven into her hull. A bad bit in the foremast was removed, new wood added. All the rigging was done over, masts scraped. When she finally took to the water again, she looked a new vessel. She was then probably the finest four-master on the East Coast.

On June 30th, the *Theoline* departed from Meteghan, bound light for Alma. With only gentle summer airs, she made slow time up the Bay, not anchoring off the New Brunswick port until July

5th. She had taken five days seven hours to cover 144 miles. Of that time, she had been anchored 58 hours, so her running time was slightly under three days.

Owing to the tremendous tides at Alma, the schooner did not go up to the wharf, but had the cargo brought out to her in lighters which made fast alongside. While shore stevedores stowed the lumber, each plank being handled separately, the crew hoisted the rigging pin rails so they would clear the deck load, lashing them to the shrouds eight feet above the fixed rails. Chains were draggd out to screw the deck lumber down. A small boat made trips to the beach with barrels to get fresh drinking water from a spring in the near-by woods. Food supplies came from the tiny port of Alma.

When finally loaded with 592,000 square feet of wood, the *Theoline* departed for Boston on July 26th. A fresh, fair breeze took her rapidly down the Bay of Fundy, passing Petit Manan 24 hours out. From then on the winds were light. The third and fourth day were spent off Portland. On the fifth day Cape Ann was sighted before fog closed in.

On August 1st the four-master came to Boston, two tugs towing her up the river to Quincy where she was to discharge. She had been six days, five hours and forty-five minutes from Alma. This was to be the last time the *Theoline* came to her home port. Not long after she was unloaded, she went to New York to load coal for St. John. Her captain was finding it more and more difficult to get men to work his old windship when steamboat owners were paying such high wartime wages. There was work for the schooner, but she could not accept the charters. In 1942 she was laid up at Bangor, Maine, for several months, then making a round trip to Baltimore for fertilizer in October. After that she took a cargo of "spuds" to New York.

About this time she changed hands again, her new owners planning on sending her to Africa with a cargo. Deeply loaded, she set out on the long voyage. It was reported that she bumped bottom near Cape Hatteras, but she got off undamaged. However, some weeks later word came from the West Indies that the fine schooner had struck a reef; it was the end of the *Theoline* as she smashed up before aid could come to her.

Zebedee E. Cliff

Built by the East Coast Ship Company of Boothbay Harbor, and launched in the late fall of 1920, the four-mast *Zebedee E.*

[57]

Cliff came too late to enjoy the large profits that the sailing ships had enjoyed a year or two before. Named after the Mayor of Somerville, Massachusetts, she was a fine vessel of 1361 gross tons and 206 feet long. In December she was towed to Boston for her finishing touches.

Shortly after her builders had sold her in January, 1922, to Crowell & Thurlow, she put to sea in the coasting trade. Less than six months later she was in difficulties when bound to Boston from New Orleans with nearly 6000 barrels of molasses. Her rudder head became twisted, forcing her into Charleston for repairs. Early in 1923, Captain Wilson Publicover took over the command of the *Cliff;* he had had the *Mabel A. Frye.* And a year or two later the *Cliff* was commanded by Captain J. L. Coombs.

In January, 1926, she was very nearly lost when she was struck by the tank steamer *Empire Arrow* of the Standard Oil Company off Miami. At the time, the four-master was bound in for that port with a cargo of lumber. At two in the morning, the sharp stem of the tanker plowed into her port side opposite the mainmast, cutting her down to her bilges. The cargo kept the schooner afloat until she was towed in for repairs.

In the fall of that year, when at Boothbay Harbor, she was ordered sold at auction to satisfy claims against her. However, she remained with the Thurlow fleet as sail was in a slump, and no one wanted her. The *Cliff* had an odd experience in 1929. While loading a cargo of plaster at the Wentworth quarries near Hantsport, Nova Scotia, in November, she was caught by a sharp earth quake which sent her reeling around, giving her a bad list. The sudden movement opened up many of her seams, and she had to be repaired before she could sail south for Norfolk.

When her owners could find no further charters for their vessel, they laid her up at Boothbay Harbor in 1932. She was still in perfect condition, but business conditions had forced her off the seas. However, in the spring of 1934, she was put back into service for a short time under Captain Robert L. Rawding. After an overhaul at East Boston, she went to Norfolk to load 2000 tons of coal for Eastport. There she furled her sails for the last time. Bernstein & Jacobson of Portland bought her in 1937, and soon after moved her to Boothbay where she joined the 'dead fleet' there.

When war broke out, the *Cliff* stirred. She was in good shape although the tides had been running in and out of her hold for several years. In the fall of 1941, she was towed to Portland. Word was passed around the waterfront that she was to be refitted for the South American trade. But nothing came of it; the Government took her over, with the *Maude M. Morey,* turning them both into breakwaters in Casco Bay, Maine. So ended a schooner which, had it not been for world conditions, might have lasted a good many more years.

Passages:

1925—arrived Boston August 25th; 22 days from Turks Island.

1934—arrived Norfolk April 29th; 12 days from Boston.

CHAPTER IV

Last of The Three-Mast Schooners

〜〜〜〜〜〜〜〜〜〜〜〜〜〜〜〜〜〜〜〜〜〜〜〜〜〜〜〜〜〜

THERE is much doubt as to when the first three-mast schooner was built, but it probably was before 1800. The last of the commercial type to be launched from a New England yard was the *Adams* in 1929. There were different forms of three-masters, each built for its own specific locality or trade. Many were center-boarders for operating in shallow waters, while others were keel vessels for the off-shore routes. The majority of the last three-masters seen in down east waters during the years just before World War II were either Maine or Nova Scotian built, the latter frequently called 'tern schooners' although the term was not often heard south of the Canadian line.

In 1939 there were still a large fleet of these schooners trading from the Bay of Fundy to New York and New England ports, as well as down to the West Indies. Within four years these survivors had passed on, either away to other parts, or had been lost, and when the war drew to a close, hardly a vessel remained; by the middle of 1948 they had all gone — 150 years had covered their rise and fall.

Here then, is the last roundup.

Albert H. Willis

Built at Phippsburg, Maine, in 1914 by Frank S Bowker & Sons, the wooden three-mast schooner *Albert H. Willis* belonged to the 'old school' with her flush deck and stanchioned railings that ran her entire length. A good sized vessel for her type, she was 567 gross tons and 157 feet long; as far as tonnage was concerned, she was the largest three-master under the Canadian flag when the war broke out in 1939.

The *Willis* had a busy life. She came in time to profit in the first World War, and following that, she continued in the coasting

trade. While still under the American flag, she had several owners, and as recently as 1937 was registered in Boston, having been
bought by Lillian E. Pezrow, for as little as $500 from the United
States Marshal at Eastport. Captain Ralph Ogilvie became her master, and three months later he purchased the schooner, putting her
under Canadian registry with her home port at Parrsboro.

The *Willis* was a lucky vessel, generally keeping out of trouble. She did get ashore off Martha's Vineyard in September, 1931,
but got off without too much damage. Later in the year she ran
into heavy weather, losing some canvas, and requiring a tow into
port when her steering gear fouled. In 1939 she struck mud in
Boston Harbor, floating clear when her deck load of lumber was
removed. However, none of these were serious problems, causing
little expense to her owners.

The *Willis* was not a particularly fast sailer, one of her best
passages in recent years being from Delaware Breakwater to St.
John in six days. A few of her other runs were as follows:
1936—arrived Portland September 17th; 14 days from New York.
1937—arrived Boston April 10th; 24 days from Hampton Roads.
    arrived New York November 22nd; 18 days from Beaver
    Harbor.
1938—arrived Parrsboro February 22nd; 19 days from New York.
1938—arrived Boston May 23rd; 6 days from Sheet Harbor.
    arrived New York August 12th; 15 days from Sheet Harbor.
1939—arrived New York May 15th; 10 days from Yarmouth.
1940—arrived New York August 16th; 12 days from Yarmouth.

In 1938 the *Willis* and the *T. K. Bentley* 'raced' from Portland to New York, the *Willis* taking seven days against the five
for the *Bentley*. In 1940 the *Willis* and the smaller *Peaceland*
came from Portland to Boston together, the *Willis* leading by an
hour at the ancthorage.

The *Albert Willis* met her end in October, 1941. In the early
war years she had found a lively business running lumber south
from Nova Scotia, frequently stopping at Gloucester to leave part
of her more than 500,000 feet of wood there before proceeding to
Boston to discharge the remainder. She was bound north light,
heading for Belliveau Cove for another load. After entering the
Bay of Fundy, she turned to pass through Grand Passage into St.
Mary Bay. Suddenly the wind dropped, leaving the schooner to
drift helplessly onto Dartmouth Ledge. As soon as the crew realized the schooner could not be saved, they removed as much as pos-

sible, but they did not have long to work. The *Willis* struck on the 25th; she was a total wreck by the 28th.

Alfred & Emily

The last three-mast schooner built in a Nova Scotian yard was the pretty tern *Venture,* designed by William J. Roué of Halifax as a training ship for the Canadian Government. Launched from the ways of the Meteghan Shipbuilding Corporation near the entrance to St. Mary Bay in 1937, she was fisherman-style with her spoon bow and spiked bowsprit. Her dimensions, 143 feet overall, 111 feet on the waterline, 27 foot beam, and 14 foot draft, were practically the same as those of the famous two-mast schooner Bluenose, also designed by Roué. She was well put together, a perfect example of the Canadian shipbuilding art, and probably the last of the larger windships to be built in that part of the world.

The war halted her career as a training ship, there being no time to train in sail in those hectic days, so she was laid up. Later on she probably made several runs to the West Indies as a freighter. Her name was changed to *Alfred & Emily,* and her port of registry became Barbados. When the war ended, she was given a thorough overhauling. In February, 1946, she was slipped and caulked. About now she was offered for sale, the asking price being $65,000. In the summer of 1947, the *Alfed & Emily* was converted into a floating cannery ship, working with the salmon fishermen in Frobisher Bay. At the end of the season she was laid up at Halifax. Early in 1948 she was fitted out as a sealer, putting out with the fleet in the spring. With Captain A. M. Shaw, Jr. in command, she pushed north through icy waters to the sealing grounds. In late March she was in Cabot Strait when she was nipped by the ice floes. Five miles from her, the auxiliary-schooner *Monica R. Walters* was crushed and sunk, but the tern worked her way clear. Again she was caught when off Cape North, and a third time when heading for Halifax. For three days she was wedged in the floes near Aspy Bay before she could get back into open water. She arrived back in port on May 1st with 2700 seal skins in her hold.

Her end came one night early in October, 1951. She was off the Strait of Belle Isle, when her engine caught fire. After a hopeless fight against the flames, her seven man crew escaped in their dory.

Alhambia

The *Bertha L. Waters* was a small three-master built in 1919 by the Bridgewater Shipping Company of Bridgewater, Nova Scotia. Only 147 gross tons and 115 feet long, she was a good deal smaller than many two-masters. Much of her earlier life was spent as a fishing vessel, but in later years with Newfoundland owners who made the most of their little vessel, she did a considerable amount of freighting as well, much of it deep water.

In July, 1933, she crossed the Atlantic from Grand Bank, Newfoundland, to Oporto, Spain, in 17 days which was good going for the vessel, deeply laden with salt fish. Later in the year, in December, she took 20 days from Burin to Oporto; she was 29 days returning to Newfoundland against the mid-winter westerlies.

In 1936 her name had changed to *Alhambia,* but she continued to sail to Spain and Portugal. In September she arrived at Lisbon 18 days out from Grand Bank, going back home in 30 days. In the following spring she varied her trans-Atlantic runs by taking a lumber cargo south to Boston, 12 days from Grand Bank. In 1938 a small engine was installed to give her a shove through calms and for congested waterways. The next two years were spent in the coastal trade, generally from Newfoundland ports to New York, taking between nine days and two and a half weeks for the southerly run.

The war brought plenty of work for the *Alhambia.* In April, 1940, she set out on a long voyage to Greece, but her hull was aged by now, and the stormy seas were too much for her. A bad leak developed. For awhile the pumps were able to control the water though not for long. It was soon obvious that the schooner was doomed. On May 11th, when in Latitude 39° 50' North, Longitude 33° 15' West, her captain and five men were rescued by the *S.S. Examiner* which took them to Gibraltar. The *Alhambia* was fired to prevent her from becoming a menace to shipping.

Alta C.

The smallest of the three-mast schooners in commercial service in New England waters during the last days of sail was the tiny *Alta C.,* no more than 62 gross tons and under 87 feet in length. Built in 1927 at Bear River, Nova Scotia, she was a pretty little thing even though she was a bald-header and had a 40 horsepower engine. She had spruce frames, birch planking, galvanized fittings, and was able to carry 120 tons of cargo. A five horsepower 'donkey' engine on deck was used for hoisting sails and working the windlass. Painted green with a black band and white topsides, she almost appeared to be a yacht until one noticed a deck load of lumber above her bulwarks.

She was a busy vessel in the lumber trade, frequently coming to Boston and other local ports from the Bay of Fundy. During her first season or two she carried pulpwood from the Minas Basin to Maine ports, being an ideal vessel for making the smaller harbors although her draft, when fully loaded, was as much as ten feet. In September, 1938, she caused quite a sensation when she carried 53,000 feet of lumber up the Ipswich River to the town docks, the first of her type there in nearly a half century. At the time, the *Alta C.* was commanded by Captain Almand Chaney who took with him his wife and fifteen year old daughter and 14 year old son.

The small tern remained in northern waters until the early war years when she was sold to the West Indies. She eventually went under the Honduran flag. In 1947 she was for sale, the owners asking $16,000.

Atlantic

Perhaps the most beautiful, graceful three-mast schooner ever built was the lovely *Atlantic* which was designed by William Gardner as a racing yacht. Constructed by the Townsend & Downey Shipbuilding and Repair Company at Shooters Island, New York, in 1903, she was 303 gross tons, 185 feet overall and 135 on her waterline. Her hull was of steel, her decks teak, and her ballast lead. Her sweeping spoon bow led up to her lengthy bowsprit which carried on the line of her sweet sheer, while aft her transome stern with its overhang completed the perfect pattern. Aloft she carried the conventional gaff rig plus a yard on her foremast; she could set 18,500 square feet of canvas.

Owned in 1905 by Wilson Marshall, the *Atlantic* was entered in the trans-Atlantic race that year, Sandy Hook to Bishop Rock, against ten other yachts. If for nothing else, the *Atlantic* will always be remembered for the extremely fast passage that she made. Leaving New York astern on May 17th, before inconstant easterly winds, she picked up speed on her second day out, and at noon on the 19th had covered 222 miles in the proceeding twenty-four hours, racing along at ten knots. The next noon showed another 229 miles, and the 21st she logged 271 miles. Then the wind dropped for some hours with the result her next noon position was only 112 miles ahead of the last one. With the return of the breeze, she was off, breasting her way through the seas at gathering speed. On the 23rd she touched 243 miles as the gusts became stronger. Her next twenty-four hours were the most outstanding of her entire career. With the wind from the southeast, the swell not too large, she tore through the water at better than fourteen knots, often hitting sixteen knots and more in the squalls. In 23 hours and 31 minutes she sailed 341 miles, an amazing showing for a fore-and-aft craft.

With Captain Charles Barr driving her onwards, she followed the Great Circle course across the Atlantic. On the 25th, with a whole gale blowing from the west, she plunged forward in a lather of spray and foam under her squaresail and fore trysail; her run was 282 miles. Another day added 279 miles, and the next 243 miles. On the 28th, she again went over the 300 mark, touching 309 miles in under twenty-four hours. The 29th found her approaching Ireland, her run to noon being 282 miles. She passed Bishop Rock Lighthouse 11 days, 16 hours, and 21 minutes from Sandy Hook. Now the wind fell light, and the last lap was a struggle for headway. On May 30th she passed the Lizard, 12 days, 4 hours, 1 minute from Sandy Hook, a record crossing by sail for the 3014 miles. She had averaged better than ten knots for the entire distance.

The *Atlantic* was in another trans-Atlantic race in 1928, Ambrose Channel Lightship to Santander, Spain. There were five yachts in her class. The two-mast schooner *Elena* was winner in 16 days, 19 hours, 49 minutes; the *Atlantic* was twenty hours and thirty-six minutes behind her. The tern *Guinevere* was six hours astern of the *Atlantic*. During the next few years, the *Atlantic* was frequently seen in New England waters. At this time she was owned by Gerald B. Lambert. In 1935 she was the 'mother ship' to Mr. Lambert's *Yankee,* the large 'J' class yacht, when she went across to England to race. The two vessels went from Boston to Cowes in slightly less than 18 days.

When World War II broke out, Mr. Lambert turned his beautiful yacht over to the Coast Guard. Later on she became a training ship for the cadets at New London, but she was more than they could handle. In 1946 the Coast Guard spent $150,000 giving her new standing rigging, new hollow booms and a jib-headed rig. A new suit of sails cost $30,000. Many of her old plates were renewed. The new rig was not becoming to the large racer, and she never regained her old speeds. After using her for a month or two, the Coast Guard decided to get rid of her. In 1948 she was sold to a New York ship broker for $18,240 although she supposedly had about 150 tons of lead ballast valued, on the metal exchange, at $350 per ton.

A year or two later local newspapers announced that the *Atlantic* was headed for the scrapyards to be broken up. However, at the last moment she was reprieved, and since that time has been laid up at Wildwood, New Jersey.

A. W. Chisholm

Although not a visitor to New England ports, the *A. W. Chisholm* frequently crossed the outer edges of the New England waters, and so deserves mention. The *Chisholm* was not a large vessel, being only 175 gross tons and 116 feet long. Built at Dayspring by F. Robar in 1920, she differed from the lumbermen of the Bay of Fundy in that she was a fisherman type with a modern curved stem, spiked bowsprit, and short step amidships.

In her earlier years she was owned by W. Duff, but later on by the Chisholm Shipping Company; her home port was always Lunenburg. The *Chisholm* had a varied career. In the early 1930's she made a number of trips to the West Indies, outward with dry fish for Puerto Rico, returning with salt from Turks. In 1933 she spent part of the summer at Canso, buying codfish from the local fishermen. The fish were split, salted, and kenched right on board. When she had a full cargo, she returned to Lunenburg. With business poor around 1936, the tern was laid up. She tried fishing in 1938, but was not successful. She was not even registered in 1939, but war finally brought her back into service.

On February 7th, 1940, the *Chisholm* with Captain George H. Corkum in command departed from Lunenburg with fish for Puerto Rico. Almost from the start the schooner met bad weather. Hurricane winds and mountainous seas battered the vessel, smashing against the old, worn out hull with terrific fury. Somehow she held together for a week; then, on the 14th, her seams aft let go, and within ninety minutes she had filled to the deck with water, driving the crew from their quarters. Her six men had to lash themselves to the spanker boom so they would not be washed overboard. In order to get food, they chopped holes in the schooner's deck above the stores, and then fished around for what they could get with a boathook. For three days they were without water until one of them succeeded in dislodging the water cask. They managed to build a fire on the roof of the deckhouse to cook their salt-water soaked potatoes. Later they had turnips which floated up below. Someone hooked a slab of pork, so they had meat, too.

All the time the gale raged about them, ever threatening to smash up their waterlogged schooner; there was nothing the men could do but wait for a passing ship. Finally, on the 18th a steamer hove in sight. She was not far from the *Chisholm*, but apparently missed the distress signals for she never stopped, leaving the discouraged men to their fate. Nine days later the Swedish freigher *Sagoland* with Captain Henrik Bang-Melchior appeared over the grey, stormy horizon, bound from India to New York. The men on the *Chisholm*, soaking a coat in gasoline, set it afire. The blazing torch attracted the Swedes who came to the rescue. Their first lifeboat was unable to get close to the sinking schooner as such tremendous seas were running. However, she stood by all night, and the next day succeeded in taking all hands off the schooner.

The *Chisholm* must have foundered soon afterwards. Her crew were landed at New York, later returning home to Nova Scotia.

Betoine

In February, 1941, a small steel three-mast schooner arrived at the Boston Fish Pier with a cargo for the local buyers. She was obviously not a 'Yankee' craft, nor even a down easter since she was quite different in shape from the usual windships seen in these waters. On her rounded counter was her name, *Betoine* from St. John's, Newfoundland.

The *Betoine* was built by W. Rubertus of Groningen, Holland, in 1918. Of 223 gross tons and 115 feet long, she was launched as the *Horizon* under the Dutch flag. However, by 1921 she was owned by the Irish Shipping Company of Dublin, and called *Ballycorus*. In 1933 she went to the Ajax Shipping Company of Poole, England, now becoming the *Henford*. She flew the Dutch flag again in 1935, and was renamed *Betoine*. In 1939 she was sold to St. John's, and for a short period was called *Grete Kure*. She was the *Betoine* once more in 1940 when she was taken over by the Marine Agencies Limited of St. John's; it was they who sent her south with fish.

A bald-headed tern, she also had engines. Forward she carried a short spike bowsprit setting a staysail and two jibs. Aft there was a house over her wheel. The *Betoine* was similar to a number of sailing coasters that had survived in the European waters. Her canvas was secondary to the engines, but was a help in heavy weather and when the winds were strong and fair.

Charles and Vernon

Built by W. A. Naugler of Bridgewater, Nova Scotia, in 1919, the tern *Charles and Vernon* was a medium sized vessel of 347 tons and 136 feet long. Registered in La Have, she was one of the many schooners in the lumber-salt trade. Under Captain Byron D. Getson, she made a good name for herself.

In later years she varied her West Indies runs with passages to New York for coal. In 1936, for instance, she loaded coal at New York in April, sailing on the 21st for Port Daniel, Quebec. After putting into Lunenburg, she arrived at her destination on May 12th. By the 17th she was discharged, and on her way south to Barbados, taking 27 days for the run. On July 4th she was headed north again, this time for Paspebiac on the Baie de Chaleur.

Commanded by Captain S. Dunphy, the *Charles and Vernon* departed from Halifax on May 19th, 1937, with lumber for Philadelphia, arriving there on April 5th after an easy passage of 17 days down the coast. When the wood was out of her, she took coal for Hamilton, Bermuda. Deeply loaded, she went down to the Delaware Breakwater to await a favorable slant. It came on April 23rd, and the *Vernon* got under way, passing out to sea. For several days previous to this, strong winds had been kicking up a heavy swell outside. Now the tern met with a hard pounding from the rough waters. The coal was a dead weight; the schooner had no give to take the shock of the waves. Less than twenty-four hours from port, she sprang a leak. The crew tried to get the pumps going, but something was wrong; perhaps they were clogged. Captain Dunphy ordered distress flags flown. Three steamers came along but none of them noticed the flags. Things were looking very bad for the windship men when the *S.S. Lake Ormoc* arrived on the scene. She was only just in time for a few minutes after the schooner crew had been picked up, the *Vernon* sank, going down some six miles from Winter Quarter Light.

Charles H. Klinck

The three-mast schooner *Charles H. Klink* was built of oak, chestnut and yellow pine, with iron fastenings. Launched from the yards of Robert Palmer & Son of Noank, Connecticut, in 1901, she

The three-mast schooners Rebecca R. Douglas and Lucy Evelyn.
The Adams, last of her type launched in New England yards.

The five-mast schooner Edna Hoyt entering Havana Harbor.

The four-mast schooner Albert F. Paul sailing light.
The four-mast schooner Albert F. Paul at Providence, R.I.

The Herbert L. Rawding was the last active four-mast schooner in the 'Down East' trade.

The four-mast schooner Alvena at New London in June, 1930.

The bow ports, seen open below the anchors, were used when long lengths of lumber or piling were to be taken as cargo. When at sea the ports would be closed and caulked. The schooner is the Anna R. Heidritter.

The four-mast schooner Helen Barnet Gring near Windward Passage on her last voyage in 1940, shortly before she was wrecked.

The James E. Newsom, launched fully rigged and ready for sea.

The Laura Annie Barnes was one of the last schooners on the East Coast to set a 'queen staysail'.

The James E. Newsom sailing light.

The four-mast schooner Edward L. Swan, formerly the M. Vivian Pierce.

right: The three-mast schooner Lillian E. Kerr at Machias in 1932. She is shown later, below, re-rigged as a four-mast schooner.

below right: The four-mast schooner Mabel A. Frye at Boothbay Harbor.

Barkentine Reine Marie Stewart laid up at Thomaston, Maine.
right: The Reine Marie Stewart, now a four-mast schooner, on the beach at Metaghan, N.S.
far right: The wreck of the four-mast schooner Snetind on Spectacle Island in Boston Harbor.

The four-mast schooner Constellation departing from Boothbay Harbor in 1934, bound for Washington, D.C.

Sunrise aboard the Theoline — the man at the wheel.

left above: The four-mast schooner Theoline entering Boston Harbor in 1941.

below: Looking aft from the bowsprit of the Theoline.

The City of New York as a bark returning to New Zealand from the South Polar regions in 1930.

The three-mast schooner Citnalta.

*The City of New York as a three-mast schooner at the Quincy Lumber
Company wharf in October, 1952*

The three-mast schooner Albert H. Willis running before the wind.

was designed to carry granite and stone in the New England trade, so was put together to withstand a hard life. Her bottom planks were huge timbers of solid oak four inches thick and sixty feet long. Her strength was increased by a heavy centerboard trunk amidships; on account of it, her main mast was placed slightly to starboard to clear it. The board itself was of massive timbers, and when down, the schooner drew 17½ feet of water. She was 522 gross tons and 150 feet long.

Her earlier years were spent in carrying stone south. With her homeport New London, she continued operating until the early 1930's. When business slumped, she was laid up at Tenant's Harbor in Maine, and it was while here that she was very nearly lost when a fire destroyed a steam lighter alongside of her. From 1936 to the recent war, she lay moored to a wharf in the Snow Shipyard at Rockland, with her sister schooner, the *George E. Klinck,* alongside of her. As the years went by, so her condition deteriorated, and her value went down. In 1938 she changed hands for $425; a year later she was again sold, this time for $85. By now her rigging was rotten, and one night during a wind storm her foretopmast snapped in the middle, the upper section hanging in her forestays. No one ever thought that she would put back to sea, but with the need for more and more ship bottoms, she was brought out of retirement by F. Gordon Carvell of St. John, New Brunswick, who put her into the lumber trade after giving her a complete refit. She came into Boston on April 23rd, 1942, with wood from Annapolis Royal. She was commanded by Captain Donald R. Glennie who had been at sea for all of forty years, all the time in sail.

After discharging, the *Klinck* went back to Nova Scotia for a second lumber cargo, this time loading at Apple River. She returned to Boston on July 27th, twelve days out, unloading at the East Milton docks. Before the summer was out, she had made one more trip, again with lumber, this time from Parrsboro, arriving on September 30th. During the fall, she took aboard another wood load at Apple River before crossing to St. John where Captain S. Zinck of Chester, Nova Scotia, took command. While the schooner lay in the mud at low tide, Captain Zinck inspected her under body. In spite of her 41 years, he found her bottom sound, not even wormed. However, he did not like the look of her timber port in the bows; it seemed her one weak point although he was not able to examine it from the inside owing to the full cargo load.

Nonetheless, he was assured that the strongbacks were all secured, and that he need not worry about it.

Sailing in mid-winter, the *Klinck* stood out from St. John, and passed down the Bay of Fundy. Once outside, they were struck by heavy weather with all the might of a January gale. Freezing winds iced the rigging with flying spray, weighted the schooner down under its weight. Suddenly, without warning, the tern began to founder with water pouring into her hold. Although he could not see it, Captain Zinck felt certain that the lumber port had dropped out; the seams opening would not have let the seas in so fast. There was nothing the hands could do but gather aft in the house, and hope the schooner would not break up under them. Before the storm let up, they were a battered wreck, the wild waves crashing across her decks, only her cargo keeping her afloat.

Two coastal planes passed over the sinking vessel but they did not seem to realize that she was in trouble. Her crew, soaked through by the freezing water, could only watch them disappear over the horizon out of sight. They had about given up hope after two more days when a third plane zoomed above them; some hours later a United States warship came to the rescue. After taking off the men from the *Klinck,* they sank her with shellfire to prevent her from becoming a menace to navigation. It took a lot of ammunition to destroy her.

The crew were put to bed aboard the Navy ship which took them into Portland. Two of her men were so badly frozen they had to go to the hospital; the remainder returned north to St. John. It had been a terrible strain on them all, and Captain Zinck, who was an elderly man, never fully recovered, passing away on December 22nd, 1945.

Citnalta
Launched in 1917 as the *Esther Adelaide,* the *Citnalta,* as she was later called, was a medium sized wooden tern of 398 tons and 148 feet long. First taking to the water at Fox River, Nova Scotia, she spent the first part of her life in the coasting trade until she was laid up in 1932 on account of the depression. Although she was in poor condition by 1936, she was bought by the Parrsboro Shipping Company who practically rebuilt her. They stripped another vessel that they owned, the old *Cape Blomidon,* to refit the *Citnalta,* her name being Atlantic spelled backwards.

Once more in service, she resumed her coasting trade, generally south with lumber to New York. She had a good turn of speed, making better than average passages. A few of her runs were as follows:

1937—arrived Boston April 19th; 9 days from Port Greville.
1938—arrived New York June 16th; 12 days from Port Advocate.
      arrived New York August 19th; 10 days from Spencer Island.
1939—arrived New York May 15th; 13 days from Apple River.

With the coming of war, the *Citnalta* found plenty of business which kept her very much on the move. In September, 1940, she struck Race Rock in Long Island Sound, but she got clear without too much damage. In December, 1941, she arrived in Boston with 415,000 feet of lumber after a very smart passage down the coast from Yarmouth, taking only thirty hours to cover the 235 miles, an average of eight knots.

A Mr. Schultz of New York bought the tern about this time, but she did not last long. Chartered to load coal at Boston for the West Indies, she set out in the spring. Hugging the coast, she again hit Race Rock. Once more she got clear, proceeding on her way, but this time she was more damaged than suspected. A leak developed, and on May 3rd she foundered between New Haven and Bridgeport.

City of New York

When Admiral Richard E. Byrd was planning his first voyage to the Antarctic, the great explorer, Captain Roald Amundsen, recommended to him the barkentine *Samson* which had been built at Arendal, Norway, by K. Larsen in 1885 as a sealer. She was very strongly put together to withstand the pressure of the ice, her hull being of the finest spruce and oak with thick inside and ouside planking on ribs that were so closely spaced that they nearly touched, making her sides some 34 inches thick. She was so shaped that if she were caught in the ice, she would rise above the pressure, clear of being crushed. She was a small vessel, only 515 tons and 170 feet long overall, 147 feet on her waterline.

Leaving her home port of Tromsoe, she put into Oslo before setting off across the Atlantic under sail and power, the latter a 200 horsepower steam engine. She had not gone far when she ran into heavy weather, so straining her boiler that it very nearly exploded. After that, she came on under sail alone, taking almost three months to reach New York. Renamed the *City of New York*, she was completely made over. Her cost to Admiral Byrd, including the alterations, had come to $165,000. She had been in poor condition, but by the time she was ready to depart for the Antarctic, she was in top shape, rotten planks renewed and bad spots corrected. She was re-rigged as a bark.

With Captain Frederick Melville in command, she departed from New York harbor on August 25th, 1928, bound south with a crew of 33 men, and 200 tons of cargo. She had her bunkers full with 150 tons of coal plus an additional 50 tons on deck. Under power, she used six tons of coal daily, making a 100 miles every 24 hours; a fair wind and her sails would help her out. Her outward passage was slow, light winds and not enough coal to do the entire trip under steam. The one time she had had a good breeze, it had driven her far off her course.

She had finally arrived at Dunedin, New Zealand, on November 26th. A week later, loaded down to her marks, the *City of New York* pushed on southward. To make better time, and to preserve her small coal supply, she was taken in tow by the steamer *Eleanor Bolling*. When they met the ice pack, the *City* would have to break a passage through for herself; she would need all her coal then. Sometimes when the wind was fair and fresh, the tow line would be cast off, and on occasion the old bark foamed along at ten knots. When the wind headed her again, the tow would be resumed.

On December 7th, a heavy gale struck the two ships, huge seas whipping out of the westward. When the towline snapped, the *City* was on her own with thirty fathoms of line hanging from her bows. All hands, groping their way forward, fought to haul it in. For two long hours they worked on the cold, exposed forecastle head, straining and pulling on the wet rope, before their task was completed. The *City* labored on, rolling her rails down but never taking solid water aboard. Her husky dogs, their kennels on deck, added their yowls to the shriek of the wind, a ghostly sound in a weird setting of flying spume and stinging spray.

Arriving at the ice pack, the *Bolling* loaded the *City* with all the coal that she could take; then the *Bolling* turned back for Dunedin. In the meantime, the steam whaler *Larsen* had joined the *City*, and she took the bark in tow, heading into the pack.

Leaving the *Larsen* in Ross Sea, the *City* came to the edge of the Barrier on Christmas Day. On January 1st, 1929, a suitable base was located; it was named Little America. When the wind-ship was unloaded, Byrd tried to take her on a trip of exploration to the eastward. The gallant bark fought her way through the ice, but as conditions were against her, he had to abandon his plans. With winter approaching fast, the *City* departed for New Zealand in mid-February, leaving the expedition at the base. For a few days it was touch and go with her as she struggled through thickening ice fields. Her coal supply was almost gone, her food stores low. If she had been trapped by the ice, her men would have faced a dreadful winter. However, she managed to get to the *Larsen* which was also about to turn north, and the whaler was able to give the bark 90 tons of coal and some provisions. Before the *City* made New Zealand, she ran into an 80-mile an hour gale, the worst of the passage. The winds built up terrific seas that smashed against the little ship. Rolling as much as sixty degrees, she fought for her life. In the engine room, the floor plates were shaken from place, and even the boiler was jarred from its base. A mountainous wave smashed the starboard lifeboat to kindling; foaming water surged across her decks. Hour after hour the storm raged, ever threatening to swamp her in the huge combers that seemed to tower about her on all sides. But the *City* was built for just such weather, and clawed her way through to safety. She spent the winter berthed at Dunedin.

On January 5th, 1930, the bark was on her way south once more, running into heavy weather almost from the start, meeting squalls of hurricane force. She had to borrow coal from a Norwegian whaler that she met near the pack. Entering Ross Sea, she was struck by the worst gale of all with gusts of wind reaching more than 100 miles an hour. Her engines could not hold her against the blasts, and she was slowly driven backwards into the ice. To save the rudder, Captain Melville swung her around, but as she lay beam to the sea, she was washed by torrents of water that swept the decks, breaking loose cargo lashed topside, sending it crashing down between the bulwarks. When she hit the ice, the old ship shuddered all over, but nothing gave. After sheltering in the pack for a day, she turned south only to meet another gale head-on, and this one nearly ended the career of the *City*. Ice began forming quickly on her hull and rigging, the spray freezing where it struck. Her crew fought to hack it clear, but it appeared faster than they could break it away. Gradually the weight bore the bark down until her decks were nearly level with the sea. Some 200 tons of ice clung to the 500 ton bark; in places it was three feet thick. Rigging lines were as large as barrels, and for the most part, frozen in one solid piece of ice. Only the end of the storm saved the ship. When the navigators were able to get their next sights, they found that they had been driven some 300 miles off their course.

The City arrived in the Bay of Whales on February 18th. After a few hectic hours of loading, she was bound north with the expedition, all within twenty-four hours. While she had been wintering, Admiral Byrd had flown over the South Pole, other flights had been made to locate mountain ranges, sled teams had pushed on to find new horizons, and Little America had become a place on the map; the expedition had been a success.

After a pause at New Zealand, the *City of New York* made the long voyage home. In time she was turned into a floating museum of antarctic exploration, and as such, she toured the Atlantic Coast, arriving in Boston in the early 1930's. Later on, she went out to the Great Lakes, appearing at the Chicago World's Fair. After that she moved to Cleveland where she remained for several years, still a show boat. For a time it seemed that she would never go to sea again, but there was a use for her in World War II. Her masts had to be sent down to get her out of Cleveland as a bridge had been erected since her arrival there.

When she was re-rigged in 1944, she appeared as a three-mast schooner. Her new owner was Captain Louis Kenedy, now of Nova Scotia. She had very little war service as she was not ready to sail until the war was practically over. With her ancient steam engines removed, she relied on her canvas alone as she ran between Nova Scotia and the West Indies. Her best run to Barbados was twenty days.

However, the *City* was built too heavily to be a good sailer; it needed a gale of wind to move her. Therefore, in the spring of 1947, Captain Kenedy took his vessel into Dayspring Harbor to have her topmasts removed, her jibboom taken out, and a 350 horsepower engine installed. This left her with only two jibs, her foresail and mainsail.

In the fall of 1952 the Captain sold his vessel to a group who planned on putting her into the Prince Edward Island potato trade, but on December 30th, when a tow line to her tug snapped, she drifted onto Chebogue Ledge outside of Yarmouth Harbor, Nova Scotia. In a short time she was a total loss.

Daniel Getson

One of the most active three-mast schooners in the late 1930's was the Canadian built *Daniel Getson* which had been launched from the yards of W. A. Naugler of Bridgewater in 1917. She was a smallish tern of 351 gross tons and 132 feet long, but she was a fair sailer and a good sea boat. In her earlier years she became well known along the East Coast as she was employed in the lumber trade out of the Bay of Fundy. When the lean times came in 1932, she was laid up.

In 1934 she was on the go again, this time with Captain Arthur Moore, who had had the *Utilla*, in command. She came romping into Boston Harbor in December with 331,825 feet of lumber, three days out from Weymouth. She had just been given an over-haul, and although she was 17 years old, she looked a new vessel. Some months later, she was back with another timber cargo. When she came to sail from Boston for Turks Island in early May, 1935, there was almost a flat calm; in ten hours she had crawled as far as Nahant, hardly outside the harbor. Captain Moore gave up, drift-ing back in with the incoming tide to await a breeze.

From Turks the *Getson* went north with salt. Then at St. John she loaded lumber for Funchal, Madeira, arriving there on August 15th, having taken 31 days for the 2470 miles, an average of 80 miles a day. She now loaded onions, and set off for Grand Turk which she made in 34 days, covering another 2920 miles at an average of 85 miles a day. With rock salt for cargo, she next took 17 days to get to Providence, 1200 miles at 70 miles a day.

In January, 1937, the *Getson* had a hard passage south from Bridgeport, Connecticut, to Jacksonville. Caught by a mid-winter gale, she was driven 400 miles off her course. Before the storm had passed, her mate had been swept overboard to his death in the angry seas. She eventually limped in 31 days out.

The *Daniel Getson* was sold American early in 1938, being renamed *Wanderthirst;* her new owner was H. L. Sutton who regis-tered her at Rochester, New York. From this time on, she seems to have remained south of New England waters. In April, 1939, she was damaged by fire at Berkeley, Virginia, but returned to sea soon after. The three-master changed flags again when she became Panamanian in 1941. A year or two later she sank in those southern waters.

Passages:

1934—arrived Madeira August 7th; 26 days from St. John.
1937—arrived Bermuda February 26th; 14 days from Jacksonville.
    arrived Jacksonville March 29th; 14 days from Bermuda.
    arrived Bermuda April 25th; 7 days from Jacksonville.

arrived Fort de France July 7th; 21 days from Jacksonville.
arrived Barbados November 19th; 41 days from Bridgewater,
N.S.

Dauntless

Robert E. Tod of the New York Yacht Club was always famous
for his yachts. One of his earlier ones, and one of his loveliest, was
the three-mast schooner *Karina* which was launched at Port Rich-
mond, New York, in 1911. Of 513 gross tons and 168 feet long, she
was a beautiful, graceful craft and a fast sailer.

One of her first races was in August, 1911, when she met the
already well-known *Atlantic,* then still in her prime. The course
was from Brenton's Reef around the Ambrose Channel Lightship,
and return, a distance of some 260 miles. The prize was the Brenton's Reef Cup which had been held by the *Atlantic* since 1905. On
the outward leg, the wind was light and fickle with shifting airs.
The fast *Atlantic* made the turn 35 minutes ahead of the Tod yacht.
During the return run, the breeze strengthened somewhat, and
the *Karina* picked up on the 'Champion of the Atlantic'. For a few
miles they sailed side by side, almost within hailing distance. Then
the *Karina* got her stride, simply walking away from her rival and
taking the race by an hour and a half. She had taken 38 hours for
the entire course, slow sailing in the summer airs.

About the time of the first World War, the *Karina* changed
hands and names, becoming the *Undaunted.* A few years later she
changed her name again, this time to *Dauntless.* In the years before World War II, she was a familiar vessel along the East Coast.
However, in January, 1942, she was converted into a cargo carrier
at the Boston Dry Dock Company. Her evidences of grandeur were
removed as she became a commercial carrier. In 1948 she was still
active in the West Indies waters, but she was now listed as a 'motor
vessel'.

Director II

In 1920 the Chester Basin Shipbuilding Company launched a
fine three-mast fisherman type schooner which was christened
D. D. Mackenzie. Not very large, she was 168 gross tons and 119
feet long. For many years she was registered in Lunenburg, S. A.
Ernst her owner. A sharp, round bowed tern, she had a good turn
of speed, capable of 16 knots, and on one occasion she went from
Portland to Lunenburg in 29 hours. Part of her life was spent in

the lumber trade, and in later years it was rumored that she had once been one of the crack schooners of the rum-row fleet.

In 1933 she was completely rebuilt at Mahone Bay, becoming a luxurious yacht. Renamed *Sachem,* she was owned by Rowe B. Metcalf. She was very nearly lost in February, 1934, when she grounded on Turtle Harbor Reef, Florida, due to a missing channel marker. A heavy swell gave her a bad shaking, but on the following day, rising seas drove her clear over the reef, back into deep water.

In 1937, renamed the *Adventure,* she was to have carried the Sanderson Expedition around the world. Each member of the crew was to have paid $3000 to cover expenses, and further funds were to have been raised by publishing a bulletin which would have gone to subscribers at $60 per year. The voyage never came off.

However, she did get to the South Seas. In 1939 she was sold to the Fahnestock family who were already noted for their sailing activities. Sponsored by the American Museum of Natural History, they planned on gathering a collection of natural settings for four or five bird groups in the museum, and at the same time, record native music of the islands. The tern, now called *Director II,* had refrigeration, electric lights, a dark room and laboratory, extensive radio equipment and diesel power to help her sails. When she pulled out into the ice-crusted East River at New York on February 1st, 1940, she was starting out on what was to have been a 40,000 mile voyage.

The later part of the month found her at the Canal Zone. A half year later she had crossed the Pacific to New Caledonia, and on from there to Brisbane, Australia, where she was hauled out for caulking and painting. Not long after, she was on her way north, heading for Gladstone, when one of her fuel tanks opened up, flooding the bilges with nearly 1000 gallons of oil; this had to be pumped overboard.

As the schooner was steering for Gladstone on October 17th, feeling her way through the reefs under power, she suddenly ground on a sand bar, shuddering to a stop. The engines were thrown into reverse, but the tern did not budge. Sail was hoisted with the hope of heeling her over; it did not work. The local pilot vessel, coming out from port, attempted to tow her back into deeper water, but she could not move her. The grounding had sprung some of the *Director's* seams below the waterline, and before long she started to leak badly. For a time the pumps were able to hold their own. However, the continued bumping on the bottom strained her hull still more; soon the pumps were flooded. The crew did not give up, and tried bailing with buckets; it was too much for them. When the salt water covered the batteries, the men were forced to give up, the gas driving them to the deck.

Gathering what they could, they took to their launch, running into Gladstone. On the next day they returned to the wreck with a large scow, hoping to use her to right the vessel. Luck was not with them. On the 19th a storm struck the area, and before day was done, the tern had broken in two, a complete and total wreck.

Edward R. Smith

Built at Phippsburgh, Maine, in 1911 by Frank S. Bowker, the *Edward R. Smith* was a large three-master of 565 gross tons and some 158 feet long, a flush-decked vessel strongly put together, a fine example of the Maine builders' art. A typical coasting schooner, she was well known along the Atlantic seaboard where she spent her entire life carrying all cargoes, although chiefly lumber and coal in her later years.

The *Smith* was occasionally in the news for one thing or another. In December, 1928, she arrived in Boston from Nova Scotia with 504,583 feet of pine planks and boards for a Cambridge firm. It was then discovered that her beam exceeded by two inches the clearance at the Warren Street Bridge so that all her cargo had to be moved by rail from Chelsea, a costly transaction. Her 1925 season gave her two trips from Portland to Weymouth with 600 tons of fertilizer, then wood pulp runs to Portland, and finally with pulp from Port Wade to Bangor at $4.40 per cord with free load and discharge. She also took 600 tons of salt cakes in bags to Bathurst, New Brunswick, the first cargo of that type to be loaded in Boston in many years.

In 1932, after lying up at New York for some time, she was sold to Captain E. Marshall Baird who lately had had the tern *William E. Litchfield* which had wrecked and burnt at Alma. Some time before, Captain Baird had been with the five-masted schooner *Nancy;* she ended her days on the beach at Nantasket after going ashore there in 1927. Often laying up during the winter months when conditions could be more than unpleasant at sea, the *Smith* was kept fairly busy at other seasons. Now and then she met with accidents. In the spring of 1937 when loaded with 800 tons of coal from New York for Camden, she had a close call with disaster. On May 6th the *Smith* was picking her way past Cape Cod in a thick fog when a steamer was suddenly sighted dead ahead. Both vessels swung, but it was too late to avert a crash, and the schooner plowed into the mid-section of the Italian motorship *Maria* which was doing about ten knots. With a splintering of wood, the bowsprit and jibboom of the *Smith* shattered, the headsails fouling about the foremast in a tangle of wreckage. Her bows were pushed in, many of the seams forward opening up. At first it was thought that the windship would founder, but when the pumps were able to take care of the inflow of the water, a tow line was given to the *Maria* who took her into Boston. After minor repairs, the tern was later towed to Camden where her cargo was discharged. She was then completely repaired.

From 1936 to 1939 she was employed chiefly in the Nova Scotian lumber trade to New York, Boston or other New England ports. Although there was plenty of work for the *Smith* in the war years, it became increasingly difficult for her to put to sea owing to Coast Guard regulations that were brought about on account of the Nazi submarines off the eastern shores. She is said to have changed hands in October, 1942, for $35,000, but she was not to last long as she went ashore on the Virginia Coast on January 24th, 1943, becoming a total loss.

A few of the *Smith*'s passages might be of interest:
1937—arrived Boston August 12th; 5 days from Yarmouth.
      arrived New York October 4th; 9 days from Alma.
1938—arrived New York September 9th; 13 days from Parrsboro.
1941—arrived New York April 27th; 2 days from Boston.
      arrived New York October; 11 days from Yarmouth.

Edwin G. Farrar

The *Edwin G. Farrar* was a fine three-mast schooner which was built at Phippsburg, Maine, in 1912 by F. S. Bowker for the old Boston firm of Rogers & Webb. She was a large schooner, probably the largest of the tern schooners on the East Coast in the last years of sail, grossing 573 tons and 158 feet long; her dimensions varied only by a few inches with those of the *Edward R. Smith*, built in the same port a year earlier.

The first part of the *Farrar*'s life was spent in the southern lumber trade, working between Jacksonville and New England. She was in her prime during World War I, never lacking a cargo and always finding plenty of work. Her large cargo capacity gave her a distinct advantage over her smaller rivals, although she herself was not considered unduly big at a time when five- and six-masted schooners were still being built and sailed across the seas. She was just one of the fleet of windships whose sails dotted the Atlantic from the West Indies to Newfoundland, a sight so common then that little attention was paid to them as they arrived and departed.

Although not often in trouble, the *Farrar* did have a close call in December, 1925. With a lumber load valued at about $28,000, she sailed from Jacksonville on December 6th with Captain K. E. Ronberry in command. After a quick run up the coast, she was some six miles south of Scotland Lightship at 3 a.m. on the 12th. The weather was clear and fine as the schooner ghosted along on the port tack. Suddenly the lookout sighted a steamer on her starboard bow. Moments later the tanker *Miller County* plowed into the bow of the *Farrar,* ripping away the bowsprit and the fore rigging, and splintering the deckhouse. The lookout, running for his life, barely escaped the deluge of falling rigging as blocks, sails and lines dropped through the night. A passing steamer radioed for help. The tern was towed into Stapleton, Staten Island, for repairs.

In early 1927, the schooner went under the British flag when she was purchased by Captain Robert Kerr of Nova Scotia. A year later she was bought by Captain C. Malcolm Wilkie who also became her skipper. She was registered in Bridgetown, Barbados, although her home port was La Have. She now entered the Nova Scotian lumber trade, generally making several trips to New York each year, and also running down to the West Indies on occasion. In October, 1933, she was considered overdue on a trip north from Barbados with molasses for Yarmouth. Unsighted for more than a month, she had been blown far off her course by storms.

On November 27th, 1935, the *Farrar* was towed into Boston with her windlass damaged. She had been bound for La Have from New York when she met heavy weather. Head winds had forced her to anchor off Handkerchief Shoal in Nantucket Sound, but when she came to get under way again, it was found that the power windlass would not work. As she did not carry enough crew to hoist sail or get the anchor up by hand, she was forced to call on the Coast Guard for help. The cutter *Mojave* towed her to Provincetown, but when repairs could not be done there, the cutter took her on to Boston. A day or two later she was on her way again.

The *Farrar* was in the news again in 1938. Sailing from Halifax with a full lumber cargo on October 7th, she headed south for Barbados. Days passed, and there was no sign of her; she was crawling along in light airs off by herself, just making a slow passage. The following are some of her other runs:

1930—arrived Boston May 25th; 4 days from Alma.
1935—arrived Boston August 26th; 3 days from St. Martin's.
1936—arrived New York July 4th; 14 days from Parrsboro.
      arrived Liverpool, N.S., July 31st; 7 days from New York.
1937—arrived Halifax June 8th; 13 days from New York.
1939—arrived La Have May 20th; 22 days from Barbados.

The *Farrar* was sold to Demerara parties in 1939, after which she carried hard pine to Barbados and Martinique. She finally loaded greenheart logs at Demerara, but burnt before sailing.

E. P. Theriault

Frequently seen passing through New England waters during the last days of sail, the tern *E. P. Theriault* was one of the most active vessels of her type, working the year round between Nova Scotian ports and the West Indies. She was built in 1919 by the Theriault Shipbuilding Corporation at Belliveau's Cove, Nova Scotia, and was averaged sized, 326 gross tons and 136 feet long. She seems to have been in the salt business most of her days; this undoubtedly helped in preserving her hull, the salt preventing any rot. As far back as March, 1921, she arrived at Boston 17 days from Turks with 13,595 bushels of salt.

In November, 1921, the *Theriault* was very nearly lost during a terrific northwest gale off the southern New England coast. Before dawn broke on the 5th, she crashed onto the rocks along the shore of Fishers Island. As huge seas pounded her hard, it did not seem possible that she would hold together long. Her crew of six, fearing for their lives, leaped overboard into the storm lashed surf, struggling through the surging waters to safety on the beach. However, the schooner, still young and strong, was able to take her punishment, and some days later the Scott Wrecking Company managed to float her clear without too much damage,

In the 1930's the *Theriault* was a noted vessel for her captain and owner was Mildred I. Wambolt, a young lady hardly out of her 'teens from La Have. After making many trips with her foster father, Captain Angus Publicover, she took over the *Theriault*, transacting all the business of the schooner, signing clearance papers, and managing the crew of one Nova Scotian and eight natives of Barbados. By this time the schooner was registered in Bridgetown, Barbados.

While Captain Wambolt was in command, the tern put in some very good passages. On one run she was 16 days from Shelburne to Barbados, and she made two passages from Bridgewater to Barbados in 17 and 13 days. She also made a 13 day trip from Bridgewater to Turks Island. None of these runs could be considered poor; in fact, several rate better than average. In February, 1933, caught out in a winter gale which ripped the sails and damaged the schooner's gear, Captain Wambolt was forced to turn and run before the blast until it let up. She was driven far off her course, but brought her vessel safely home.

The *Theriault* was often on the casualty list althought never for anything very serious. In early 1935 she was picked up off Nova Scotia, and towed into La Have, 38 days out from Turks. This had been an exceedingly hard weather passage of one storm after another. The tern *Esthonia*, which had sailed with the *Theriault*, was listed as overdue, but she crawled into Lunenburg on January 12th. The three-mast *Nova Queen*, also at sea during this period, was never seen again, presumably foundering.

In the fall of 1935, the *Theriault* was taking a lumber cargo south when she developed a leak which forced her to return to port. A year later she had another bad trip from the West Indies, 37 days at sea; she had to put into Riverport for repairs. On March 14th, 1937, she completed one of her longest trips, 46 days from Turks to Lunenburg. Soon after sailing she had lost her rudder, and for thirty-three days the schooner was steered by her sails alone. On March 1st, when 300 miles southeast of Cape Hatteras, she had been given supplies by the Dutch steamer *Amazone*.

In 1938 mutiny struck the crew of the *Theriault*. Now under the command of Captain George Corkum, she was loading salt at Turk's Island when the crew refused to work, saying the ship was leaking like a sieve, and that only her gasoline pump was keeping her afloat. They added that she was unseaworthy, and that if the pump, which was nearly worn out, should stop for any length of time, she would sink like a rock with such a heavy cargo as salt. Finally the crew deserted over the side, leaving Captain Corkum, his mate, and ship's boy aboard. The Captain tried to ship a crew of natives, but the word had got around about the non-stop pump; no one would join him. It would have been too expensive to ship out a new crew from Canada; there was nothing to do but sail short handed for home. Captain Corkum and his two men and the chugging pump took the tern the 1400 miles to Lunenburg without further ado, arriving there on November 17th, three weeks out.

Early in the war years, the *Theriault* was sold to parties in Jamaica. Not long after, she was caught by a Nazi submarine off the Cuban coast. At the time, the tern was loaded with lumber from Florida for Jamaica. The Germans chased away her crew, and then put a bomb aboard, blowing off her stern. In time the wreck drifted ashore on the Cuban coast where she was salvaged, and towed into Havana for repairs.

By now the *Theriault* was hardly recognizable as the smart sailing ship which the New England waters knew. Now owned by B. P. Gancedo of Havana, she was called *Ofecia Gancedo*. Her topmasts and bowsprit had gone, and she carried only a wisp of canvas; she was a motor vessel.

Below are a few of the passages that she made under sail:
1937—arrived Barbados November 19th; 34 days from Halifax.
1938—arrived Demerara March 28th; 18 days from Halifax.
    arrived Bridgewater July 3rd; 15 days from Barbados.
    arrived Barbados September 27th; 32 days from Halifax.
1939—arrived Bridegwater April 27th; 24 days from Barbados.

Esthonia
    Originally built as the *Vincent A. White* by T. White & Son of Alma in 1918, this tern was for many years, part of the Parrs-boro fleet. She was a fine vessel, and a good carrier. In his book, 'Sailing Rigs and Rigging', Mr. Harold A. Underhill uses her as an example of the 'down east' terns, writing:
    "The *Vincent A. White* was a product of New Brunswick, so it is only natural that timber should be used for her con-struction. She is a typical vessel of that coast; the standing bowsprit and jibboom, treble bobstay, and the booms on the fore-staysail and jib, all stamp her as belonging to the land of 'Wooden Ships and Iron Men'. Her hull too is typical; the deckhouse right forward with the foremast up through it; the raised quarterdeck with turned wood rails and boat in davits over the stern, and the modern stockless anchor at her bows."
    Once in her earlier days, she joined the Western Ocean schooner fleet that ran between Newfoundland and Spain in the

fish and salt trade. The *White* returned to the westward in thirty days.

She remained in the registry as the *Vincent A. White* until 1927. Shortly after this, she changed hands, and was renamed *Esthonia,* owned by the Esthonia Shipping Corporation of Halifax. She ended her days in the West Indies salt trade, a hard run for any vessel, especially for an aging wooden one. In early 1935 she completed a long passage from the Indies to Lunenburg. She and the *E. P. Theriault* had sailed together from Turks Island. Storms drove her far off her course, and she was overdue before she came wandering in from the sea several days astern of the *Theriault.*

In the fall of the year the *Esthonia* ran into severe weather near Nantucket when bound for Bangor with rock salt. As the storm grew worse, the rudder was snapped by the raging seas. Lying helpless in the trough of the waves, the schooner was battered and beaten. Leaks developed along her seams. The screeching wind carried away her canvas. There seemed little hope for her crew of ten, but then the Norwegian tanker *South America* came out of the gale. With some fine seamanship, the Norwegians managed to save all hands. On October 26th the *Esthonia* foundered.

Evelene Wilkie

Although the tern *Evelene Wilkie* was not a visitor to New England ports in recent years, she deserves mention as she frequently passed through New England waters during her many voyages between Nova Scotia and the West Indies. Built by J. A. Balcom & Company of Margaretsville on the Bay of Fundy, she was a medium sized three-master of 405 gross tons and 138 feet in length.

Loading lumber at Parrsboro in September, 1918, she sailed to Barbados on her maiden voyage. From there she went to Turks to load for Nova Scotia. Her second passage, again south with lumber, was a lengthy one for she crossed the Equator, going down to Bonaceris on the River Plate, taking 75 days for the run which was good going considering the distance and her bulky cargo. She next loaded Argentine corn which she took across the Atlantic to Las Palmas in the Canary Islands, proceeding from there light to Turks where she again picked up salt for Lunenburg. By the time she had arrived back in Canadian waters, the shipping slump had already set in, and despite the fact that she was still a new vessel, she was laid up for a time.

When she went back to sea, it was to run between the Gaspe and Barbados, outward with cargoes of lumber, shingles, and fish, returning north with molasses and sugar. Sometimes she altered this run by taking lumber to U.S. ports, and hard pine from the Gulf ports to Cuba and the other islands. In recent years the *Wilkie* traded regularly in the lumber-salt run, loading in winter at Bridgewater and Lunenburg. She made 35 round trips to the West Indies in succession. Although none of her runs were exceptionally fast, neither were they slow, and she seems to have been a remarkably steady earner for the Evelene Wilkie Shipping Company of La Have who managed her through all these years. In her later years she never seemed to lack cargoes.

Perhaps 1938 is a typical example year for her numerous runs. Sailing from Lunenburg on February 21st, she went south through mid-winter storms to Barbados, taking 24 days for the passage. On March 25th she departed for Turks Island, running light. She was back in Lunenburg on April 21st, 19 days out. She took on lumber at Bridgewater in May, and a little more than a month later had discharged at Barbados. By the end of October, she had been to Nova Scotia, unloaded salt, taken on lumber, and returned to the Indies. On November 30th she was back in Lunenburg, 21 days from Turks.

In January, 1939, both the *Wilkie* and the four-mast *James E. Newsom* left Lunenburg on the same day for Barbados. The tern arrived there on February 12th, 16 days out, while the larger vessel did not come in until the 14th. In June, that same year, the *Wilkie* left Bridgewater the same day the *Jean F. Anderson* departed from La Have. The latter took 17 days to Barbados, a day less than the *Wilkie* needed for the slightly longer distance.

During the years from her launching until 1941, she had had but one master, Captain Ernest A. Wilkie, and it was undoubtedly due to his thorough knowledge of the North Atlantic in all its moods that the *Wilkie* was able to operate for so long without any serious weather damage or other troubles. He will long be remembered for his dramatic rescue of the tern *E. C. Adams* in December, 1935. Sailing a day behind the *Adams* from Turks, the *Wilkie* ran into heavy seas and winter gales as she worked her way north through the Gulf Stream, winds and spray lashing across her decks while towering combers sent her plunging and reeling onward but making little speed along her course. One day, not too far from the George Banks, the *E. C. Adams* was sighted flying distress signals, her hull waterlogged and her port bow stove in by the pounding waves. Captain Howard Corkum on the *Adams* had been attempting to work his sinking vessel into the fishing grounds with the hopes that a fisherman would be able to take off her crew, but so far they had only sighted nothing but the grey seas that for ever battered them, threatening to overwhelm their schooner, and send her to the bottom. They were loaded with salt, and if it clogged their pumps, nothing would save them.

Although the gale had departed, great seas were still running high when the two schooners met. Captain Wilkie had to bring his tern into position to effect the rescue, heaving to not too far from the doomed *Adams*. It took fine seamanship on his part plus the heroic work of his crew as they handled the lines on the pitching deck. Before leaving the *Adams,* her men fired her to prevent her from becoming a menace to navigation should she perhaps stay afloat. As it was, she did not last long, disappearing in the deep, wild waters while the *Evelene Wilkie* carried on for her home port. This was probably the last rescue made of a sailing ship crew by another sailing ship crew.

Captain Wilkie kept his schooner until 1941. The year before the tax by the Canadian Government had gone up to 75 per cent of one's earnings. He finally got discouraged when he found that all his work was not bringing in any money. In May he sold her to Jacobs Commercial & Shipping Company of Kingston, Jamaica, where it was still possible to operate a windjammer at a profit. Staying on as master, Captain Wilkie loaded a final lumber load, and once more turned to Barbados. From there he went over the old familiar road to Turks Island. This time he took his salt south, discharging at Kingston. And now, after 32 years with the *Evelene Wilkie,* Ernest Wilkie left her to return to his home in Nova Scotia.

After the war the *Wilkie* was still operating in the West Indies, but she no longer relied on her sails for when Jacobs sold her in 1946, an engine was installed, and she became a motor vessel. Nonetheless, behind her was a great record, one of faithful service through the years. She had outlived most of her contemporaries, and was a shining example of the Nova Scotian built schooners.

CHAPTER V

More Terns

~~~~~~

BUILT at Canning, Nova Scotia, by Lockwood & Hatfield in 1920, the tern *Fieldwood* was some 483 gross tons and 154 feet long. Most of her life was spent in the Nova Scotia-West Indies trade with lumber and salt, and she would make an occasional trip to New York for anthracite. She was an able vessel with a fair turn of speed.

For many years the *Fieldwood* was commanded by Captain Harris Oxner who seems to have done very well with her. However, the schooner got herself into a little trouble in 1929 when she was caught in a wintery blow in early February while loaded with salt from Turks to Lunenburg. At the height of the storm, she lost her rudder somewhat northwest of Bermuda. The U.S. Coast Guard, finding her helpless, had to tow her in for repairs.

A series of bad storms swept the North Atlantic in the winter of 1935, and once again the *Fieldwood* was caught out in a severe gale. Winds of hurricane force ripped the mainsail to shreds. Pounding seas once more disabled her rudder. Oddly enough, her position was not too far from where she had had her similar accident six years previously; the month, now, was January. As the schooner was battling the storm, all hands were below with the exception of Captain Oxner who was on deck watching over his vessel. Suddenly, without warning, a mammoth sea came racing out of the flying mists, rearing its foamy crests high above the tern. She struggled to lift to its height, but did not quite succeed as a torrent of water crashed with a roar along her decks with its wild force. The receding seas swept the decks bare, taking the captain with them; he was never seen again. A few days later the Coast Guard *Argo* picked up the *Fieldwood* not too far from the coast, towing her into New Bedford with her flag at half mast.

After minor repairs she went on to Boston, and later to La Have. Captain John B. Wilkie now took command. On April 20th,

1936, she arrived at La Have 24 days from Turks; on June 22nd, she was at Bangor, again from Turks, this time taking 25 days. In the fall of the year she made a couple of round trips to New York for coal. In the summer of 1937, she got stuck in a blow off the Nova Scotian coast, and was forced back into Halifax for repairs to her leaking hull. Christmas that year found her at sea; on December 29th, she arrived at Hampton Roads, 28 days from Halifax. Loaded with coal, she took 18 days to go south to Gaudeloupe, anchoring there on the last day of January, 1938. After a stop at Turks, she went north to Liverpool.

On December 13th, 1938, the *Fieldwood* sailed from Port Hawkesbury loaded with wood shingles and dried fish for Barbados. Captain E. L. Croft, who now commanded her, had six men with him, and a bulldog named Yummie. Right from the start they had heavy weather, the North Atlantic in its winter mood, ugly and wild. On the second day out the pumps broke down as the storm grew worse. Already the schooner was leaking as her seams worked open in the rough waters. To ease the load of their vessel, the crew dumped overboard the deck cargo, at the same time setting a course for the steamer lanes. She could not fight her way back to port against the westerlies which were now at gale force. With her small radio out of order, there was no way to call help.

On the 17th, a Saturday, the schooner filled with water, the seas breaking right over her. Only her strong construction held her together. With the food water-soaked, the crew was forced to live on canned goods, but they had no fresh water as the tanks in the cabin were under six feet of salt water. All hands huddled on deck in the bitter wind; there was no protection, and they had no fire. They were constantly soaked by the icy seas as comber after comber rolled down on them. None ever thought he would sight land again, expecting the schooner to break up under them momentarily.

Saturday passed, then most of Sunday. During the dark hours they sighted a ship, but she did not see them, passing on through the night. All day Monday they searched the wet horizons for signs of smoke. As the sun began to sink, they knew that they could not last another night; it seemed the end for them. It was then that the *S.S. American Farmer,* a passenger-cargo ship commanded by Captain H. A. Pedersen came out of the dusk. Sighting the foundering schooner, the *Farmer* hove to while a life-

boat in charge of Chief Officer James T. Knowlton was lowered to make the rescue. Knowlton and his men took their lives
in their hands as they set out in their mere cockleshell through
the arching seas, but their fine handling saw them safely across
to the windship. All hands and the dog were safely picked up, and
taken back to the *Farmer*.

The last seen of the *Fieldwood* was some 200 miles southeast
of Halifax. Her men were landed at New York. Later Captain
Pedersen received the Distinguished Service Medal of the United
States Lines for his handling of the rescue, and each member of
the lifeboat crew were also decorated as well as getting $25 each.

Frances Parsons

The tern schooner *Frances Parsons* was built in 1919 at Chev-
erie, Nova Scotia, by G. M. Parsons, being one of seven schooners
in the Parson's fleet. She was a smallish vessel, only 270 gross
tons and 112 feet long, but she carried a good load for her size. She
was not a fast schooner although sturdy and strongly built for the
lumber trade in which she was employed a good part of her life.

The *Parsons* had her share of mishaps through the years. On
January 30th, 1925, she drove ashore on King's Point near Southwest Harbor while awaiting the weather. She was light at the
time, and there was a driving blizzard which caused her to drag.
She was in a dangerous position, but the Coast Guard stood by,
and towed her clear. On July 2nd, 1933, when she was bound
down east in ballast, she grounded on the south shore of Penikese
Island in Buzzards Bay during a heavy fog. At first there was no
danger, but when the wind blew up to gale intensity, the schooner
was pushed up on the rocks which gave her a terrific beating. The
Coast Guard were unable to help as the tide ebbed, leaving the
schooner firmly ashore. However, some hours later, after the turn
of the water, she was pulled off without too much damage.

In the late summer of 1939 with Captain Karl Williger in
command, she lost her fore topmast in a breeze. On the next passage, she was caught by a heavy gale as she came down the coast
loaded with 270,000 feet of lumber, even her decks piled high,
bound for New York. She was off the Maine coast when a 50
gallon barrel of gasoline which was lashed on deck broke open,
soaking the lumber with fuel, leaving none for the pumps. Then
the seams began to let go, the seas pouring into the vessel. The
crew, pumping by hand, could not keep up with the flood. By

the time the Coast Guard cutter *Chelan* had picked her up to tow her into Rockland for repairs, she was a sorry sight with three of her sails in ribbons, her rigging damaged. Instead of going on to New York, she discharged later at Quincy.

After this she was laid up on the beach at Parrsboro, and would probably have remained there but for the war as she was getting along in years. In June, 1941, she was bought by Captain Medley Blenhorn from the estate of Edmund Willigar. After repairs, she continued in the home trade with lumber cargoes to New England ports. In the summer of 1942, now commanded by Captain John Taylor of Parrsboro, she got caught in another nasty breeze which proved too much for her aging rigging, and she lost her spanker, jibboom, and fore topmast.

In 1943 the *Parsons* was sold to parties in the West Indies as Canadian taxes were making it unprofitable for her owners to continue operating their windships. However, she did not last long. Bound south loaded with dried fish and whiskey, she ran into a heavy spring gale. For five days the little schooner fought for her life, but she was old and tired, too frail now to take the pounding of the Atlantic in its mad fury. Finally, on April 22nd, when 450 miles east of the Virginia Capes, she foundered as her crew took to their boat. For three days her men were adrift before they were picked up and rescued.

Not only was the *Parsons* the last of the Parsons fleet of Walton, Nova Scotia, but also the last of the Willigar fleet of which she had been part for many years. Some of her runs follow:
1936—arrived Boston June 15th; 9 days from Alma.
    arrived Boston July 18th; 6 days from Belliveau Cove.
    arrived Boston October 26th; 26 days from Alma.
1938—arrived Providence August 5th; 22 days from Point Wolfe.
1942—arrived Boston June 8th; 11 days from Parrsboro.

Frederick P. Elkin

The tern *Frederick P. Elkin,* was launched as the *Seaman A.O.* in 1919 from the ways of S. M. Field of Cape d'Or, Nova Scotia. Registered in Parrsboro by her first owner, A. O. Seaman, she was a fair sized vessel of 470 gross tons and 152 feet long, very similar to her many sisters that were built at about the same time around the Bay of Fundy and Minas Basin. She changed her name about 1923 when she went to St. John's registery.

Throughout the years she had managed to keep on the move,

not only in and out of New England waters, but to the West Indies as well. Her cargoes had been lumber, coal, salt, and the like. Much of the time she had kept clear of trouble, and so avoided undue stresses and strains. In November and December, 1935, when she was on a passage from New York to Nova Scotia, she met very severe weather off Cape Cod, finally struggling into Gloucester Harbor on December 2nd, 19 days out from New York. The *Minas King* came in with her, 12 days from City Island. When the *Elkin* finally made Yarmouth on December 8th, Captain Haughn declared that he had passed through the three worst storms of his career. However, apart from losing her foresail and some minor rigging damage, the tern was unscathed.

The three-master was given a thorough overhaul at Meteghan in 1939 so she was ready for the coming war years. She brought a load of spruce to Milton, near Boston, in September, 1941, from Sheet Harbor. Her last call in Boston was in April, 1942, again with lumber from Sheet Harbor. Following the war the *Elkin* worked chiefly around the West Indies with an occasional jaunt to the Chesapeake to load coal for Bermuda or Barbados. Although she was still well kept up, she was now showing her age with a decided hog. In July, 1948, when she sailed out from Newport News bound for the West Indies, she was the last windship to carry coal from the Bay. A year later her sailing days ended when her old hull, now worn out, was broken up in Barbados.

Passages:

1936—arrived Bangor May 11th; 26 days from Barbados.

arrived Boston July 25th; 8 days from Sheet Harbor.

1937—arrived Barbados May 20th; 25 days from St. John.

1939—arrived Yarmouth December 14th; 27 days from Barbados.

1947—arrived Baltimore July 13th; 15 days from Nassau.

General A. W. Greely

The Shelburne Shipbuilding Company in Nova Scotia launched the tern *Donald II* in 1919. Only 215 gross tons and 109 feet long, she had a spike bowsprit, no jibboom, but a full set of topmasts. She was strongly built and was a good sailer in a heavy wind. On one occasion she ran from Cape Sable Light to Rugged Point Light, Barbados, in 19 days. Another time, with a full load of lumber, she went from Louisberg to Bridgetown in 26 days.

The *Donald II* was generally employed in trade between the

Maritime Provinces and the West Indies. In 1929 she went as far south as Maceio on one trip. She frequently visited Newfoundland ports (she was registered at St. John's for many years), the Gaspe, Cape Breton, and thereabouts. Lumber, fish, and salt were her usual cargoes. In 1936 the tern was converted into an auxiliary twin screw although she retained her canvas as well.

In January, 1937, she came into Boston with 155,091 feet of lumber for a local concern. In February, when bound for New York, she caught fire off Sandwich. The blaze was extinguished with the aid of the tug *Joseph A. Moran*. After passing through Cape Cod Canal on February 16th, she arrived at New York three days later after a heavy weather passage.

During the next few months, the *Donald II* was made over into an arctic exploration ship. On May 3rd she was re-christened *General A. W. Greely* as she lay at her wharf in Port Newark. On July 3rd, when she sailed north with the MacGregor Arctic Expedition to study meteorology conditions in the polar regions, she carried a refrigerator and an ice cream freezer. On her way up the coast, she met a northwest gale which smashd at the small, overladen schooner. Her bowsprit was carried away, her decks swept clean, and three feet of water sloshed in her hold. When salt water flooded the drinking water tanks, the crew had to drink beer for more than a week until they could put into port to replenish their supplies.

September found her at her base of operations, Reindeer Point, Greenland. On the 6th of the month a howling storm with wind of 80 to 100 miles an hour blew the schooner away from her anchorage, driving her out into huge seas. At the height of the gale, a fire broke out in her engine room, making her engines useless. When the weather had moderated, the small boats from the *Greely* had to be used as tugs to get her back inside the harbor. On September 30th another storm forced icebergs into her basin of refuge, the ice crushing against her wooden hull. With the temperature at 11 degrees below zero, the men fought to keep their vessel in place. The pressure snapped two 10-inch hawsers before the wind shifted, easing the situation.

After spending the winter frozen in the ice at Reindeer Point, the tern did not get clear until July, 1938. On her trip south, she was caught for three weeks in more ice in Baffin Bay; she was badly strained by the ice pack. By the time she made St. John's she had to put in for repairs as she was leaking so badly after her experiences. Almost three weeks had passed before she was ready to carry on southward. Sailing in September, she was just in time to catch the full force of the infamous New England hurricane which she rode out 150 miles from Cape Cod. The wind ripped away some of her canvas, but she managed to take the blow without too much additional damage. She finally staggered into New York on October 4th. Considering that she had been built as a typical down east tern, she had stood up to the rugged conditions in remarkable fashion, certainly a feather in the cap of her builders.

In 1940 the *Greely* was sold to the Venezuelan Government for service in the West Indies.

George E. Klinck

Slightly larger than the *Charles H. Klinck,* the *George E. Klinck* was another heavily constructed three-master designed for the stone trade. Built by Michael B. McDonald of Mystic, Connecticut, in 1904, she was a centerboarder of 560 gross tons and 152 feet long, one of the bigger schooners of her type. Her earlier years were spent mostly between Maine ports and New York, south bound with heavy stone slabs for building construction or paving stones, and returning north with coal when she could get a charter.

Once in May, 1924, her owners thought she had foundered during a trip from Vinalhaven to New York. Sailing on the 2nd, she was not sighted for three weeks; an average run would take a week to ten days. However, she was safe, just fighting her way against stormy headwinds. The following April she was given a complete overhaul at Rockland, caulking, a new Oregon foremast, headstays, and such. Later she took paving stone from Long Cove to New York.

She kept in fairly regular service until the early 1930's when she was laid up, first at Tenant's Harbor and later at Rockland. When she changed hands in 1938 for $160 she was in very poor condition aloft, and her hull was beginning to give in places.

The war years brought her back to life. In late 1940, she was towed to Southwest Harbor by her new owners, Jay Bushway of Marblehead and Lennox Sargent of Southwest Harbor. Here she was given a complete overhaul and refit. Her rotted stern was taken off, a complete new one taking its place. Her rigging was checked, the spars scraped down. She was modernized in every way with comfortable quarters for her crew, electric light, ship-to-shore telephone, and the like. A new suit of sails were made for her. Lastly, the schooner was painted. By the time she was ready for sea, she looked a new vessel. Even the gold scroll work about her bows shone, and her figurehead, the head of an eagle, was touched up. Very few of the last schooners had anything in the way of ornamental work about their bows, and the eagle head was almost unique.

The *Klinck* was ready to sail in January, 1941. Her new commanding officer, Capt Lewis McFarland of Trenton, Maine, had gathered together seven men to serve with him. His mate was a Dane who had been at sea all his life, and who had had three ships go down under him. At least one man in the crew had never been to sea before, but with the demand for sailors so great, Captain McFarland had to take anyone who was willing to serve in a windjammer.

Departing from Rockland on January 29th, the *Klinck* ran down the coast. She stopped at Vineyard Haven on February 2nd before pushing on south to Jacksonville where she arrived February 13th, nine days from Vineyard Haven. After taking aboard a load of southern pine, she sailed for Portland on March 3rd. Soon she ran into bad weather which gradually grew worse as she came north.

She was 150 miles southeast of Cape Hatteras when she began to show signs of opening up. For hours the schooner had been buffeted by heavy seas which jarred her from end to end. In the early evening of March 7th, a wave larger than the rest came racing out of the gloom, smashing head-on with the schooner. She staggered for a moment as she fought to rise to the crest, and her long bowsprit lifted to the skies as the wild foam slid past on either side in a deluge of flying spray. The damage had been done for her forward seams began to open. The *Klinck* had two gasoline-powered pumps on board but one of these had been put out of action by a sea that had boarded her earlier in the day. Now the remaining pump could not be kept up with the flow of water as it poured in through the openings. At seven o'clock Captain McFarland ordered an "S.O.S." call to be sent out on the ship-to-shore telephone, but it was then discovered that the set had been smashed by the seas that were now boarding the tern with increasing frequency. Sometime after ten o'clock, when it seemed certain that the vessel would not hold together until morning for the 60-mile-an-hour wind was whipping up the seas steeper and steeper, the crew brought out a dozen parachute flares that they had. The first one shot aloft into the black, cloud filled sky, a bright beam of light which was their one ray of hope. One light after another, the flares hovered above the doomed vessel. As the last light was burning out, the running lamps of a vessel were sighted in the darkness; rescue was on the way.

Not long after, the *Klinck* was suddenly bathed in the beam of a spotlight from the huge aircraft carrier *Wasp* of the United States Navy. As the carrier was working into a position to lower a boat, an extra strong gust struck the *Klinck,* throwing her over onto her beam-ends as she lay broadside to the rollers. With the boiling foam smashing across the leeward deck, the crew clung to the windward railing, wondering if they would go down with help so near. Fortunately, the old masts could not stand the strain, and one by one they snapped, permitting the sinking schooner to right herself. Captain John W. Reeves, Jr., of the *Wasp,* realizing that the schooner would shortly be battered to bits by the combers, placed the bows of the carrier against the *Klinck* so that a Jacob's ladder could be dropped to her decks. With the two vessels rising and falling in the rough waters, it took much courage for the *Klinck*'s men to work their way across her sloping decks to start up the dangling rope ladder. In fifteen minutes four of them had got aboard that way. One of the men, Gerald Windam, was snapped off the rope before he was able to board the *Wasp,* falling between the two ships, but a green sea flipped him aboard the tern unhurt.

Without warning, the schooner now drifted away from the carrier. Captain McFarland and three men were still awaiting their turn to be rescued. As a last resort, the *Wasp* lowered a motor whaleboat under the command of Chief Boatswain H. O. Warren with a crew of volunteers. The tiny boat, lifting and diving in the mountainous seas, edged its way close to the hulk. They did not dare get too near for fear they would be smashed to bits alongside the larger wooden vessel, but they were able to throw lines and life jackets to the men on the *Klinck.* Then, one after another, the men jumped from the schooner into the water to be hauled into the lifeboat. Captain McFarland was the last to leave his ship. Soon they were all on board the *Wasp,* suffering from exposure but with little other hurt.

The *George E. Klinck* did not last long, and was soon knocked to bits by the gale. Old shipping men felt that she had been given too heavy a cargo after her refit, before she had time to settle down. The strain of the seas had pulled her open; she had not had a chance to get a hold of herself. She was last seen with her decks awash in Latitude 35° 02' North, Longitude 74° 21' West.

Guinevere

The *Guinevere* was a handsome three-mast steel schooner-yacht which was built by Lawley's at Neponset, Massachusetts, in 1921. Practically a duplicate of the *Visitor II* launched ten years earlier, she was a medium sized vessel of 508 gross tons and 171 feet long, and was one of the first large yachts to use engines with electric drive in connection with diesel power. Under canvas alone, she was a smart sailer, capable of reeling off the knots. In the 1928 trans-Atlantic race from Ambrose Channel Lightship to Santander, Spain, she placed third behind *Elena* and *Atlantic,* with a passage of 17 days, 22 hours. Her two best 24-hour runs were 285 and 243 miles.

After an inauspicious start in life when she grounded in Buzzards Bay shortly after leaving her builder's yard, she was long a familiar sight along the East Coast. Her owner for many years was Edgar Palmer of New York.

World War II found the schooner with the U. S. Navy, but unlike so many other auxiliaries that the Navy took over, she kept her canvas although her topmasts were removed, and her spanker was cut down to a riding sail. Well armed and with 150 men in her crew, she was used as an escort for the slow convoys across Massachusetts Bay and for patrol duty in the Caribbean.

At the end of the war, she was turned into a cargo ship in New York, sailing south in July, 1946, to take up her new work in the West Indies.

Hazel L. Myra

The *Hazel L. Myra* was a small sharp 'Novy' tern which frequently passed through New England waters on her passages from Canada to the West Indies. Built by the Bridgewater Shipping Company in 1920, she was 223 gross tons and 109 feet long.

In the 1930's she was registered in Bridgetown, Barbados. A most active schooner, she was generally in the lumber-salt runs to the Indies although she varied this in 1936 and 1937 by making passages to Madeira.

Her end came in 1938. In February she was bound from Turks Island with salt when she sprang a bad leak during a storm which had smashed her rudder. The *Myra* was very nearly foundering when the British steamer *Cavalier* sighted her. As Captain F. Acker and his crew of five abandoned the tern, they put a torch to her to prevent her from becoming a menace to shipping. She sank about half way between Bermuda and Florida.

Passages:

1936—arrived Madeira August 31st; 27 days from Riverport, N.S.

1937—arrived Barbados April 9th; 24 days from Bridgewater, N.S.

arrived Paspebiac May 24th; 33 days from Barbados.

arrived Madeira September 5th; 39 days from St. John.

arrived Bridgewater November 19th; 29 days from Barbados.

Helvetia

The *Helvetia* was a fine three-master built by I. L. Snow of Rockland, Maine, in 1905. A large vessel of 499 tons and 157 feet in length, she was constructed of oak frames, longleaf pine planking, fastened with iron and copper. For many years she hailed from Rockland with Snow her owner who put her in the coastwise trade. The first World War boosted her earnings, and so, too, did the Florida land boom a few years later.

In July, 1918, it was feared that she had been sunk by German submarines as she took so long on a passage from Maine to New York. When she did turn up, her captain reported a lack of wind all the way. On December 13th, 1922, she departed from New York for Charleston, South Carolina, with 470,000 feet of lumber. When she did not arrive, she was listed as overdue. After a derelict schooner had been sighted on January 17th off the Virginia Capes, her crew were given up as lost in the storms. However, on January 27th, the *Helvetia* sailed into port, 47 days from New York. Captain L. A. Greenwood was able to read his own obituary in the current newspapers. Continuous gales had driven her far off course. Once she had been only 100 miles from her destination only to be driven seaward again. On her next voyage, bound for Boston, further gales whipped her, washing overboard 50,000 feet of her deck load of lumber. But she was a staunch vessel, taking little damage herself.

By the 1930's, the schooner was finding it ever more difficult to locate charters; her owners knew that she was not earning her keep. In 1933 she was sold by the U. S. Marshal to Kenney & Company for $755. A year or two later she was owned by Edwin F. Pettegrow of Larrabee, Maine. For a time she worked in the

THE LAST SAIL DOWN EAST

Nova Scotia lumber trade, but she was not too successful at it. In April, 1935, she took 21 days to sail from Salmon River to New York, spending much of the trip sheltering from the weather. In May, 1936, she was 8 days running from Alma to Boston with lumber; then she took another 8 days to go to New York in June. In August she needed 21 days to get from Alma to Boston, dodging storms part of the time at Jonesport. Her last trip to Boston under sail was in July, 1937. On June 10th she had sailed from Salmon River, crossing over to Alma to complete loading. On the 24th she left the New Brunswick port, next putting into Rockland early in July for shelter. She finally made her destination on the 9th. Not long after this, the *Helvetia* was cut down to a towing barge, then owned by the Maine Seaboard Company. She remained in Maine waters for several years, but in 1943, as a scow-barge of 514 tons, she was transferred to the Panamanian flag. She was said to have been still afloat in 1948.

Henry H. Chamberlain

The three-mast schooner *Henry H. Chamberlain* was an "old timer", having been built by F. S. Bowker at Phippsburg, Maine, as far back as 1891. A shallow draft vessel, she was 246 gross tons and 122 feet long. Fastened with wooden treenails, there was not a metal nail in her hull. For 46 years the tern was active in the local coasting trade with lumber and coal cargoes. In her earlier years her home port of registry was Bath, but later on it became Calais.

The Chamberlain was a good sea boat. In 1898 she weathered the terrible gale that lashed the New England coast, the storm that sank the *City of Portland* with a heavy loss of life. There were times when she was able to make good speed, and it has been said that she could get up to 14 knots if the conditions were in her favor. For the greater part of her life she was owned by Captain Wasson who managed to steer her through the years without too many troubles or difficulties, yet keeping her most active.

The tale is told down east that one of Captain Wasson's sons was killed in her by the main topmast which had rotted away at the foot, and suddenly fallen to the deck during the course of a voyage. From that time until her sale, the topmast was never replaced.

In 1937, when the tern was about worn out, Captain Wasson sold her to Canadian parties. She did not last long. On November 14th, bound from Fourchu, Cape Breton, for Halifax, she was hit by a blinding rain squall. Before it had cleared, the old schooner had crashed on a ledge off White Point, Nova Scotia. The captain and his crew of five were rescued after they had clung to the sea-swept reef for four hours, but the *Chamberlain* was a total loss.

Irene & Myrtle

The *Irene & Myrtle* was a small three-master which was launched as the *McLean Clan* at Mahone Bay, Nova Scotia, in 1920. Built by the McLean Construction Company, she was only 285 gross tons, and 125 feet in length, but she carried the typical coasting rig with her three topmasts and bowsprit with jibboom.

Until the second World War she was active in the down east lumber trade between the Maritime Provinces and the New England ports. In October, 1929, she was purchased by Captain Thomas Antle who renamed her *Irene & Myrtle* after his two daughters. Captain Antle had commanded the schooners *Orozimbo,* the fast *Sarah Eaton,* and other coasters in the local trade, so was well known in these waters.

The *Myrtle* had two 60 horsepower engines put in her hold to give her an extra shove through calms and for entering and leaving ports. However, she was not entirely an auxiliary as the engines were not always in working order, and many of her passages were done under sail alone. And in later years, it was said, the Canadian Goverment removed the propeller from the small tern because her captain did not have a ticket for power, and refused to remove the propeller himself.

During the 1930's, the *Myrtle* was a frequent visitor to Boston and Gloucester, generally making her first trip south each year in April when the ice had freed her from her winter berth; she would lay up in November or December for the coldest months although there were some seasons when she never stopped working. Fully loaded, she would generally take some 220,000 feet of spruce. For the most part, her passages were on the lengthy side, but she sometimes turned in a fast run. In the fall of 1931, she went from Boston to Windsor, loaded with fertilizer, in 50 hours dock to dock; she returned to Boston with lumber from St. Martin's in four days. When she arrived in Boston on June 18th, 1932, she brought in one of the last lumber cargoes before the new import tax went into effect — a tax that many thought would end the down east lumber trade for the Canadians, but the demand for wood kept the schooners going regardless of the price. Once in

[99]

1931 she was suspected of having a cargo of liquor under her lumber load, but a thorough search cleared her of the charge.

By 1940, the *Myrtle,* with an engineer aboard, was making more use of her engines, and her topmasts had been removed. In August of that year she was overdue on a trip to Gloucester from Parrsboro with as much as 300,000 feet of spruce, a huge load for her. When she was unreported for 17 days, the Coast Guard sent out a message for all ships to keep an eye out for her, but the schooner was safely, slowly ambling down the coast, having sheltered at Southwest Harbor during a breeze outside.

Captain Antle died suddenly when the schooner was at New London in the late summer of 1942. His son and one other hand carried on alone, bound for Nova Scotia with a cargo of coal. An amusing incident took place when she arrived at the Cape Cod Canal. Coming in under power alone, she was permitted to proceed, the Coast Guard thinking that she would pass through the canal before the tide would change. However, they had not figured on her weary engines. As the *Myrtle* passed the lookout station on the western end of the canal, the C.G. lookout reported by phone to the eastern end that the schooner was on her way. Two hours later the eastern end phoned back to know what had happened to the schooner as she had not yet arrived there, only some eight miles distant. An investigation showed the *Myrtle* in mid-canal, engines going at top speed, all sail set to a fresh breeze, just holding her own against the strong current against her.

Shortly after this, the *Irene & Myrtle* joined the U.S. Navy as the *Irene Forsyte.* Her commander, Lt. Richard Parmenter, has written the following about her:

"In August, 1942, I was instructed to take under consideration the feasibility of fitting out an armed schooner for anti-submarine work in the Caribbean where some 26 or 28 small schooners had previously been sunk by German submarines, mostly by gunfire. As you are aware, there were virtually no American three-masters of recent date and after a survey of the American schooner *Lucy Evelyn,* which was in frightful condition and I believe has since been in serious trouble several times, our attention was turned to Canadian schooners which, although built of soft wood, were far more recent. We inspected the *Frances Parsons,* the *Peaceland* and the *Irene & Myrtle* which at the time was making her way back to Yarmouth, Nova Scotia, with a cargo of coal, and which we found lying in New London harbor. She appeared to be in the best shape of any of the schooners mentioned, although a complete absence of hanging knees made me feel that tie rods would be a necessity if any heavy machinery was installed.

"The ship was at that time in possession of the Antle family. Captain Antle had died in New London in mid-summer of 1942, and his son, age about 25, and one hand were attempting to work the ship back. After protracted negotiations with the Canadian Government, the United States secured the vessel for a little over $15,000 with the understanding that her cargo would be transferred to the *Frances Parsons*, then unloading in Gloucester, in order that the families around Yarmouth would get their coal for the winter. She was towed from Gloucester to New London on the sixteenth of November, 1942, and delivered to the Thames Shipyard for conversion. At this time she had in her in line of machinery one 40 HP gasoline engine, one 60 HP gasoline engine, both broken down, and one 'bull dog' in the forecastle for operating the anchor and hoisting sail. I don't think I have ever seen a filthier vessel or one with more bedbugs. As the winter of 1942-43 dragged on, it became apparent that the conversion would take a longer time than was anticipated, and the entire submarine situation changed. The Germans were no longer operating in the Caribbean, but were bunched in mid-Atlantic north and south of the Azores, and it was finally decided to disguise the *Irene* — now the *USS Irene Forsyte* — as a neutral fishing schooner returning from the Grand Banks to Europe. This plan was arrived at after scrutiny of Intelligence photographs, and a European schooner, which did not differ in profile too much from the *Irene,* was selected. It was apparent that all of New London knew the ultimate role that the *Irene* was to play, and consequently the conversion to the specific neutral schooner would have to be done away from the shipyard. The schooner chosen was known only to myself, and one or two higher officers, who warned that the State Department had not been consulted, and that if we were captured, the Navy would be forced to disclaim any knowledge of the ship or her crew.

"We sailed in August, 1943, with the materials for altering the profile stowed away on board, and left New London in broad daylight without camouflage and under lower masts, all guns showing and painted the standard Navy gray. We anchored behind Great Point, Nantucket, after dark in thick weather, and by morning the guns had been concealed, the profile altered, topmast sent up and the ship painted white (in accordance with German regulations for neutral vessels). We rode out a very heavy gale in the vicinity of Nantucket and sailed for South America on a track which would carry us well across the Atlantic. The ship had been armed with one 4" gun, one 40mm, two 20mm, and a 16 barrel rocket thrower. We carried radar, sound gear, and two 500 HP Diesel engines had been installed.

"Unfortunately, the installations of these heavy engines, which was against the judgement of many people including myself, very radically altered her trim, so that instead of running on a nearly even keel and drawing about 11' as was her normal loaded draft, she now drew 14'6" aft and 9'3" forward. This made her handling under sail extremely difficult, and four or five days after sailing we encountered a very heavy gale, and had to ride it out broadside to, as it was impossible to control her running before it, or to make her lie to, even with the trysail set on the mizzen. The ship opened up and water gained on the pumps, and it was questionable whether or not we could get control of the situation. After the gale had passed, I requested permission to run into Bermuda for repairs which were effected in the dockyard there, and sea trials were held in the neighborhood of Bermuda, and a large improvement in the sailing qualities of the ship were effected by leaving some twenty tons of stores, mostly engine room, behind.

"We operated in the vicinity of Bermuda for awhile, but by this time the 'baby flattops' were clearing the Atlantic, and we were finally ordered back to New York, and all the Q-ships were decommissioned, two of them being turned over to the Coast Guard as weather ships.

"The *Irene* was loaned to the Maritime Commission, and served as a training ship, I think until the autumn of 1944. I next heard of her in the autmn of 1945 at which time she was lying in Brooklyn being converted, it was said, for the China trade. That venture never came off, and when next I heard of her from sources I do not recall, she was in New Orleans.

"Incidentally, if she is ever hauled out, there is a copper plate under the heel of the mizzen which gives the names of her five officers and thirty-one men . . ."

After the war the *Irene & Myrtle,* as she was best known in New England waters, was still in commission in the West Indies in the freight trade. Under the Honduran flag, she reverted to her first name, *McLean Clan,* and then later became the *Santa Clara.*

She was lost in December, 1950, when her tired seams opened up off La Ceiba. There she foundered.

Below are a few of her passages of her lumber days:
1933—arrived Boston March 25th; 10 days from Parrsboro.
1934—arrived St. John May 20th; 4 days from New York.
1936—arrived St. John October 15th; 15 days from Boston.

Jean F. Anderson

One of the better known tern schooners operating out of Nova Scotian ports was the speedy *Jean F. Anderson,* owned for a time by Captain Publicover. Built at Port Wade in 1919, she was a medium sized, sharp vessel of 396 tons and 140 feet long. Her entire life was spent freighting cargoes along the East Coast, from the Indies to Newfoundland. One voyage might find her going south to a United States port with lumber, the next trip might be north with coal for Harbor Grace, and then a jaunt to Turks for salt.

A few of her passages are listed:
1926—arrived Boston July 30th; 12 days from Gaspe.
1936—arrived Halifax October 14th; 28 days from Barbados.
1937—arrived New York May 14th; 16 days from Bridgewater.
        arrived La Have June 7th; 11 days from New York.
1938—arrived New York April 17th; 9 days from Bridgewater.
        arrived Demerara September 5th; 18 days from Bridgewater.
1939—arrived Barbados June 4th; 17 days from La Have.

For the most part, the *Anderson* was a lucky vessel, but she did make the casualty list once or twice. In October, 1930, when bound light through a dense fog from New York to Boston, she hit the shoals at Monomoy Point. Although a strong southwest breeze was blowing, she did not pound badly. Some hours later the Coast Guard pulled her off, just in time as a full gale struck which she rode out at anchor. In December, 1936, she crawled into Bermuda after ripping some of her canvas during a bad gale on a voyage from Charlottetown, Prince Edward Island. Some of her livestock cargo was lost. In February, 1938, she was again caught out in a winter blow, this time 150 miles off Sable. She fought her way through terrific seas that battered her from all sides, but she managed to make Halifax, 35 days from Turks Island. Once more she had suffered torn canvas and broken spars.

The *Anderson* arrived at Portland, Maine, from Clark's Harbor, Newfoundland, on July 24th, 1939. While there, she loaded

246,000 feet of lumber. After waiting a week for wind, she crossed the Gulf of Maine to White's Cove for an additional 200,000 feet of lumber before proceeding to Funchal, Madeira, a long voyage for the aging vessel.

Her end came in December, 1941. In May of that year, she was sold to parties in the West Indies for, it was reported approximately $15,000, a good price for a 22-year old vessel built of soft wood. In December the *Anderson* was bound south from Lunenburg to the West Indies. Shortly after entering the Caribbean, she was struck by a smashing hurricane that wrenched the hull open with its force. Soon the tern became a waterlogged hulk with only its rigging above the foaming seas. For five days and nights the crew clung to a boom, 'like crows sitting on a roost'. Finally, a British steamer sighted them, and took all hands off their perilous position.

The last captain of the *Anderson* was St. Clair Geldert of Lunenburg.

John Bracewell

One of the oldest existing terns was the *John Bracewell,* launched in 1878 from the Bath yards of Goss & Sawyer who were well known for the numerous full-rigged ships that they had built. Strongly constructed, the *Bracewell* was a fine looking craft in her younger days, with a pleasing bow, the stem piece painted with scroll work running up under the front of her long bowsprit and jibboom. Although her lines were full amidships, she had a clean run aft to an attractive stern.

The *Bracewell* was not a large vessel, being some 394 gross tons and 113 feet long. For many years she was owned by B. F. Nealley who registered her in Portsmouth, New Hampshire, in 1900, and in Rockland twenty years later. About 1921 she was taken over by the C. A. Small Company of Machias who ran her for about a year. Her next owner was C. Morrison of New York. In 1924 she went under Canadian registry, then managed by L. A. Rowe of Parrsboro. In spite of her age, the *Bracewell* kept active until around 1937; in June, 1936, she took a cargo of lumber to Bangor, Maine, from Nova Scotia. However, she was too small to successfully compete with other terns, and she was too old to have an engine installed; a power plant would have shaken her to bits in no time at all. She was laid up on the beach in Parrsboro Harbor, and there she disintegrated.

She was very typical of the hundreds of three-masters that were built in the latter part of the nineteenth century, and which were known all over the world. Unfortunately, most of the *Bracewell's* history has been forgotten. The coasting men who sailed her did not keep much in the ways of logs, probably never thinking that anyone would be interested in their ship more than a half century later. As she had outlived her builders and most of her crews, there was no one to turn to for information; the story of her life has passed with her.

J. T. Wing

It is a strange fact, but the last of the commercial windjammers on the Great Lakes was formerly a 'down east' lumberman, which ended her days as a marine museum in Detroit. Launched as the *Charles F. Gordon* in Weymouth, Nova Scotia, in 1919, she was first owned by her builders, Beazley Brothers, who operated her in the lumber trade. She was a typical Nova Scotiaman of 431 gross tons and 140 feet long, carrying the usual rig of the tern schooners.

During the slump in shipping after the first War, she entered the lucrative rum running trade along the East Coast, carrying cases of liquor south to a point off the three-mile limit where she would be met by fast moving power craft that would speed the precious cargo ashore under cover of darkness. All went well until she was put ashore on a southern key. Captain J. O. Webster bought her in 1922. After repairing and re-rigging her at a cost of $3000 in Miami, he operated her as an American vessel, named after himself.

Under Captain Edward Long, she continued in the coasting trade as long as he could find business. In November, 1930, when the demand for lumber had gone, he was forced to lay her up after trying every lumber shipping port in the Maritimes for a cargo to New York. In May, 1931, when bound from Yarmouth to New York in ballast, she went ashore on Green's Ledge, Connecticut. At the time she seemed a complete wreck, but a month later she was salvaged and taken in Noank, Connecticut.

Grant H. Piggott purchased her in 1935, rebuilding her, replacing worn planks, strengthening her old hull, overhauling her standing rigging, replacing her running rigging and sails, so that by the time she was ready to sail she was very nearly a new vessel. Heading north, she left New England waters for the last time as she made her way for the St. Lawrence River to enter the Great Lakes. Renamed *J. T. Wing*, her first load for the Lakes was pulp wood which she took on at Rimouski, Quebec, and delivered to Port Huron, Michigan, arriving there on August 14th, 1936.

During the next three years she was a familiar sight as she plod the Lakes, deep laden with lumber, cedar, pulpwood and logs, from the Canadian ports around Georgian Bay and Green Bay of Wisconsin to ports on Lake Huron, often going down to Detroit to discharge. In all the Lakes, she was the very last sailing ship to carry cargo, a far cry from a half century before when the Lake ports were often a forest of masts in the days of wooden ships and iron men.

In 1939 the *Wing* became a training ship of the Kalamazoo Sea Scout Squadron through the efforts of Frank F. Ford, their Commodore. Once more the schooner was done over, this time fitted out for a complement of 100; in her commercial days she had sailed with a crew of six. Below decks steel stanchions were set up for the boys' hammocks, while aft cabins were arranged for 14 officers. Her galley was done over, made large enough to take care of a 100 hungry mouths at each meal time, and six large iceboxes were installed to keep food fresh. She did not need large fresh water tanks; they could draw their water from over the side — so different from the schooner's saltwater days. She was renamed *Oliver H. Perry* after the Naval Officer who had won the smashing Battle of Lake Erie, in 1813.

The first cruise of the *Perry* took her through Detour Passage, St. Mary's River to Sault Ste. Marie, and then on into Lake Superior, returning via the Straits of Mackinac. Her 97 boys had a chance to see a real windjammer under sail, could thrill to handling lines, take their trick at the wheel, stand watch, and learn the ways of sailors. Under Captain John Mattison, an old-timer who had begun his sea-going career in Finnish square riggers, following that with many years on the Lakes aboard the ancient lumber schooners, the boys had an ideal man to lead them for he had a vast knowledge of the sea, and there was little that he did not know about the Lakes.

Most of the *Perry's* cruises were uneventful although now and then she would get into some minor trouble. Once she was aground for a spell, and on another occasion she was becalmed and fog-bound for four days which was all part of the sailor-scout life, but which had the boys' families worried when the Chicago Daily

Tribune headlined "SEA SCOUT SHIP LOST". On her first cruise in 1940, she met some breezy weather, one time being hit by a 50-knot squall. During her third cruise, which was from Chicago to Milwaukee, she raced through choppy seas which did no harm to the ship, but caused many a scout to wonder why he had ever left dry land. When she was 35 miles northeast of Milwaukee, a blinding rain squall struck. The weather suddenly turned bitterly cold, hail filled the air. The old schooner fell over before the blast until water gushed in through her freeing ports. With a roar, her spanker ripped up. At the height of the storm, a water spout raced towards the windship, but when it was fifty feet away, it split in two, with half crossing her bows while the other part just missed her stern. The squall settled down into a fresh gale with heavy seas and a biting wind, but the *Perry* was an able vessel, coming through with minor damage. During another storm later in the season, the tern logged 12 knots as she raced for home, slowly catching up to one of the large ore steamers, and easing ahead of her. Later she raced a powerful Ford tug with two barges, and for fifty miles the schooner led the way, showing that she still had a good turn of speed.

The *Perry* remained a training ship until the end of the 1941 season. With the war on, the schooner went back to work in early 1942 when she again became the *J. T. Wing,* and now owned by the Chippewa Timber Company of Sault Ste Marie, Michigan. Once more she carried pulp wood and logs, making her last commercial voyage in the summer of 1943 when she took timber from Manitoulin Island to Detroit. Then she was laid up.

In 1945 she was bought by several ship lovers who presented her to the City of Detroit, and plans were made to turn her into a marine museum devoted to shipping on the Great Lakes. She was moved to a site at Belle Isle, serving as a museum for the next seven years. By 1956 rot had set in. She was too expensive to keep up so it was voted to do away with her. After her hold had been filled with 2000 gallons of fuel oil and old tires, tracer bullets set her afire, so closing the Great Lakes windjammer days.

Leona and Marion

The three-master *Leona and Marion* was a handsome vessel of 313 gross tons and 134 feet long. Built by the Job Shipbuilding Company of Machias in 1920 for C. A. & B. F. Small Company, she was designed to carry salted fish from the smaller Maine ports to the larger markets. In later years she was also employed in the lumber trade from Nova Scotia to New England ports and down to New York. For a number of years she was commanded by one of the seafaring Wasson family, Captain Alvin Wasson.

In November, 1937, she was sold to the Mullark Shipping Company of Halifax, then going under the British flag. Loading lumber at Bridgewater, she sailed south to Barbados, arriving there on January 6th, 1938, after a slow passage of 32 days. When she had discharged, she went light to Turks, departing from there on January 23rd with 300 tons of salt for Lunenburg. At first the weather was pleasant, and she made good time on her northern run until she was off Cape Hatteras where she began to meet wintery weather. By the time she had made Nantucket waters, a full gale was blowing with the Atlantic becoming ever rougher.

Rearing and plunging, the *Marion* tried to run before the storm, but the strain was too much, and on February 4th, her foremast carried away. Before the wreckage could be cleared, the main topmast also snapped off. Practically helpless, the schooner took a terrific beating from the foam-crested combers which time after time crashed against her wooden hull. In a short time, when the seams began to go, the crew realized that their ship would not last long. Captain Skinner sent up flares into the night, their one hope as it was far too rough for their one small boat. About 9:30 p.m. on February 6th, the tanker *Harry F. Sinclair,* sighting the darts of light in the wild murk, raced to the rescue. Within an hour all hands and the pet cat were taken off the doomed *Marion* which was set on fire to prevent her from becoming a menace to navigation. Soon after, the little schooner sank; her crew were put ashore at Boston on the following day.

Marine

The *Marine* was a good-sized tern of 390 gross tons and 147 feet long, built by Beazley Brothers at Weymouth, Nova Scotia, in 1919. She had a fairly active life, spending most of her later years in the lumber trade from 'Novy' to New England ports. She does not seem to have been very fast, sometimes taking as much as three weeks and more to come down the coast. She did quite well for herself in July, 1937, when she arrived at Boston in less than nine days from Apple River. In December of that year she was two weeks from Moncton to a point off Winthrop, near the entrance to Boston Harbor, where she anchored. Although there was very little wind, a heavy ground swell was running, the aftermath of a heavy storm that the schooner had weathered on her trip south. While awaiting tugs to tow her in, she was badly strained by the violent rolling, her seams opening and letting the water in. However, her lumber cargo kept her afloat until she was pumped out before docking. After spending Christmas and New Year in port, she departed for Parrsboro on January 3rd, 1938.

That was the last trip of the *Marine*. Upon her arrival at Parrsboro, she was laid up; she never sailed again. If she had been sufficiently seaworthy, she would have gone back into service in the recent war, but no one cared to take the chance, so she never left the harbor.

During the last years of her active life, the *Marine* was registered in Charlottetown, her owners being the Willigar family, with Captain Murray Willigar in command.

Mary B. Brooks

With the exception of the *Venture,* which was built as a training ship, the *Mary B. Brooks* was the last tern schooner of her class to be launched in a Canadian down east yard. Built by W. D. Foley of Digby County, she first took to the water in 1926; she was to replace the *Westway* which had been wrecked the preceding year. Named for the wife of Captain William Brooks who was her skipper, she had been on the ways for 5½ years owing to the shipping slump. She was not a large vessel, only 243 gross tons and 99 feet long, but she was rather handsome with her hull painted grey to the deck line, and her bulwarks painted white.

For some ten years the *Brooks* traded pretty regularly in the lumber trade from the ports around the Bay of Fundy down to New England and New York. As a rule she laid up during the winter months when the weather was bad, and the northern harbors iced over. Her maiden voyage had been to Portland.

In 1938 the tern left Meteghan after she had been given an overhauling, bound for the West Indies. On April 5th she arrived at Havana where she was sold to local buyers, going under the Cuban flag. During the next few years she was seen around Cuban ports and also at Mobile, Kensington, Nassau, and Bermuda in the West Indies trade. However, she did not last long, for shortly after war was declared in Europe in 1939, the *Brooks* was wrecked off one of the salt islands, her bones bleaching in the hot sun.

Her last appearance in New England was by way of the movies when she appeared as a background in "Bahama Passage" with Sterling Hayden and Madeline Carroll in 1941 and 1942. Much of her paint was gone by then, her bottom badly holed, planks missing, and it seemed that the next tropical storm would surely break her up.

Some of the *Brooks's* passages were as follows:
1929—arrived Boston April 4th; 8 days from Weymouth.
1934—arrived Boston July 24th; 7 days from Weymouth.
1935—arrived Boston May 22nd; 3 days from Weymouth.
    arrived Boston July 1st; 4 days from Weymouth.
    arrived Boston August 7th; 5 days from Weymouth.
1936—arrived Providence April 22nd; 29 days from Weymouth.
1937—arrived Boston May 26th; 3 days from Weymouth.
    arrived Perth Amboy, October 21st; 6 days from Boston.

After this last passage, she never came into another New England port.

Migrant

The *Migrant* was one of the last large schooner-yachts to be built. Designed by Henry J. Gielow, Incorporated, for Carll Tucker of the New York Yacht Club, she took to the water in 1929 from the George Lawley yards at Neponset. She was 223 feet long overall, and was able to set 15,825 square feet of canvas.

The *Migrant* was beautifully fitted out below deck with seven staterooms, each with a private bath. Her main living and dining saloon which extended the full width of the yacht amidships had a wood-burning fireplace as an added touch. Her outward appearance was somewhat spoiled by her large deckhouses, but these added greatly to the comfort of her owner and his guests. Below deck she had a 1000 horsepower diesel which could drive her at 13 knots.

During the recent war, the *Migrant* served with the U. S. Navy. Her foremast removed, she was used for patrol and escort duty. Later she was a freighter in the West Indies, frequently bringing bananas to Miami from Colombia; she was listed as a 'motor vessel' then.

Minas King

Often seen in New England waters in the years preceeding World War II, the tern *Minas King* was a regular visitor to Vineyard Sound as she traveled back and forth between Nova Scotia and New York. Built by J. S. Creelman at Bass River in 1918, she was one of the larger tern schooners, being 550 gross tons and 154 feet long. Although she was not particularly fast, she seems to have been a reliable vessel, and managed to keep fairly busy taking lumber south and coal north.

Late in 1935, the *King* went through a severe dusting on a passage from New York towards her homeport, Parrsboro. Sailing on November 20th, she ran up Long Island Sound, through Vineyard Sound, and over the Shoals. Off Cape Cod she met very ,bad weather, having to fight her way across the Bay to shelter at Gloucester. The *Frederick P. Elkin,* which had left New York on the 13th, arrived there on the same day. When the weather had moderated, the *King* put to sea again, but was driven into Portsmouth by another gale. She sailed from there on December 11th, and was not heard from until she came into Rockland on the 21st after a third gale. In the end, she was towed on to Yarmouth, arriving there the day after Christmas, having taken more than a month for the 500 mile trip.

The following spring the *King* had a close call off Quoddy Head. Eleven days out from New York with 600 tons of coal, the tern was caught by an easterly gale that drove her towards the rocky coast. Captain George Merriam, who had his wife and a crew of seven with him, ordered the anchors dropped, but they did not catch a hold on the bottom, the schooner slowly dragging in the tremendous seas. Coast Guardsmen on shore, sighting the signal flares from the windship, attempted to launch their surf boats, but found the seas too rough to get out. The cutter *Ossipee,* berthed at Portland, was called to come to the rescue. It was a long run for the cutter, and only a shift in the wind saved the *King* from being grounded to bits on the sharp ledges along the beach. She was later towed into Johnson's Bay on May 15th, before proceeding to discharge. She then crossed the Bay to Port Greville for repairs, and to load lumber.

She departed from Port Greville on September 4th, bound for New York; the day before, the *Minas Prince* had sailed from St. John, also for New York. Although both vessels had the same weather, the *Prince* arrived at her destination on September 11th, 8 days out; the *King* did not turn up until the 25th, having taken 19 days for the run. She made a still longer passage to New York some months later, taking 59 days from Beaver Harbor, much of the time being spent weathering at Jonesport and Portland. The *Minas Prince* arrived the day after her, after a 55 day trip from Digby; they may have arranged to spend Christmas together at Portland.

Some other runs of the *Minas King* follow:

1938—arrived Parrsboro March 10th; 38 days from New York.

arrived New York May 19th; 15 days from Port Greville.

arrived New York July 25th; 17 days from Parrsboro.

arrived New York September 30th; 18 days from Apple River.

1939—arrived St. John June 22nd; 7 days from New York.

The *Minas King's* sailing days came to a close soon after the start of war when she was bought by the Dominion Coal Company of St. John, who used her as a barge for some time. She was finally towed outside the harbor there, and beached as a hulk.

Minas Prince

One of the best known Nova Scotian tern schooners that frequently visited New England waters in the days before the recent war was the large *Minas Prince,* a vessel of 511 gross tons and 148 feet long. Built during the first World War, her keel was laid in the yards of J. E. Pettis at Spencer's Island, Minas Basin, in 1917, to the order of Captain Wallace Smith who had organized a company and sold shares in the new vessel. Her lines were taken from those of a schooner that had been built some years earlier, the *Charlevoix,* which had proved so successful that fifteen copies of her were built between 1918 and 1920. The Pettis brothers, William and J. E., built the first three-mast schooner on the Bay of Fundy, and they became the leading builders of this type of vessel.

The *Minas Prince* was launched on March 4th, 1919. Captain Smith had watched his vessel on the ways, and he had seen that only the very best material went into her. She had a hard wood bottom, and spruce and hard pine top planking; her ceiling was of Douglas fir and spruce.

The maiden voyage of the *Prince* began on July 17th, 1919, when she departed from Parrsboro with 610,000 feet of lumber for England. She discharged at Liverpool, took on 100 tons of ballast, and was back at Parrsboro in sixty days to the hour since she had sailed from there. Her second voyage was the same run, this one being completed in 72 days. In the winter months she took pine to the West Indies, returning with salt. Her record load of salt was 24,000 bushels. In the summer of 1920 she went back on the England run, doing three round trips, averaging 70 days. She was once only 14 days from England to Parrsboro, shore to shore; on another trip she needed 47 days to get home. Later in the year, the *Prince* set up something of a record when she sailed light from New York to Mobile in 12 days. She had raced down the Atlantic seaboard at better than thirteen knots, and she was off Tortugas in nine days, but from there on she had not had the right winds so was slowed considerably over the last leg of the passage. She loaded hard pine there, some 457,000 feet being her limit with the heavier woods. She once carried 632,000 feet but that was the lighter spruce. The heaviest cargo that she ever lifted was rock plaster, 926 tons of it which really set her down to her marks, and then some.

In March, 1929, Captain Smith purchased the shares of the tern from Hugh Gillespie & Company, who had been the major holders; he continued to sail as her captain for the next eight years. At the end of the year, the *Prince* had a rough passage from Boston to Wolfville with 430 tons of fertilizer. She lost her foresail, fore-staysail, and jib, ripping her mainsail, carrying away her mizzen topmast, and straining her hull, as well as having her steering gear damaged and much deck gear destroyed. She was partly re-built in 1932 in Parrsboro.

The *Prince* hit the headlines of the Boston newspapers in December, 1933. After discharging a lumber cargo, the schooner was being towed out into the harbor through two or three draw-bridges by the tug *Eileen Ross*. Suddenly a gust of wind carried the two vessels, side by side, into the draw of the New Haven railroad; there they wedged in the narrow opening. The accident took place shortly after mid-day as the tide was falling. Tugs and fire-boats tried to pull them free without success, although at one time it appeared that their straining lines would pull the schooner apart. When the five o'clock rush hour came, all trains to the Cape were held up, some 25,000 persons being delayed. Not until nearly midnight did the tide rise sufficiently to permit the two vessels to get clear.

This had been an unlucky voyage for the *Prince*. With Wallace Smith sick, his son Douglas had taken charge. After loading at Alma, the schooner had lost part of her head gear when a tug held on too long to its hawser. Later, when she was entering Boston, passing through the same draw, she was the indirect cause of two trains crashing, one smashing into the rear of another that was awaiting the draw to shut.

After this, the *Prince* returned to her quiet ways, passing up and down the coast fairly regularly. She was one of the fastest schooners that remained, seldom making a bad run unless forced into a harbor of refuge to wait out a storm. Some of her passages follow:

1925—arrived Boston May 26th; 3½ days from St. Stephen.
1929—arrived Boston April 25th; 3 days from Parrsboro.
1936—arrived New York May 10th; 23 days from Apple River.
     arrived New York September 4th; 18 days from Moncton.
     arrived St. John October 13th; 16 days from New York.
     arrived Boston December 1st; 22 days from St. John.
1937—arrived New York September 11th; 8 days from St. John.
1938—arrived New York December 4th; 9 days from Parrsboro.
1939—arrived Boston April 25th; 3 days from Parrsboro.

In 1937 Captain Wallace Smith died. The new owners of the tern were Martin Gavin and associates of Parrsboro. Towards the end of the year she sailed for New York with lumber, but did not arrive until January 18th, all of 55 days out. She had come by way of Beaver Harbor, Machiasport, and Portland, storm dodging all the way. The *Minas Prince* was not too lucky in 1938. In March when on her way from New York to Parrsboro, she was caught in a gale off Monroe Island. Her rudder was damaged, and some of her canvas was ripped away by the force of the wind. When the Coast Guard picked her up, her crew were short of provisions, and nearly worn out.

The *Prince* was laid up the latter part of 1939 to await better charters. In January, 1940, she was bady damaged by fire, but she was repaired at Parrsboro. The war brought her back into service again. Her last passage began on September 13th, 1940, with rock plaster for New Haven. She had hardly cleared the Bay when she met the tail end of a hurricane sweeping up the Atlantic from the Bahamas. Huge seas of ugly green-grey water bore down on the schooner, crashing across her decks in a swirling foam. With a thunderous roar, the staysail and jibs carried away. The mainsail, still set, brought her broadside to the swell. Huge waves broke aboard, smashing her pump. The crew fought to make repairs, but they had no sooner got it operating again when further seas swept over them, this time destroying the pump as the receding waters carried parts of it overboard. As water seeped in, the *Prince* began to go down by the head. Fearing the hatches would blow off at any minute, letting the schooner sink like a rock, the crew took to the small boat. The only food that they had with them was twelve cans of tomatoes. After a time, when they saw that the *Prince* was staying afloat, they reboarded her, put her off on the other tack, and let her tow the boat towards port.

The gale passed, and the next day brought calm seas. The men had been using hand pumps, but they were exhausted after hours of work; they could not go on much longer. They went back to the small boat. The *Prince* slowly towed them on although her rigging had become slack; perhaps her masts had jumped off their steps. They also thought that the fore piece had pulled out.

With no one at the pumps, the *Prince* slowly filled and sank, going down on Sepember 18th, some sixty miles southeast of Nova Scotia. Thus passed one of the greatest terns of them all.

Her crew was picked up by a steamer which took them into port.

CHAPTER VI

And Still More Terns

O F THE tern schooners working along the New England
coast, the *Peaceland* was one of the most active, and probably the last of her type to come into Boston with lumber from
Nova Scotia. Built by the Annapolis Shipping Company of Annapolis Royal in 1919, she was on the smallish side, being only 228
gross tons and 112 feet long. Owned for many years by Captain
Walter Wasson, she was bought in 1930 by the Ogilvie family with
Captain Hilton Ogilvie taking command; her homeport was
Parrsboro.

The *Peaceland* spent the greatest part of her later years on
the Nova Scotia-New England run with lumber, working from the
Bay of Fundy to Boston, Gloucester, or Portland, doing several
trips in the summer months, and laying up during the winters.
Below are a few of her typical passages:

1924—arrived Boston May 27th; 5 days from Parrsboro.
1935—arrived Boston July 11th; 5 days from Alma.
        arrived Boston September 23rd; 10 days from Alma.
1936—arrived Boston June 1st; 9 days from Alma.
        arrived Boston July 13th; 8 days from Alma.
1937—arrived Boston May 14th; 7 days from Parrsboro.
1938—arrived Boston June 10th; 13 days from Alma.
        arrived Parrsboro September 25th; 13 days from Boston.

Fully loaded, the *Peaceland* could carry some 250,000 square
feet of lumber, much of it stacked high on her deck. Her arrival in
port was often heralded in the local newspapers with an adver-
tisement showing a picture of her at her wharf, with an announce-
ment: "NOW UNLOADING . . . Schooner *Peaceland* with a cargo
of white spruce direct from the great timberlands of the Apple
River country in Nova Scotia. . . . This sturdy first growth lumber,
sold most everywhere at premium prices because of its scarcity,
is offered here in Gloucester at prices oftentimes less than is paid
for ordinary lumber."

As the *Peaceland* sailed in the summer months when the winds were light, she seldom found herself in trouble. However, in May, 1939, she struck Mosquito Island, off Port Clyde, in a dense fog. For a time she was in grave danger of pounding to bits on the sharp rocks. However, a high tide and the efforts of the Coast Guard cutters *Argo* and *Travis,* a patrol boat and a tug, floated her clear without too much damage.

The *Peaceland* had a good turn of speed, and could hold her own with the other terns of her size. On May 27th, 1924, she entered Boston Harbor in company with the schooner *Margery Austin*. Both had come from Parrsboro, the *Austin* sailing on April 26th, and the *Peaceland* on May 22nd. The latter had made the round trip, Boston to Parrsboro to Boston, in three days less than it had taken the *Austin* to come one way. Still, in 1929, the *Peaceland* required 41 days to cover the run from Parrsboro; for three weeks she had been forced to shelter at St. John while a gale blew outside the entire time. The *Peaceland* and the *Mina Nadeau* had come from the Minas Basin to Cape Ann together within hailing distance all the way; the latter had gone on to New Haven.

On August 17th, 1936, the *Peaceland, Marine and Mary Brooks* arrived in Boston together. The *Marine,* from Alma, well up the Bay, had taken 12 days; the other two, the *Brooks* from Weymouth, and the *Peaceland* from Windsor on the Avon River, had taken 11 days. The *Peaceland* certainly sailed the longest course of the trio. In November, 1940, she raced the *Albert Willis* from Portland to Boston; Captain Ralph Ogilvie was in command of the *Willis* and his brother Hilton still on the *Peaceland.* The smaller tern carried 228,000 feet of lumber, while her larger sister was laden with more than double that amount, all of 537,000 feet. Getting under way at 8:30 a.m., the two schooners ghosted along together out of Portland Harbor, the wind so light that it took them until 11 o'clock to pass Cape Elizabeth, only seven miles from their anchorage. As long as the breeze was gentle the *Peaceland* held her own, but once outside, the *Willis* began to walk away as the wind came up. In the afternoon, the schooners were forced to take in their topsails as the weather turned bad, but they continued to drive down the coast in a flurry of foam. Such a sight as two lumbermen under press of canvas will never be seen again along the New England coast; this was probably the last race. The *Willis* anchored in Boston Harbor late that evening with the *Peaceland* just an hour behind her, a good showing for the little schooner. The *Peaceland* had completed her sixth trip to Boston that year, something of a record for the Nova Scotiamen.

The *Peaceland* last came to Boston in 1942. On May 7th, she sailed from Parrsboro, sheltered at Jonesport around the 13th, and made Boston on the 19th. Her next trip of the season was Yarmouth to Boston in June, taking seven days. In July she was six days for the same run. She was back in Boston on September 8th, and for the last time, on October 17th. She is the last commercial windjammer from overseas noted in the Boston Customs House book of arrivals.

Not long after this, the *Peaceland* was sold south. Sometime in 1943 she foundered, it is said near Cape Hatteras, going down with all hands. The little schooner, which had done so well in New England waters, was too old to fight the stormier seas outside; she must have just opened up in a heavy gale.

Rebecca R. Douglas

One of the oldest three-mast schooners operating in New England waters when the recent war broke out was the veteran *Rebecca R. Douglas* which had been built by Kelley, Spear & Company of Bath, Maine, as far back as 1894. Of 475 gross tons and 138 feet long, with hard pine planking on oak frames, she was fitted with a centerboard that was 18 feet long, 12 feet wide, and six inches thick. When lowered it added some ten feet to her draft. As the centerboard well was almost in the center of her keel, the mainmast had to be stepped slightly off to port to clear it. The board was hoisted by gear attached to the mainmast. When the schooner was loaded, one man could handle the board as it would float up, but when she was light, at least two men had to haul on the tackle to lift it.

During her earlier years, the *Douglas* worked around the Chesapeake Bay in the lumber trade, and it was about this time that another deck was added amidships as protection for her cargoes of kiln-dried lumber, so that her below-deck cargo space was quite considerable while she could carry little or no deck load. This added superstructure rather spoilt her appearance, although it did give her considerably more strength.

In the 1920's, C.A.&B.F. Small took over the schooner, using her chiefly between New England ports and New York, south with lumber or potatoes, returning north with coal. In 1926 she was nearly lost when, on September 17th, she collided with the *S. S. Eastern Crown* in Pollock Rip Slue. The schooner's bow was almost cut right off, but she managed to stay afloat until she could be towed into port for repairs.

When the shipping slump struck in the early 1930's, the *Douglas* was laid up at Machiasport. As she was getting to be a very old vessel by then, it seemed that she had reached the end of her active days. Her sails had been taken off, and her booms were bare. The boat was missing from her after davits. Her grey paint was stripping off her hull, while rust streaks ran down from her chain plates. Moored away from shore, with chains out fore and aft to hold her, she was a sad sight.

However, she returned to service in 1937 when Captain Burtis M. Wasson purchased her. Captain Wasson, Canadian born but an American citizen, had been in sail for a half century. For thirty-one of those years he had been owner and captain of the *Henry H. Chamberlain,* another tern, which he had just sold before buying the *Douglas.* Few men knew the Atlantic coast as he did, a most useful knowledge when running in fog or heavy weather. He was a most careful man, never taking unnecessary risks. He had the best crew that he could find. His eldest son Alvin was chief mate, another son Harold was second mate. Two other sons, Paul and James, acted as able seamen, while Paul's wife went as stewardess. Then, in 1940, Reid joined the crew; he was Captain Wasson's 13th grandchild, only a few months old.

The *Douglas* was now kept busy. After a refit, she appeared as good as new, becoming one of the smartest down east coasting schooners. Life on board was happy, all hands living aft, leaving the crew's quarters forward empty. However, she was not always lucky. On the night of June 27, 1939, when off Fire Island Lightship bound from Jonesport to Port Reading, New Jersey, without any cargo, she was in a crash with the *S.S. David McKelvy.* The weather had been clear with good visibility, and no doubt each vessel had sighted the other. Captain Wasson followed the rule that a sailing ship has the right of way over a steamer, but this time the steamer failed to alter course. However, the damage was not too serious. The *Douglas* lost her headgear and was smashed about the bows. When she arrived at Port Reading, repairs were made. She then took on a coal cargo, taking it to Seal Harbor in five days. In spite of her age, the *Douglas* was not a slow vessel, and her record shows several fast runs. In October, 1939, she was only eleven hours from **Vineyard Haven** to Gloucester even though she was deeply loaded with coal; her average speed for the distance had been ten knots. In December she had been six days from Port Reading to Southwest Harbor. After that she was laid up until the spring. In April, 1940, she took fifteen days to trip from Machias to City Island with lumber. She returned from Sandy Hook to Seal Harbor in four days, another very fast run. In August she swept from Machiasport to Boston in two days, again with lumber.

One of her slowest passages took place in January, 1941, when she was all of 31 days from South Amboy to Jonesport. However, nineteen days of this period were spent at anchor at Vineyard Haven awaiting a break in the weather. Perhaps her best run was in October when she took coal from Sandy Hook to Bass Harbor in two days, seventeen hours. The wind was right for her, and she had raced along at her best speed.

When the *Douglas* was surveyed in November, 1942, she was found to be in excellent condition considering her 48 years afloat. There was a little rot here and there, but nothing that could not be remedied at too great an expense. However, Captain Wasson thought it best to sell his vessel with such high prices prevailing, and on January 1st, 1943, the *Douglas* was sold to the Douglas Navigation Corporation of New York for $20,000.

Taking aboard 300 tons of paper at Searsport for Baranquilla, Colombia, she sailed on March 12th, southward bound. After putting in at Rockland, Boothbay Harbor, Gloucester, and Vineyard Haven, she arrived at Brooklyn on March 29th to load the remainder of her cargo. With Captain Walter Wrightson in command, she left New York on May 1st. She had new sails, shining white, and she made a fine picture as she left the land astern.

Outside the weather was moderate, but the breeze was gradually picking up all the time. Off the New Jersey coast a 60-foot Coast Guard picket schooner, a former yacht, came alongside, but the *Douglas,* only under her three lowers and two jibs, quickly left the smaller schooner astern. All evening the breeze freshened as the barometer dropped, and by the 3rd a heavy gale was blowing with winds of sixty miles an hour lashing the area. As the seas rose, they pounded the tern, and before long she was opening up, water seeping in through the cracks. Perhaps if Captain Wasson, who knew all her tricks, had been there, she might have been saved, but instead she slowly foundered. Off Cape May her crew gave her up to the sea, taking to their small boat. However, when this boat capsized in the heavy seas, Captain Wrightson and all but two of his men were drowned.

The passing of the *Rebecca R. Douglas* brought to a close the sailing ship era of the State of Maine for she was the last coastwise sailing vessel owned there. At the turn of the century there must have been hundreds of her type trading from various Maine ports; today there are none. The deep-water ship has gone.

Ronald C. Longmire

The *Ronald C. Longmire* was a Nova Scotian tern which was built by W. R. Longmire at Meteghan in 1920. Quite noted for her speed, she was some 183 gross tons and 102 feet long, certainly not a large vessel, but a handsome one. Most of her life was spent in the lumber trade from the Maritime Provinces to New England ports and New York with a jaunt to the West Indies for salt every now and then.

On one of her first trips to Boston with lumber in December, 1921, she was frozen to her wharf at Weymouth, not getting clear until mid-March. Twelve years later she was again caught by the ice there, this time in Dorchester Bay where she was held for nearly two weeks.

When she was a new vessel, she did some smart sailing along the coast. One of her best runs took place in 1925 when she swept into Boston in late April only 48 hours out from Church Point, Nova Scotia, a distance of 275 miles. She was loaded with 153,176 feet of spruce lumber and 1748 bundles of laths. On another occasion, in August, 1930, the *Longmire* and the *Peaceland*, both from Parrsboro, arrived in Boston on the same day; the former had taken six days, the latter eight days for the run.

The *Longmire* was commanded by Captain William Burns for many years. In the early 1930's Captain Frank C. Rangdale had her, but when he was injured by a fall aboard her in 1934, Captain Arthur Moore, who had recently commanded the ill-fated *Utilla,* took over.

The tern had one of her few serious accidents in February, 1937. At the time she was 22 days out from Boston when she ran ashore near Digby. However, she was on the beach less than a week, being successfully refloated; she repaired at Belliveau Cove.

In the early part of 1939, the *Longmire* was sold to buyers in the West Indies. From then on she worked in the southern waters until September, 1943, when a hurricane hit her while she was on passage from Abaco to Jamaica. She went down with all her crew.

St. Clair Theriault

The *St. Clair Theriault* was a medium sized three-master built at Belliveau's Cove by P. A. Theriault in 1919. She was 331 gross tons and 135 feet long. Although registered in the Canadian books during her earlier years, her home port later became Bridgetown, Barbados, her owners finding it less expensive to operate out of the southern port. However, she continued her usual trading, generally lumber south to the Indies, returning home with salt; she would sometimes make a trip to Boston or New York when charters were offered.

She was not a lucky vessel, often in trouble but managing to survive. In 1933 she sailed from Barbados bound for Pictou. Days passed without her being reported, and in time she went on the overdue list. It was then that she put into Halifax for shelter from a fall storm, little the worse for wear. Some months later, in January, 1934, she crawled into Barbados after a hard voyage from Pictou. During a winter gale her full deck cargo was washed from her decks by the raging seas; it was a wonder that she was not more damaged herself. At the end of the year, she was carrying lumber from Campbelltown to the Indies when she bumped a reef off the New Brunswick shore, opening up her seams, and sending her into Pictou for repairs.

The *Theriault* went through a series of misfortunes in 1936. In January she hit a bridge in the south of Cape Breton Island. Badly leaking, she was towed into St. Peters to be patched up before towing to Canso, her destination. She was a long time overhauling, but finally set out to get another cargo. She had not gone far before she was in the midst of a fierce gale which ripped several of her sails, and broke her spanker boom. She had to go back to the shipyard for further repairs. After this, she made a round trip to the States with lumber, this time dodging the perils of the sea although a few months later she was back in trouble again. She had picked up a cargo at Yarmouth, sailing for Lynn with her deck piled high with wood. The trip south, done in three days, had been uneventful, and Captain John S. Smith was beginning to feel that at last his vessel was in for a spell of better luck. As the schooner arrived off Graves ledges at the entrance to Broad Sound in lower Boston Harbor, shortly after midnight on October 26th, a strong westerly wind combined with a rapidly flowing, incoming tide drove her toward the Swampscott rocks. Captain Smith tried to work her back to sea, but it was too late, and within a half hour she had struck the reefs. There was not a great deal of swell running so no great damage was done. Before flood tide, the crew carried out her anchor, and at high water they were able to kedge her back into the channel. Although she was leaking badly, there was no danger of her sinking with the lumber cargo. The mate went ashore to phone for a tug, and not long afterwards, she was towed into the safety of Lynn harbor. It was said along the waterfront that if the schooner had struck the rocks a few feet further up, she would have been a total loss.

The next two years found the *Theriault* keeping busy. In 1938 she crossed the Atlantic to the River Moy in Ireland. Her end came in February, 1939, while on another Atlantic crossing. Her seams opened up at sea in Latitude 48 degrees North, Longitude 6 degrees West. As her crew were rescued, they fired the tern to prevent her from becoming a menace to navigation. Below are some of her passages:

1933—arrived Madeira July 9th; 38 days from Halifax.
1937—arrived Boston August 30th; 15 days from Apple River.
1938—arrived Moy River September 11th; 26 days from Pictou.

Stewart T. Salter

The three-mast schooner *Stewart T. Salter* came from the B. G. Dyas stocks at Parrsboro in 1919. A small vessel of 252 gross tons and 115 feet in length, she was typical of the Nova Scotian lumber schooners, just one of the many once so numerous in the down east waters. Owned by Captain Charles Salter and others for many years she traded regularly between the Bay of Fundy and the New England ports. She was not always lucky but she managed to come through all her troubles.

In April, 1929, she was caught in a bad blow off Cape Ann while heading for Boston with 240,000 feet of lumber from Apple River. She was 25 miles distant from Gloucester as her jibs began to rip. Heavy seas, smashing against her deck load, made it impossible for her crew to get at her pumps, and before long, with her seams opening, the tern was waterlogged. However, the fishing dragger *Mystic* happened along. With some skillful maneuvering, she was able to get a tow line across to the tern, giving her a lift to port where the *Salter* was pumped dry. Later a tug took her on to Boston to discharge and make repairs.

A month later the Nova Scotiaman was in trouble again. On May 6th she went hard ashore on Cape d'Or at the entrance to the Minas Basin on her way up to Parrsboro. This time she was badly damaged, the jagged rocks ripping off much of her shoe and keel, and tearing her planking. Mostly underwater, she was buffeted by the tides, her rails smashed, her stern battered, her houses gutted and her sails and gear destroyed; her fore-topmast came crushing down in a tangle of wreckage. She was a sorry sight when she was later refloated and towed around to port. However, a few weeks in the repair yards had her looking as good as new again.

In May, 1938, the *Salter* had what was probably her closest call with destruction. Leaving St. John on May 11th with 300 pilings below deck and 700,000 laths topside, she eased her way down the coast bound for the site of the New York World's Fair which was then being erected. She first met signs of bad weather on the 15th some 60 miles southeast of Portland. Captain Allan B. Taylor who was in command and Captain Joseph N. Pettipas who had bought the vessel two months before both realized that this was going to be more than just a summer breeze, and had much of her canvas furled. The *Salter* had been fitted with a 180 horsepower engine; this was giving her a boost. However, by six a.m. the rising seas had flooded the engine room, shutting off the motor. She tried to ride the storm out under sail. Her fore-staysail was blown to ribbons by the 70 mile-an-hour winds. Sea after sea crashed across the vessel, turning her into a waterlogged hulk in less than an hour. Her pumps, choked, were useless.

The crew crouched on the after cabin roof, clinging on amidst the swirling seas. Below deck, the pilings took charge, crashing and smashing back and forth, gradually opening up the vessel still more. The laths were washed away to leeward. Days later a fishing captain reported that it had taken his vessel nearly 24 hours to pass through a sea of floating laths.

In the late afternoon, the oil tanker *Harvester* sighted the *Salter,* and offered to take her in tow, but Captain Taylor requested a call for the Coast Guard. Seven hours later the *Algonquin* arrived. In the glare of the cutter's searchlights, a boat was put out to go alongside the floundering schooner, but she found it too rough to get close. The *Salter*'s men were forced to leap from the cabin top. In this manner the Coast Guard were able to save all hands. The next day a tow line was put aboard the tern, and she was taken into Gloucester.

As she lay alongside a wharf, the *Salter* appeared a shambles. Pilings had broken throught her planking in places, her after cabin and forward houses were demolished. Deck fittings were smashed. Her rigging was slack, as if her masts had come un-stepped. A report sent to the insurance companies stated that the stern post was apparently broken, rudder port burst, wood ends started from the stern post, masts dropped four to six inches, practically all seams opened, rudder driven into the stern of the vessel some six inches, and several planks broken above and below the waterline. She was condemned as a total loss, and Captain Pettipas collected some $4000 from the insurance companies; he stood to lose money as he had the vessel under-insured.

As the schooner was lying at a pier running up a wharfage bill, the Court ordered her sold to cover her expenses. An official appraiser valued her as worth $640. At her first auction the top bid was $155, but the Court would not accept that. At a second auction, the top bid had dropped to $25. At the third auction held, Captain Pettipas bought her back for $270. After a caulking job, the tern was towed to Boston, arriving there on February 21st, 1939, 286 days from St. John, some 300 miles away!

When the piling was discharged, further repairs were made. Some months later Captain Pettipas with his son and another boy sailed the *Salter* to Meteghan, the three of them handling the tern on a 19-day trip, nine of which were spent in Rockland while a gale blew outside. Some months after, the Captain sold the vessel for a reported $7000. She continued in service along the coast. One of her last visits to Boston was in October, 1941; by this time she was pretty much of a power vessel, her sails being very secondary.

In 1945 her name was changed to *Caroline*. She was now a full-powered motor vessel, with no canvas at all, owned by the Bradford Iron Works of Wilmington, Delaware.

A few of her passages as a windship follow:
1931—arrived Boston June 12th; 3 days from Apple River.
1936—arrived Boston July 13th; 9 days from Alma.
  arrived Boston October 24th; 18 days from Alma.
1937—arrived Boston December 3rd; 13 days from Apple River.

Thomas H. Lawrence

The last commercial windship built in Boston to see active service was the three-mast schooner *Thomas H. Lawrence* which was launched from the yards of R. Crosbie & Son of East Boston in 1891. A medium sized vessel of 375 gross tons and 134 feet long, she was owned for many years by E. P. Boggs who had her registered in Boston in 1900, and in Detroit 20 years later. In 1930 she was owned by F. G. Boggs, registered in Wilmington. F. A. Julie was her owner in 1935, and Rockland was then her homeport. G. B. Gordon had her next, but in 1939 she was taken over by the Pioneer Transportation Company, her homeport once again becoming Boston. However, by this time she was finished, never seeing service in the war.

During the 1930's, the *Lawrence* was kept busy along the Atlantic coast from the West Indies to Canada. Despite her age and run-down condition, she was amazingly active, generally managing to keep clear of troubles and accidents. A few of her runs were as follows:

1932—arrived Boston September 15th; 5 days from Belliveau Cove.
1934—arrived Havana, Cuba, May 8th; 13 days from New York.
      arrived Georgetown, S. C., June 6th; 6 days from Havana.
      arrived Boston November 26th; 11 days from St. John.
1935—arrived Boston April 24th; 5 days from St. Martin's.
1936—arrived Boston February 26th; 6 days from St. Andrews.
1938—arrived New York August 30th; 23 days from St. John.

In 1939 the *Thomas Lawrence* was given a complete refit at Rockland. Much of her rigging was done over, in some places turnbuckles replacing deadeyes and lanyards, so that she was a mixture of ancient and modern. She was given new hatches, and much other new wood where it was badly needed. Her bottom was caulked before painting. When she was ready for sea, she looked like a new vessel although an eight inch hog spoilt the sweep of her sheer.

Her owners planned to enter her into the Cape Verde trade between New Bedford and the Islands with passengers and cargo. Passenger fares were to have been $60 one way, $100 round trip. Sailing empty from Rockland to load at New Bedford, the old schooner slid down the shoreline in late August. As she approached Massachusetts, a heavy northeast gale came in from the Atlantic, driving her down on a lee shore. As the water rapidly shoaled off

Plum Island, Captain Antonio Perry let go the anchor, hoping that it would hold him off the beach, but when the chain snapped, the tern was left to drift helplessly before the blasts, completely out of control. A second anchor proved useless, just dragging over the bottom. After bouncing over three sand bars, the *Lawrence* finally flung herself on Crane's Beach, Ipswich, where it seemed that she would be a total loss. At low water she was almost dry; at high water she was still too far ashore to pull clear.

Hope of saving the tern had just about gone when a lighter with sandsucker equipment dug a channel to her, enabling the Coast Guard to tow her back into deep water. The next seven months were spent at Chelsea, Boston, where she was given a refit. Her rudder, which had been smashed in the grounding, was mended; her seams were again caulked.

On April 23rd, 1940, she departed from Boston bound for Jacksonville to load a general cargo for the Islands. A few days later she put into New Bedford as she was leaking. Here she was condemned by the Government inspectors who stated that she was not seaworthy. For a time she lay at anchor; then a gale struck her, driving her ashore again. Her sails and all moveable gear were removed, and she was abandoned as a hulk. Sometime later, boys set her afire, charring the hull although the spidery rigging continued to stand after the blaze. The schooner never moved again. Before the war was over, she had been pretty well broken up, and by 1947 only parts of her ribs and keel showed above low water.

So passed the *Thomas H. Lawrence.* She had been launched in the heyday of sail, when square-riggers were still common, and fore-and-afters were found in every harbor along the coast. The fifty years of her life saw almost the complete decline of windships, from the peak of the era to its end.

T. K. Bentley

About the largest of the Nova Scotia-built terns was the *T. K. Bentley* of 509 gross tons and 160 feet long. Constructed by T. K. Bentley at Advocate Harbor in 1920, she was owned by Bentley & Pugsley for many years, registered at Parrsboro. She spent her entire life in the down east lumber trade, and during her last years, generally between Canadian ports and New York with an occasional trip in to Boston.

[127]

When still a young schooner, the *Bentley* very nearly had her career cut short. On January 4th, 1922, she was traveling at nine knots in the dark off Cape Cod when the huge battleship *North Dakota* was sighted on a collision course. Having the right of way, Captain Leonard Berry of the schooner held his course. The navigator of the battleship, failing to realize the speed of the schooner, did not bear off, and the two vessels came together with a terrific crash. The *Bentley* lost her headgear as well as getting holed above her waterline. The battleship also had considerable damage as her training systems of the guns were thrown out of adjustment, the shutters and elevators ceased to function, and her starboard whaleboat was demolished. A Navy tug came out from Boston to tow the schooner in to port for repairs.

The *Bentley* was in another crash in October, 1928, this time with the U. S. Coast Guard cutter *Mojave* in Massachusetts Bay. Although the cutter was judged at fault, the schooner owners did not get a check from the United States Government to cover their repair bills until September, 1930.

The *Bentley* was in yet another accident on October 5th, 1933. She was anchored in the East River when the strong tides there caused her to drag anchor. The schooner's stern first smashed into a motor yacht off the New York Yacht Club at 26th Street. Then her bow swung around, striking another vessel before she drifted clear. Further down stream, her stern fouled the anchor cables of a houseboat. Eventually, tugs rushed out to pick up the runaway, and she was towed to Newton Creek where it was found that she had suffered but little damage.

In later years the *Bentley* was owned by Captain John J. Taylor who had commanded her for some time before purchasing her. He made some good passages with her just before the war even though her soft wood hull was aging rapidly. In 1937 the *Bentley* had an interesting 'race' with the *Albert H. Willis*. Leaving Apple River on November 3rd, the *Bentley* put into Portland to await the weather. Here she was joined by the *Willis* which had left Beaver Harbor on the 4th. As soon as the conditions improved, both schooners set off on November 15th for New York, all sail set although the seas outside were still running high. The *Bentley* seemed to make the best of the rough going, sweeping across the Bay, around Cape Cod, and down the Sounds to City Island, arriving there on the 20th; the *Willis* did not come in for another two days. While the Bentley was the longer vessel by two feet, the *Willis* was a considerably larger one, with a far greater tonnage.

Some other passages of the *Bentley* follow:

1936—arrived St. John July 24th; 10 days from New York.

arrived New York October 27th; 19 days from Parrsboro.

1937—arrived New York April 2nd; 20 days from Parrsboro.

arrived St. John October 4th; 8 days from New York.

1938—arrived New York May 7th; 10 days from Apple River.

arrived New York July 7th; 11 days from Apple River.

arrived New York September 1st; 8 days from Parrsboro.

arrived New York November 6th; 11 days from Parrsboro.

1939—arrived St. John June 16th; 8 days from New York.

This latter run was about the last passage of the *Bentley* for soon after she was laid up at Parrsboro to await better times. She had about reached the end of her days now for the life of the soft wood Canadian vessels was seldom more than twenty years. It is said that the *Bentley* did load once again, but she had got no further than Yarmouth when she began leaking so badly she had to put into port. The lumber was discharged there, and in time she returned to Parrsboro. Although war cargoes were bringing nice profits, the *Bentley* was considered too far gone to be of any further use. After she was sold to a Mr. Schultz of New York, she was condemned, and left on the beach. Not long after, she flattened out, and the ice of the following winter carried her bones away.

Vema

Formerly the *Hussar III*, the three-mast schooner *Vema* was one of the most handsome sailing yachts along the East Coast in the days before the recent war. Built at Copenhagen in 1923, she was a large steel vessel of 533 tons and 202 feet long overall. She had a good turn of speed under sail, and with the help of her engines made two fast trans-Atlantic passages. In May, 1932, she went from Montauk Point to Bishop's Rock, a distance of 2750 miles, in ten days, twenty-one hours; a year later she did the same passage in ten days, ten hours. The story is told that on one of her homeward trips she was struck by a squall which laid her on her beam-ends with her canvas in the water, but she managed to shake herself clear without serious damage.

The *Vema* was bought by the United States Maritime Service

in 1941 for use as a training ship, and acted as such during the war years. In 1953 she was purchased by Captain Kenedy who was going to put her into the lumber trade but instead chartered her to Columbia University for oceanographic research work. Later Columbia bought the vessel, and has used her since in research in waters around the world. As a yacht the *Vema* set 13,000 square feet of canvas. Her main truck was 131 feet above her deck; her main boom was 71 feet long. Today she is hardly more than a pure power vessel.

Victory Chimes

A frequent visitor to New England waters when the Nova Scotian lumber trade was at its height in the early 1930's was the tern *Victory Chimes* which had been built by J. A. McDonald of Cardigan, Prince Edward Island, in 1918. A smallish vessel of 397 gross tons and not quite 130 feet long, she was owned and commanded in her later years by B. E. Merriam with her homeport at Parrsboro.

The *Chimes* was not slow as some of her sisters, and had several creditable passages to her record. In May, 1935, she sped from Albert, New Brunswick, to Pawtucket, Rhode Island, in four days with 320,000 feet of lumber. On her run east, she had gone from Vineyard Haven to Albert in three days. The time consumed going and coming, together with taking on the wood, was less than 12 days. Captain Merriam believed this to be the record.

The *Chimes* was very nearly lost in 1931 when she was bound south with a full lumber cargo. Sailing from Parrsboro on July 1st, she had had a slight leak at the time, but her power pump had had no trouble keeping up with the flow. With a fresh summer breeze blowing, she made good time until the pump broke down. For eighteen hours Captain Merriam and his crew of eight worked the hand pumps, but the leak was too much for them. By the time the schooner was off Rockport, her rail was awash, the hold flooded, with only her cargo keeping her afloat. The Coast Guard cutter *Antietam* took the waterlogged vessel in tow, bringing her into Boston where she discharged her load and was repaired.

The *Victory Chimes* had an odd end. She was lying at her berth in Parrsboro where the tides rise and fall as much as forty feet. Somehow she managed to work herself over to the edge of the bar on which she rested normally at low water. As the tide went out, she gradually heeled over on the bank before falling on her side. Her bulwarks fell in from their own weight, and she became a total loss although most of her gear was saved. As late as 1940, her remains could still be seen, but it was hard to believe that the pile of weed-covered wood had once been a trim tern.

Village Queen

The *Village Queen* was one of the several very small three-mast schooners that ran in the local lumber trade south from Nova Scotia. Only 184 gross tons and 90 feet long, she was built in 1923 by F. A. Robar at Dayspring for Captain Publicover.

On one occasion in 1936 when the *Queen* had brought a lumber cargo to Boston, she lay alongside the *Laura Annie Barnes*. At that time Andrew Publicover was in command of the small tern, and his brother William was with him; his father was aboard the four-master with eight other members of his family. It was a day of reunion for the Publicover clan.

The *Village Quee*n last came to Boston in September, 1936. Two years later she was driven on a lee shore near Cape St. Mary's, becoming a total loss.

Wawaloam

One of the very few steel schooners to pass through New England waters in the last days of sail was the 142-foot *Wawaloam* which had been built in Holland in 1918. A three-master, she was originally a North Sea trader under the Dutch flag, but in 1923 she was made over into a luxurious yacht, sailing under the U. S. flag in the South Pacific. After several years she was laid up, but in 1939 Captain L. Kenedy of Conquerall Bank bought her while she lay at Philadelphia, turning her into a cargo vessel again.

With the help of his mate, two schoolboys and his wife, Captain Kenedy did all the work that was needed, laying new decks, giving the schooner new spars, sails, and rigging, and fitting her with topmasts. She had an aged engine below deck; this was replaced with a high speed Gray 165 horsepower diesel which gave remarkable service, shoving the schooner along in a calm at six knots when she was deep with 550 tons of cargo in her. She turned out to be a good sailer if loaded or partly loaded, being narrow and with good lines, but when she was light, Captain Kenedy said that she was like a balloon on top of the water.

The *Wawaloam* was placed in the Nova Scotia-West Indies

lumber-salt trade. A sixteen day passage was about average for her although she once made Barbados in fourteen days; her engine was a great help when the wind was light. Captain Kenedy liked his steel schooner, but she was not to last long. He wrote of her end:

> "A sub stopped us August 6th, 1942, 460 miles south of Cape Race, Newfoundland, and sank her with gunfire. They first shot the masts out of her with three well aimed shots. The captain of the sub took me aboard for a while and asked me her name, etc., and gave me a box of rockets and flares and asked if we needed food or water. He was quite polite and we felt good to get off with a whole skin. Next day we had a southerly gale shifting to west, and as we were in the Gulf Stream a bad sea made up. The mate's dory was dumped end for end, and I took all hands into my dory, seven in all plus a dog. We used the other dory as a sea anchor and breakwater to windward which was very much help. Next day we bailed out the swamped one, and sailed northwest toward Nova Scotia. Six days later, having sailed 300 miles and being handy to Sable Island, we were picked up by the neutral Eire steamer *Irish Rose* after shooting off some of my German rockets."

Captain Kenedy's description does not tell of the hardships that he and his men suffered as they bobbled around in the tiny dories in the wild Atlantic. Only those who have weathered a Gulf Stream storm can know how really nasty it can get there, huge seas curling and breaking with terrific strength behind them. That a deeply laden dory, her gunnels only inches above the water, could live under such conditions was due entirely to seamanship of her captain and his six men; only their thorough knowledge of small boat handling saved them.

William Bisbee

The three-mast schooner *William Bisbee,* built by the I. L. Snow & Company of Rockland in 1902, was a staunch coaster of 309 gross tons and 133 feet long. She belonged to the old-style type of windship with her long bowsprit and jibboom, martingale, towering topmasts, her tiller on deck in the open directly under the wheel spool, and her lines in general.

She was very nearly lost in February, 1921, when she was caught in Massachusetts Bay in a heavy blizzard while she was bound from Port Johnson, New Jersey, to Boothbay Harbor with 350 tons of coal. Driven far off her course by the gale, the *Bisbee* was forced to anchor near North Scituate. Soon, with her anchors dragging, the tern slowly backed towards a series of rocky ledges off the beach. When the Coast Guard sighted her flares, they put out their surf boat into the foam-capped seas, but there was nothing that they could do for the helpless vessel. Somehow, by the greatest of luck, the schooner missed the ledges although her anchor took a hold on them, stopping the schooner 500 yards from the beach and destruction. A day or two later a tug was able to take her into Boston for repairs to damage that was done by the pounding waves.

After nearly 35 years of trading along the New England coast, she was sold in 1936 to Ye Mystic Krewe of Gasparilla who renamed her *Jose Gasper* after the famous pirate of that name. Berthed at Tampa, used as a club house by Ye Mystic Krewe, her complement was listed at 288 — all members of the club; when she had sailed out of Rockland in the early 1930's under Captain Charles R. Trynor, she had had a six man crew. In 1953 when her old hull was in very poor shape, she was replaced by a new vessel, especially built for the Krewe. The dying *Bisbee* was left to rot at the river's edge, abandoned.

CHAPTER VII

Two-Mast Schooners

~~~~~~

NUMEROUS nautical writers have stated that the first schooner was a vessel which was launched at Gloucester in the early eighteenth century, and as she took to the water a bystander said: "See how she scoons!" However, contemporary prints before this period depict two-masted craft with the schooner rig; actually, its exact origin is rather obscure. William Falconer in his Marine Dictionary of 1769 writes of the schooner: "a small vessel with two masts, whose main and foresails were suspended by gaffs reaching from the mast toward the stern; and stretched out below by booms, whose foremast ends were hooked to an iron which clasped the mast so as to turn therein as upon an axis, when the after ends were swung from one side of the vessel to the other. This vessel was generally a fast sailer, and principally employed in trade by those who made speculations where dispatch was requisite". His description would also cover the last of the commercial schooners.

The two-mast schooner was a very common vessel in the New England waters during the last century, and as commercial craft, have survived, to a certain extent, to this day. The deep-watermen have practically gone, but a handful of bay coasters and river sailers are still to be found down east. Some of them are very old, others comparatively young.

Anna Sophia

One of the last commercial schooners built in Maine yards was the two-mast *Anna Sophia,* a good sized vessel of 200 gross tons and 102 feet long. Launched at Dennsyville, Maine, in 1923, she was in the local coasting trade for quite a few years, frequently tripping down the Sound to New York to load coal for Maine ports. A good part of this time, she was commanded by the well-known Captain "Ben" F. Pascal.

In some respects she was a hard-luck craft for she was often in difficulties. In March, 1924, she stranded in Vineyard Haven during a strong gale, but was successfully refloated not long afterwards. In April she was caught in another storm when bound from New Jersey to Rockport, Maine, with 240 tons of coal. After her topsail sheet parted, the flogging sail whipped her fore-topmast right off the mast, and in falling carried away her jibs. Now she began leaking, and the pumps had to keep going steadily for three days until she made port. In December, 1931, she was caught off Pollock Rip in another bad storm. Her signals of distress, which were hoisted when her cargo shifted, were not noticed by passing vessels, and her crew were forced to drink rain water caught in the sails before the Coast Guard finally picked her up.

In February, 1934, she was very nearly lost in a mid-winter gale off Cape Cod. Then in command of Captain John Peabody, the *Sophia* was bound from New York to Lubec with 275 tons of coal. The third day out found her off Nauset with a strong northwest wind blowing and sub-zero temperatures. Flying spray was rapidly icing up the schooner, slowly bogging her down with its weight. A sudden squall had ripped her frozen sails and snapped off her fore-topmast which hung in a tangle of wreckage from her top. The pounding seas opened the seams of the vessel so that soon she was leaking faster than the crew could pump. Captain Peabody, seeing that his vessel was being helplessly driven off-shore with every chance of foundering in deep water, gave the order to abandon ship after hoisting distress signals. Somehow his four men managed to put over their dory, a tiny thing amongst the waves.

On shore, the Coast Guard had sighted the call for help, but it was not easy to answer. All along the beach and for a hundred yards off-shore, thick ice floes ranged with the swell; there was not an opening to launch their surfboat. Beyond the ice, the freezing *Sophia* crew tried to keep their dory head to the wind, but they were slowly being carried seaward. With time now an important factor, the Coast Guard men dragged their surfboat on its carriage through the sands up the beach to a point two miles from their station where the ice was thick, perhaps strong enough to take their weight. Boatswain George Nickerson directed his men to launch their long, thin white boat. Time and again the ice threatened to smash in the planking, but somehow the Coast Guard boys shoved the pans away from the sides. Once in the clear, but breaking, seas, they took to their oars, and in a short time had overhauled the dory with the schooner men, all of whom were now suffering from exposure. A line was passed between the two boats; then began the hard three-quarter mile tow back to shore. An hour later the boats neared the beach. The wind had cleared away ice from a small landing spot on the sands, and here the two crews brought up, chilled through but safe.

In the meantime, the Coast Guard cutter *Dix* had raced to the scene. She found the *Sophia* badly battered but still afloat. After a great struggle with the elements, the Coast Guard towed the two-master around into the safety of Provincetown Harbor. Some days later she was towed on to Gloucester where she got new rigging before proceeding for Lubec.

In December, 1935, the *Sophia* was again close to destruction when she went ashore in Penobscot Bay. She was eventually refloated and towed to Rockland where she was beached in a badly damaged condition. In October, 1937, she had to be towed in from the sea to Boston, again after a battering from the seas. In 1938, June this time, she was again on the casualty list after striking the rocks off Harwood Island near Jonesport. For three days the Coast Guard tried to free her without success. A wrecking crew had to be called to refloat her.

In 1939, the *Anna Sophia* went to Rockland for the last time to be given a complete refit. It was rumored that she was going south for service on the Orinoco River under the Venezuelan flag. Not long after, she was fitted with power. In 1941, she became a motor vessel, renamed *Amendra*. In 1942, she went under the Honduran flag, and was still listed as active in 1948.

Annie and Reuben

The *Annie and Reuben* was the last of the regular granite-carrying windships in New England waters. She had been built by R. S. Hunt at Bath in 1891. A two-master of 129 gross tons and 87 feet long, she was most ruggedly put togther with very heavy beams and planking that would stand up to hard usage.

In spite of her beamy appearance, the *Annie* was a pretty fair sailer, and handled well under canvas. Owned by the John L. Goss Corporation who operated her in connection with its granite quarries at Stonington, Maine, the schooner was commanded by Captain John E. Duke for many years. His mate, Manton Gray, had been with him for eighteen continuous years. They generally sailed her right to her wharf without the aid of tugs, just using their yawl boat astern to give her a shove through the bridge draws.

Early in 1920, the two-master took over two months to sail from Stonington to Boston, but this was most unusual. She had been forced into Boothbay Harbor with her sails ripped in the winter storms, losing much time there. A week at most would have been much nearer her normal time for the run.

Fully loaded with stone, the *Annie* would be deep with about 200 tons in her hold and on deck. On one trip in 1924, her first of that season, she had several blocks of twenty tons, and one block of 33 tons which required a floating derrick to move it from the schooner to a flat car. Nearly always sailing from Stonington, the schooner, as a rule, came to Boston although from time to time she visited many of the other New England ports. She continued in this trade until 1943. After the war broke out, she added scrap metal to her cargoes, coming into Boston with old boilers, pipes, and car rails.

In March, 1943, she was sold to New York parties who planned to use her in the Florida-Cuba trade. However, she never made it. On March 23rd, she foundered off Seaside Park, New Jersey, as she went south to take up her new duties.

One of the down east yarns connected with the *Annie* was that the waterfront folk of Portland used to refer to her as a barometer for whenever she dropped anchor there, they knew a storm was brewing.

Australia

Although never a trader in New England waters, the *Australia* today is one of the exhibits at the Mystic Seaport Museum. Built as the *Ella Alida*, 55-foot schooner, at Patchogue, Long Island, in 1862, she was under the British flag less than a year later, registered at Nassau as the *Alma*. In October, 1863, she was captured by the *U.S.S. Seneca* which caught her running the blockade. Sold at auction, she became the *Australia*, owned in Georgetown, D.C. Her U.S. registration number was "25", by far the lowest of any vessel active in recent times.

Her working years were spent freighting around the Chesapeake Bay, crabs, oysters, lumber, steel slag, and the like. Much later she became a yacht owned by the DuPont family who, in 1951, turned her over to the Seaport Museum where she has been on display ever since. She is an interesting example of one of the many small schooners which were so numerous around Long Island Sound a century ago.

Bloomer

The 51-ton schooner *Bloomer* was probably the oldest remaining New England-built coasting vessel after World War II, having been launched at Eden, Maine, in 1855. She was rather oddly constructed as she had a very steep step just forward of her mainmast, spoiling her appearance when near at hand, but not noticeable from a distance. A half century ago she was registered at Ellsworth, but her papers later were issued at Rockland.

In the 1940's, the *Bloomer* has not been particularly active although she appeared to be still in fairly good condition, and still sported her topmasts. She has since gone.

Bowdoin

Among vessels of Arctic fame is the yacht-like schooner *Bowdoin* which was built for Donald B. MacMillan by Hodgdon Brothers at East Boothbay in 1921. On the small side for her rigorous life, she is only 66 gross tons and 75 feet long. However, in spite of her size, she is very strong. MacMillan had planned her at a time when he himself was trapped in the ice only 700 miles from the Pole. He knew the type of vessel needed to combat the ice-filled waters of the north.

From the year of her launching until the recent war, the *Bowdoin* made annual trips north, and it is said that she covered some 250,000 miles during these expeditions. She did not always find the going easy. In 1923-1924 she was frozen in the ice for 320 days at Refuge Harbor, North Greenland. Other times found her sitting at odd angles on unknown reefs or atop hidden ice floes, but she always got clear in time. Well looked after, she has been kept in perfect condition. She generally wintered at Boothbay Harbor or near-by each year.

During the war years, the schooner was on Greenland Patrol with the U.S. Navy. For a part of the time, she was based at South Strom Fjord on Greenland, the island's northern-most air field station. When peace returned, the MacMillans were able to resume their travels. In June, 1947, the *Bowdoin* sailed under the auspices of the Chicago Geographic Society on an expedition that took her through Davis Strait and up Baffin Bay to 79 degrees North, 600 miles from the North Pole. There the ice fields stopped her, but she had already been further north than she had ever been before.

The *Bowdoin* again departed for the North in June, 1948, with 72-year old MacMillan still in command This year the voyage was under the auspices of Bowdoin College and the Cleveland Museum of Natural History. Among the sixteen persons making the trip was Mrs. MacMillan who was sailing north for her sixth time. The scientists aboard planned to do field work in geology, botany, ornithology and mineralogy, while other members of the crew gathered specimens for a proposed Arctic Museum at Bowdoin. In 1959 the schooner became a Mystic Seaport Museum exhibit.

Emma

The *Emma* was a small two-master of 54 gross tons and 63 feet long. Built at Stockton, Maine, in 1871, she spent her life in New England waters, mostly around the Penobscot, in the general cargo trade. In her old age she made an occasional jaunt down to Cape Ann with fish or lumber.

During one such trip in late September, 1938, from Rockland to Rockport with a cargo of soft-wood edging, she was caught in a sharp, forty-knot breeze off York, Maine. When her edging shifted, the old schooner started taking water. Captain Elmer M. Greenlaw succeeded in working his damaged vessel into Rockport while his two-man crew worked steadily at the pumps for 24 hours. Later, the Coast Guard towed her around to Gloucester for repairs.

In January, 1940, the *Emma* was caught in a northeast blizzard off Vinalhaven. Before she was able to get into shelter, she was swept onto a rocky ledge, becoming a total loss. Captain Greenlaw and his crew escaped by dory, rowing into the near-by harbor.

Endeavor

The last commercial schooner built in a Maine shipyard was the handsome *Endeavor* which came from the Stonington and Deer Isle Yacht Basin in 1938. Of 55 gross tons and 70 feet long, she could carry about a 100 tons of cargo. Fully rigged with topmasts on both her masts, she was very similar to the many small coasters which once numbered in the hundreds around New England waters a half century and more ago. She had no power, relying just on her canvas to take her from port to port.

The *Endeavor* made her first run in the early fall of 1938 with

Captain Albert M. Shepard in command. For many years he had had the two-mast schooner *Enterprise*. When she became too old for cargo carrying, Captain Shepard had planned this new vessel. None had been built for sixteen years as it was considered that the railroads and trucks had killed the windships' trade, but Captain Shepard felt he could make a go of it. There was often a cargo of salt fish for Gloucester from eastern Maine ports that he could get, or a load of salt or coal from Portland to take down east to some small harbor. Then, too, there was always the pulp wood trade on the Penobscot Bay. At the turn of the present century there were probably 70 sail in these waters; in 1938 there remained only a handful to get the business. There should be no lack of charters.

In 1939 the *Endeavor* was reported missing during a December passage from Port Clyde, Maine, to Gloucester and Boston with fish. When the Coast Guard took up the search after she had been out three weeks, they found her at anchor in Boothbay Harbor, some twenty miles from her starting point. Bad weather had kept her holed up in small coves all the way down the coast. Then, as the weather improved, she skipped across the Bay to Cape Ann in three days. She had left Port Clyde on November 28th; she arrived at Boston on January 10th.

During the war, the *Endeavor* was purchased by a New York party who gave her power. In 1946 she was sold to Honduran interests, joining the West Indies fleet.

George B. Cluett

The schooner *Giant King,* built in 1920 by Boehmers at La Have, Nova Scotia, was a typical fisherman-freighter of that period. She was a strong, well-built vessel, of 199 gross tons and 127 feet long, a good carrier and weatherly.

In April, 1930, she was purchased by the International Grenfell Association which was already well known in northern waters for its fine missionary work. Renamed *George B. Cluett* and given an engine, she replaced another schooner of the same name. With her homeport at St. John's, the *Cluett* frequently came to Boston to load oil in drums, school supplies, hospital and food materials, building equipment, and the like. Sometimes she would take live cattle aboard for the missionary herds at the head base, St. Anthony, Newfoundland. In 1939, she loaded an electric ironer which was paid for with money that the sixty orphan children at St. Anthony's had collected from summer tourists.

Although the *Cluett* had given good service plans were made early in the war years to replace her with a new, larger vessel. The *Cluett* had been forced to make several round trips each season; the new vessel would be able to take the season's supplies north in one voyage.

George Gress

Before the turn of the present century, there were quite a number of small schooners in the New York brick trade; amongst them was the *Peter Mehrhof* which had been launched in 1885 far up the Hudson River at Athens. Named after her first owner to whom she had been given as a wedding present, the *Mehrhof* hailed from Newark, New Jersey, for some years. Built as a "bricker," she was given a very heavy construction, her deck beams as large as those of any three-master, and her decks were unusually beamy to take a good deck load. She was 67 gross tons and 79 feet long with a 25 foot beam and only a 6 foot depth. She had a handsome bow with its overhang and carved trail-boards.

In later years the *Mehrhof* became the *George Gress*, named, so the story has been told, after a South Street crimp, but, as likely as not there was more fiction to the yarn than truth. Captain Parker J. Hall bought the schooner, changing her homeport to Sandy Point, Stockton Springs, Maine. It is said that he sailed his two-master for fifteen years singlehanded, seldom getting into trouble although on one occasion he split his main boom before he could get the sail off during a squall. He had a small gas engine to help with the anchor and hoisting the gaffs. He also had to look after her centerboard. Perhaps the most extraordinary thing about Captain Hall was his age — in 1948 when he passed away on August 23rd the newspapers said he was 86 years old.

A year or two before the war, the *George Gress* was in poor shape. Her stern was so hogged that it appeared to be falling off. Her deck beams were rotten, her seams were filled with Portland cement and her foremast was soft. About 1939 Captain Parker sold her to a boy who hoped to turn her into a party boat, but a year later she was back in the pulp wood trade which had always kept her busy during her years in the Maine waters. On September 16th, 1940, she was caught in a 50-mile-an-hour gale that drove her up on Hardy's Point, near Bar Harbor, smashing her to bits, and scattering her cargo of forty cords of pulpwood, the summer's work of her young three-man crew, about Frenchman's Bay.

Katie D. Seavey

The *Katie D. Seavey* was a beamy, bluff-bowed schooner which had been launched as the *Joanna Durgain* at Brooksville, Maine, in 1902. She was a small vessel of 66 gross tons and 65 feet long. Most of her life was spent about the Penobscot and near-by waters. She was frequently seen at Bangor, coming up the river almost hidden under her deck cargo of pulp wood. It was not unusual for her to take 22 cords in her hold, and another 38 cords on deck. Just before the recent war, she was getting $1.25 per cord to lift it at Belfast for Bangor. Although it would take three days to load, she could discharge in three hours by dumping the wood into the river.

There were times when she would take a charter that would give her a trip to Gloucester. On several passages she carried 160,-000 pounds of salt hake from Prospect Harbor to the Cape Ann port. She would hug the coast when outside so that if the weather changed to threatening she could dodge into a sheltering nook as it breezed up too much. In spite of her appearance, she could sail right along.

Although still in the Register as late as 1946, she was actually lost when she went ashore on the north side of Cuttyhunk Island in the winter of 1942.

Lavolta

At the edge of the Pioneer Village in Salem, Massachusetts, propped up in a dirt pit, was a strange looking craft with the name *Arbella* on her stern. With a high poop, gaudy painted sides, three spider-web like masts and yards and lateen, she was meant to represent the good ship *Arbella* which brought settlers to America in the 17th century.

In 1930 when plans were being made to celebrate the local tercentenary, the old schooner *James L. Maloy*, a coaster built in 1864, was purchased with the idea of turning her into a replica of the historical *Arbella*. However, when on her way to Salem, the *Maloy* filled with water, and was later beached. As she was too far damaged for further use, the committee then chose another old coaster, the *Lavolta* which had been built at Ellsworth in 1870. A vessel of 168 gross tons and 104 feet long, she once brought a lumber cargo to Boston from Port Greville, Nova Scotia, in less than four days. She was a pretty little craft with a clipper-bow and a long bowsprit and jibboom.

The *Lavolta* was done over completely, being changed into a freak craft which was unable to sail under her new rig. She was towed to Plymouth, and later to Boston and Salem. As there was no demand for coasting schooners when the celebrations were completed, the *Lavolta* was not given her original rig; instead, she was laid up. Sometime later, when the Salem Pioneer Village was made, the vessel was incorporated into the scheme. Although she was in no way accurate as far as likeness towards the original *Arbella,* she did give the casual tourist a faint idea of what a 17th century vessel might have looked like. She was eventually broken up.

Regina

The schooner *Regina* was built in 1891 at Machias for the local freight trade. Very similar to the hundreds of other vessels of her type, she was 116 gross tons and 87 feet long. Although her earlier days were inconspicuous, she became quite famous in her old age for she was purchased by Booth Tarkington, the well-known author, who used her as a studio near his estate at Kennebunk, Maine.

For many years the *Regina* rose and fell with the tides in her special cradle alongside her wharf. Following Mr. Tarkington's death during the war years, the two-master rapidly deteriorated, and by 1948 she was in very poor shape, and so was demolished.

William C. Pendleton

The *William C. Pendleton,* was one of the oldest vessels in the post war issue of "Merchant Vessels of the United States", having been launched at Westerly, Rhode Island, in 1857. A small schooner of 33 gross tons and 57 feet in length, she had been active for some ninety years in New England waters, the greater part of the time being registered in Maine, at Boothbay, Rockland, and now Belfast.

In the years before the recent war she was generally to be found in the pulp wood trade, her wide, spacious decks being suitable for deck loads. By 1939 she had been given an engine, but still used her canvas as well.

Although the *Pendleton* was not active in 1948, she was yet afloat, made fast at Stockton Springs. She did not last long after this.

William H. Jewell

When the second World War broke out, the oldest sailing vessel actively trading in New England waters was the blunt-bowed, square-sterned *William H. Jewell* which had been launched at Nyack, New York, in 1853. She was not a large vessel, only 46 gross tons and 62 feet long, nor was she pretty with her stubby lines, but at the same time, she was an interesting little schooner of a type of a bygone era.

No doubt in her earlier years she was employed in the New York brick trade on the Hudson, her wide deck being ideal for a goodly load. The latter part of the *Jewell*'s life was spent on the Penobscot where she was a general cargo vessel loading pulp wood, coal, potatoes, and the like. In later years she had a small engine below deck to help her in and out of port, and through calms. In 1939, she was given a new Buick engine to replace her old two-cylinder "putt-putt".

The *Jewell* was finally lost in her 93rd year. A terrific storm, said to have been the most savage within the living memory of the coast folk, lashed the Maine shores towards the end of November, 1945. It was too much for the old-timer, and she foundered off Rockland a few days later.

William Keene

Another of the very old schooners which were still active in the late 1930's was the ancient William Keene that had been built at Damariscotta, Maine, in 1866. Typical of her period, she was some 60 tons and a bit over 68 feet in length. With a semi-clipper bow, she had a long straight keel, a beam of twenty feet, and fair lines aft. In her later days she carried a main-topmast but none on her fore; forward she had the old-style bowsprit and jibboom.

During her youth, the *Keene* was registered at Machias, but for many years Portland was her homeport. She was employed in the local freight trade, occasionally making a trip south to Gloucester with fish from Maine ports. She needed a hefty breeze of wind to make her go, but when she got it, she was a good sailer.

After about three quarters of a century of active life in New England waters, the *Keene* was purchased by the Peter Paul Candy Company in 1942, and for a time was used to carry coconuts from their Honduran buyers to their plant in Florida. Later on, she was taken over by their coconut dessicating plant in Arecibo, Puerto Rico, in order to run between Honduras and San Juan in Puerto Rico. However, when the *Keene* arrived at San Juan, it was found that she was too late as two power boats were doing the job. She was sold to a man in Mayagues who was planning on using her as a fishing schooner.

The *Keene* underwent repairs in the Navy Dock in San Juan. By this time she had had engines installed to help out her canvas. During a trial run in early 1948, the gears were stripped on the motor, and she was laid up at Mayagues.

In the years before railroads connected New England ports, the chief means of transportation was by water, and many small windships earned their way by carrying passengers up and down the coast. Today the few remaining two-masters that are owned in Maine also earn their keep in the passenger trade, taking out summer tourists on weekly trips which cover the Penobscot Bay and Blue Hill Region. Although these schooners have their own crews, the dude-sailors enjoy giving a hand aboard ship, doing much of the steering and hauling on lines.

The accomodations of these little craft are plain but comfortable. The cabins which have been built into what was once the holds are generally fitted with two, three or four bunks with box springs and comfortable mattresses.

The days are spent lolling in the sun as the schooner eases across the waters. No plans are made as to evening designations for the schooners always make the winds fair, going where it sends them as there is ever a pretty little port at hand come sundown. The dudes swim over the side in the chilly waters, or perhaps cast a fish line into the depths. It is all fun for them.

The largest, and first, fleet of dude-schooners was owned by Captain Frank Swift who organized "Windjammer Cruises" in 1935 when he sent his first vessel out from Camden. In later years there were others, Frederick B. Guild, Donald P. Hurd, Donald B. Snyder, Dick Parshall, Havilah S. Hawkins, Frank Elliott, Anne White, to mention a few, who were in the business. In the early days rates for a week's cruise were $38 which covered meals, cabin and general accomodations; in 1947, with costs much higher, the rate was $60, and today it is nearer $120 for the week.

The following are some of the schooners which were in the 'dude trade':

Adventure

Launched from the James yard in Essex, Massachusetts, in 1926, the *Adventure* was a handsome 107-foot auxiliary schooner, much like the Grand Bankers of a half century earlier although her rig was a good deal shorter, and she wore no bowsprit.

Working out of Gloucester and Boston during her active fishing career, the Adventure was the last of the fleet to put to sea for dory fishing, and when she eventually left the Banks it was not because she was old but because the coming younger generation of fishermen refused to face the hardship and hazards of that type of fishing. Captain Jeff Thomas, who was her first skipper, died on board while on the Banks in 1934. He was replaced by Leo Hynes who remained with her until she gave up fishing in 1953. During the nearly twenty years that Captain Hynes had her, she was a most successful vessel, a money maker.

There was one occasion, though, when tragedy struck. In March, 1939, she was on the northern edge of Georges Bank during the worst storm of the winter, the winds screaming in excess of fifty miles an hour, when a monstrous sea smashed across her stern, sweeping away before it the pilot house. Two of the crew, William Nolen and Alexander Muise, went with the wreckage, never to be seen again. Captain Hynes himself was flung into the scuppers, breaking two of his ribs.

Four years later the *Adventure* had a very close call. Out bound from Boston in a dense fog she and a sister schooner, oddly enough, *Adventure II,* which was heading in for the Fish Pier with a big catch, collided almost without warning. The stern of the latter was sheared right off, and she sank in minutes, but there was no loss of life.

In 1954, the *Adventure,* now owned by Donald P. Hurd, entered the "dude trade", probably the most able vessel of the entire fleet. With her engines removed, to meet Coast Guard regulations, her sail area increased, and completely refurbished below, she is today, inwardly, a far cry from the fishing vessel she once was, but outwardly a tall, handsome Gloucesterman, one of the last of the Grand Bankers. In 1964 she worked out of Rockland, Maine, and out of Camden in 1965.

Alice S. Wentworth

Launched in Norwalk, Connecticut, way back in 1863 as the *Lizzie A. Tolles*, a typical small freight schooner of the period, a rather handsome vessel with a clipper bow and pleasing sheer, she was 68 gross tons and 73 feet long. A center-board schooner, she spent her earlier years hauling brick from the Hudson River area and also cargoes of coal and oysters. In 1903 Captain Arthur Stevens purchased her, took her to the Wells River in Maine where he hauled her, and then completely rebuilt her. Indeed, when he relaunched her in 1905, and renamed her after his niece, Alice Stevens Wentworth, she was considered a new vessel, and was reclassified, appearing in the ship registers as such.

For the next forty years the *Wentworth* traded along the New England coast, even as far south as New Jersey. In the early 1930's she claimed Vineyard Haven for her homeport, later changing to New Bedford. In the years before World War II she was a most familiar sight around Vineyard Sound and along the road to Nantucket. Although she was a pretty lucky vessel, there were many times when she had her troubles with wind and weather. Just one example was in February, 1930, when she attempted to sail from Boston to Nantucket with 200 tons of coke. Breaking out the anchor on a Sunday, she got outside the harbor, but had to put back on account of the wind. She tried again on Monday, and again put back. The same thing happened Tuesday. The captain gave Wednesday a rest. When he tried on Thursday, the Coast Guard had to tow him back in. She eventually got on her way properly on Friday. With a break in the weather, she could have done the trip in a matter of hours.

The best known skipper of the *Wentworth* was Zebulon N. Tilton who kept her busy for 35 years. There were many tales told of his uncanny seamanship, tales which increased each year as the tourist season got under for the summer folk were fain to believe anything that they might hear. One of the more amusing anecdotes told of the time Captain Zeb was conning his schooner through thick fog with a young boy up in the eyes of the vessel on lookout. Suddenly the boy shouted aft that there were ducks ahead. The old man hollered forward: "Be they walking or be they swimmin'?". When the boy called back that he thought they were walking, the captain yelled:

"All right, then, me lad, ready about and hard alee!", thus taking his vessel back into deeper waters.

At one time in 1939 when financial difficulties held the schooner to her wharf, sympathetic well-wishers raised funds to put her back to sea. Amongst those who helped the captain out were James Cagney of the movies and Katherine Cornell of the stage. The *Wentworth* was put in good shape again before the skipper resumed his trading. Later in the year he made plans to marry again for the third time, but fair winds kept the schooner so busy the ceremony was continuously put off until January, 1940. Captain Tilton, at the age of 75, finally retired from the sea in 1942 after sixty years in windships.

For a time the *Wentworth* was sailed by Captain Parker J. Hall who had formerly had the *George Gress*. Still known as the "Lone Mariner of the New England Coast", he generally sailed single handed. Captain Parker retired in 1944 after a passage from Nantucket to Gloucester. As usual he was alone; at the time he was 84 years old!

At the end of the war, the *Wentworth* gave up freighting to turn to the more lucrative passenger business out of Maine ports. At one point she was owned by Captain Guild, later Captain Hawkins had her, and lastly, Anne White who took her down to Vineyard Sound waters. In the early fall of 1962 the schooner took quite a pounding from a hurricane which caught her while sheltering at Vineyard Haven. Several months later, when unattended, she sank at her winter berth alongside a wharf at Woods Hole. Subsequently raised, the century old vessel has again been in financial difficulties, and in the spring of 1965 her future was in doubt. However, in April she was purchased at a public auction by Anthony Athanas for $13,500. Owner of the Pier 4 restaurant in Boston, Mr. Athanas plans on using her as an attraction and showpiece, moored alongside his pier.

Annie F. Kimball

The *Annie F. Kimball*, a handsome schooner which was launched at Boothbay in 1886, was quite small, only 41 gross tons and 59 feet long. As a trading vessel, she once called Deer Island her home port, later Boothbay, and then Jonesport. One of her last cargoes was 190,000 pounds of salt hake which she took from Prospect Harbor to Gloucester in the early fall of 1935. Not long afterward, she was purchased by Captain Swift, becoming one of

The tern E. P. Theriault at a Boston wharf.

The Oliver H. Perry, a Great Lakes Sea Scout training ship.

The George E. Klinck, left, was strongly built for the lumber trade.
above: The last moments of the three-mast schooner George E. Klinck,
photographed from the deck of the U.S. Aircraft Carrier Wasp as the
survivors climbed the Jacob's Ladder to safety.

The Irene Forsyte, last "mystery ship" of the U.S. Navy.

The terns Marine and Francis Parsons at Parrsboro in 1939.

The tern Minas King towing up the East River, New York.

The tern Peaceland awaiting a breeze at Gloucester.

right: The Minas Prince drifting along.

The Thomas H. Lawrence, launched at East Boston in 1891, was the last Boston-built merchantman to trade under canvas.

The small Nova Scotia tern Village Queen.

Vema in her early days with the Lamont Geological Observatory.

left below: The Rebecca R. Douglas at anchor in Gloucester Harbor.
right: The William Bisbee when she sailed in New England waters.

The Adventure, last of the dory fishing schooners out of Boston and Gloucester, today carries passengers out of Camden in the summer.

The bluff bows of the Katie D. Seavy; pulp wood piled on deck.

The Arbella at Salem.

The Alice S. Wentworth in the days when she was a cargo carrier, above, and below right, with passengers out of Camden.

above right: The Shenandoah, latest addition to the New England windship fleet and below, the old-time ship's card used to advertise her cruises.

above, far right: The Liberty, the last all-sail Boston pilot schooner.

The Victory Chimes—last three-mast schooner in New England waters.
right: The Yankee II outward bound from Gloucester, bound around the world.
The Albatross during the filming of 'Twilight for the Gods'.

The champion of the Grand Banks fishing fleet, the Bluenose. This same picture is on the Canadian ten cent piece.

above right: The fishing schooner L. A. Dunton.
below right: Yankee I sailing from Gloucester in 1939.

The last racing Gloucesterman, the Gertrude L. Thebaud in 1938.

*Furling the jib on the Gloucesterman Thomas S. Gorton,
last of the all-sail fishermen.*

the first vessels of his new fleet, fitted out for ten passengers. For many years she had been considered "the pride of the Penobscot", and for a period was *"the"* schooner of the Swift group.

By the time World War II was over, the *Kimball* was a tired vessel, showing signs of age. When cost of repairs became too steep, the Captain retired her, and she was left to die, abandoned by the beach in Camden Harbor, slowly going to bits.

Clinton

Built in 1886 at Millbridge, Maine, on Pleasant Bay for the general freight trade in local waters, the *Clinton* at one time was registered at Machias, then later became a Rockland vessel. Although her life was far from humdrum, what with soupy fogs, and rock filled waters, she had an uneventful career. In later days she was given an engine to give her a hand when needed.

When Captain Swift took her over he fitted her out to carry eleven passengers. The smallest vessel of his fleet, she was only 31 gross tons and 52 feet long. In the early 1950's the two-master was taken over by Dick Parshall who used Castine for his base of operations. In 1955, after hauling at Stonington, she was found to be too rotten to carry on, and died right there at the shipyard.

Enterprise

The *Enterprise* was launched in 1909 at Deer Island for Captain Albert M. Shepard. One of a fleet of at least seventy vessels that used to call at Portland to load for the smaller ports down east in the days before the motor truck had ruined the trade, she was an average sized vessel of 57 tons and 70 feet long.

Captain Shepard, a great believer in sail, managed to keep his vessel busy when the other windships were finding it more and more difficult to locate charters. During the summer months he would load pulp wood from the islands in the Blue Hill area to take up river to Bangor. In the winter months he would run his schooner to Gloucester with salt fish, or coal north from Portland to one of the islands or a tiny harbor off the beaten path.

In 1927 the *Enterprise* sank in Portland harbor after she had been hit by a steamer. However, she was raised and beached for repairs, returning to work before too long. In 1937, when Captain Shepard felt that his vessel was beginning to show signs of wear after so many years of heavy cargo hauling, he ordered a new schooner, the *Endeavor*. Some time later Captain Swift purchased the *Enterprise,* converting her into a passenger vessel. In October, 1957, when her hull was in poor shape and it was obvious that she could not pass the stringent requirements of the new Coast Guard regulations, Captain Swift had her hauled out on the beach at Camden, and set afire.

Eva S. Cullison

The *Eva S. Cullison,* built at Baltimore, Maryland, in 1888, was a typical Bay craft, one of many in the oyster and fish trade in those waters. First registered at Baltimore, she later hailed from Philadelphia. In the late 1940's she became a part of the Swift fleet. Oddly enough, she and the *Enterprise* were almost exactly the same size, nearly to the inch, 70 feet long, 21 foot beam, and a six foot depth.

After Captain Swift had retired the *Cullison* she became headquarters for the Rockland Coast Guard Auxiliary, moored to the wharf there. Later still she found her way to East Brunswick where she became an attraction in Simpson's Animal Park. In 1962 she changed hands again. While her new owners were towing her down to Gloucester, she very nearly foundered off Cape Ann, the Coast Guard taking her into Rockport. There she is today, a dying hulk. In the 1965 spring town meeting, the townspeople refused to vote funds to have her removed.

Grace & Alice

One of the last three schooners to trade regularly out of Portland, the *Grace & Alice* was a small schooner of 31 tons and 52 feet long. Built at Calais in 1910, she was a general trader in the down east waters for more than 35 years. John Peabody of Jonesport was her master for quite a period; she was owned by Fred B. Small, also of Jonesport, in 1933. Captain Guild added her to his fleet after World War II, but she did not last long in the dude trade. Laid up for the winter in 1950, in Carney Island Cove, she was stripped by vandals. It meant her end.

James A. Webster

The *James A. Webster* came from South Brooksville, Maine, in 1890, a good sized schooner of 74 tons and 86 feet in length. She was a good looking vessel with her two topmasts stepped and all canvas set. A raised poop with a stanchioned railing on either side, very similar to the larger three- and four-masted vessels, gave her an air of distinction.

In her earlier years she was registered at North Haven, then later at Rockland. In 1933 she was owned by Albert A. Webster who worked her in Maine waters in various cargo runs. When she became a passenger schooner, she was owned by James S. Walter who had her based at Port Washington, New York. Each Monday morning in the summer months she would slip out of Manhasset Bay, heading eastward up the Sound, putting into the harbors along the Connecticut shore each evening. Saturday afternoons would find her arriving back at her base with her landlubber passengers.

The *Webster* was up for sale in 1947, and apparently retired from the trade at that time.

Liberty

The last of Boston's all-sail pilot schooners was the strongly built *Liberty* which was launched from the yard of John Bishop at Vincent Cove, Gloucester, in 1896. Of 118 gross tons, 93 feet long, she was not a particularly handsome vessel as she was designed with very high bows which were most desirable when hove-to off shore in bad weather, keeping her decks dry.

Although the *Liberty* must have covered thousands of miles in her cruising off the Boston Lightship, she was probably never more than 100 miles from her homeport during her first thirty-five years. When she was still a young vessel she was given power, and her tall sailing rig was greatly reduced with her bowsprit cut off and a small triangular mainsail. However, when she became a "dude" in 1933, much of her canvas was put back on.

In the fall of 1934 she took a party to Newport to see the International yacht races being held for the America's Cup; she was there again in 1937 during the last "J" boat series. She spent a good deal of time taking out girl-scouts, the girls running the vessel. One trip took her south to Lewes, Delaware, on a treasure hunt for a sunken brig which was supposed to contain great wealth, but her backers did not return wealthy.

When World War II broke out, there was talk that the *Liberty* had been chartered to take supplies to Pitcairn Island in the Pacific, but she never got there. Owned in Miami in 1942, she was wrecked in early January, 1943, in 21 degrees 59′ North, 71 degrees 53′ West, just to the north of Haiti.

Lillian

The oldest vessel of the Swift fleet was the ancient *Lillian*, built in Boothbay in 1876, at a time when square-riggers were still being launched, and even a few of the true clippers were still lingering on. A smallish schooner of 43 tons and 56 feet in length, she was a lofty craft, carrying a good spread of canvas. First a fishing schooner and then in the general freight trade about the Maine coast, she changed hands from time to time, long outliving her first owners. In the 1890's she was registered at South West Harbor, in the 1930's at Eastport. Sometime in the interim she was given a small engine of 20 horsepower to give her a boost when the going got too light.

In 1939 the *Lillian* was converted into a passenger vessel with accomodations for sixteen. She had a spacious hold which was ideal for cabins. At first it was planned to cruise Maine waters in the summer, and the southern waters in the winter, but war time conditions prevented her from going south. Captain Swift took her over not long after this, and ran her for several years. In 1952 she worked out of Belfast, mostly on day trips. She was eventually beached and dismantled at Sandy Point on the Penobscot in 1955.

Lois M. Candage

The *Lois M. Candage* was launched in 1912 at Blue Hill where the water is deep and cold, and the forests come down to the sea. She was a small freight schooner of 44 gross tons and 59 feet long, built for trade in the local waters, around the many islands and short coastal runs. She was given a small "kicker" engine so she could work her way in and out of many of the small nooks and holes where she was apt to pick up her pulp wood or other cargoes.

In the early 1930's the *Candage* was owned in Eastport, but by 1940 she had joined the Swift fleet. A few years ago, after her active sailing days were over, she was taken to Damariscotta, where she was made fast to the wharf of the Saltwater Farm Pier Restaurant as an attraction for the guests. She was still there in 1964.

Lydia M. Webster

The *Lydia M. Webster* was a chunky little schooner of 47 tons and 58 feet long, built at Castine in 1882. She was not a very handsome vessel with her very nearly straight stem and not much sheer. However, she was a busy little craft in her youth when there was still plenty of work for the sailing coasters. She was first registered at Castine, later at Belfast.

The *Webster* was one of the first vessels of the Swift fleet, giving good service for several years. However, in 1945, when Captain Swift decided that her upkeep was not worth her value as she was worn out, he had her hull stripped, and scuttled her bare hulk off Mark Island.

Mabel

The *Mabel* of 40 gross tons and 54 feet long was built at Millbridge in 1881. For well over a half century she sailed in New England waters carrying cargoes from port to port. Strongly built, she weathered the years in amazingly good condition, remaining sound and tight in spite of her years and hard work.

Captain Swift added the *Mabel* to his fleet after the second World War, one of the last additions to his fleet. He sold her in the late 1950's. Berthed at Stonington, she became a floating home for a Rockland educator and his family. In 1962 she again changed hands. Later her new owners were towing her down the coast, bound for Boothbay when she started taking water. She was forty miles east of Portland at the time. A call was made for the Coast Guard, but it was too late; the old-timer broke up and sank. Her two owners were rescued.

Maggie

The schooner *Maggie* was built in Dorchester County, Maryland, in 1871. Like most of the Bay sailers, she was a shallow draft vessel, having a depth of less than six feet although she was 72 gross tons and some 87 feet long. For many years she was in the Bay freight trade, and as lately as 1945 was registered out of Baltimore.

In 1946 she joined the dude-schooner fleet in Maine waters, working out of Rockland. Like her sister passenger schooners, she had left behind the days when she carried dirty, smelly cargoes. She was now spotlessly clean with her accomodations plain yet comfortable, and not even the most fastidious could find cause to complain. Donald Hurd ran this vessel before he refitted the *Adventure*. The *Maggie,* worn out, not worth repairing, died at a wharf in Rockland. Her remains were burnt in March, 1965.

Mary Day

One of the younger men to enter the windjammer cruise business was Havilah S. Hawkins, a man with a great love for ships and the sea. Owner and captain of both the *Stephen Taber* and the *Alice S. Wentworth,* he spent twelve years studying the trade. Then he designed the *Mary Day,* outwardly a coaster with traditional lines, but on the inside planned for her passengers, cabins with full head room and full clearance to sit up in every berth. She has two single cabins, six double cabins and four triple cabins. In the main cabin there is a fireplace and an old-fashioned organ.

Launched in January, 1962, built entirely of oak, the *Mary* Day is 83 feet on deck, 23 foot beam, and carries 3600 square feet of sail. Although fitted for topmasts, she does not carry them at the present time. In the summer months, she works out of Camden.

Mattie

Launched as the *Grace Baily* at Patchogue on the south side of Long Island, New York in 1882, the *Mattie* was a clipper-bowed, square-sterned coaster, a handsome craft with a pleasing sheer which flowed into a bowsprit and jibboom. A schooner of 58 tons and 72 feet long, she spent her earlier years working out of Great South Bay with numerous other vessels of her type. She changed her name in 1906.

In later years she joined the coasters off the Maine shores, and for a lengthy period carried fish from Maine ports to Gloucester. She was also seen in Boston during the 1930's when she brought hard wood in, as much as fifty cords at a time. She was always a neat looking schooner, making a pretty picture under sail as she glided across the blue waters, gently heaving to the swell.

The *Mattie* was one of the first schooners of the Swift fleet, and was long a favorite. In spite of her years, she has been able to hold her own against her younger sisters. When Captain Swift retired a few years ago Captain Jim Nisbet took over the fleet, and has been running the *Mattie* ever since.

Mercantile

The youngest vessel of the Swift fleet is the *Mercantile,* built at Deer Isle in 1916. Some 41 tons and 71 feet long, she spent her first years in the freight trade, registered at Rockland early in the 1930's, and later at Providence, Rhode Island. Captain Swift purchased the two-master about the end of World War II. Captain Nisbet had her active in 1964.

Shenandoah

The latest addition to the passenger-carrying fleet is the *Shenandoah*, an "extreme topsail clipper schooner", launched at South Bristol, Maine, in February, 1964. Based on the plans of the *Joe Lane*, a fast United States Revenue Cutter built in 1849, she is 108 feet overall, 23 foot beam and 10½ foot draft, setting 7000 square feet of canvas. Unfortunately, owing to a misunderstanding of Coast Guard regulations, Captain Robert S. Douglas of the Coastwise Packet Company, owner of the schooner, was not permitted to operate commercially during 1964; all passengers whom he carried went as his guests. The *Shenandoah*'s homeport is Vineyard Haven on Martha's Vineyard, and her cruising grounds are to the west of the Cape.

Stephen Taber

One of the best known dude-schooners in the Maine waters today is the pretty little *Stephen Taber* which was built at Glenwood New York, in 1871 for the brick trade. Not a large craft, only 46 tons and some 63 feet in length, she was ideal for her work, being very handy and easy to sail.

Her later years found her in the pulp wood trade around the Penobscot Bay area where it was not an uncommon sight to see her during the 1930's laden with logs that seemed to almost bury her under their weight for they would be piled high above her railings. Undoubtedly she would have stayed in this business if the more profitable dude trade had not offered better chances. At the end of the war she was made over into a passenger vessel.

Captain Guild, who once owned her, wrote at the time: "She is without doubt the best vessel of her type afloat today as she has been completely rebuilt in the past ten years. . . . Known as the 'Queen of the Coasters', she is unusually fast and handles beautifully . . . Off the wind she can usually trim about anything anywhere near her size, and showing her heels to schooner-yachts I take more or less for granted usually, much to the surprise and consternation of their owners."

During 1964 the *Taber*, now owned by Captain Jim Sharp was based at Camden. In her 94th year, she is a very remarkable vessel.

Listed here with the dude schooners is one three-master:

Victory Chimes

The *Victory Chimes* began life as the ram *Edwin and Maud,* built at Bethel, Delaware, in 1900. Very heavily constructed of Georgia Pine and live oak, she is over 200 tons and more than 126 feet long. 'Rams' were, technically, sailing barges, so designed that they could pass through the Chesapeake and Delaware Canal with heavy lumber cargoes. Their beam was limited to the 24 foot width of the locks. They were flat sided and flat bottomed, but they could sail, and at one time there was quite a fleet of them in the Chesapeake. Many of them went 'deep water' in the coast wise trade, and one even crossed the Atlantic to Spain with a cargo of oak staves.

The *Edwin and Maud* was renamed *Victory Chimes* in 1954 when she came to Rockland to join the cruise schooners. With 13 double staterooms, one three berth room, and three four berth rooms, she is not only the largest passenger-carrying windjammer on the Atlantic coast today, but probably the only three-master working under sail alone. At one time Frank Elliott ran her; today she is Capt. Guild's.

In addition to the above vessels, there were three two-masters which were based in New England ports but sailed to far away places with their paying passengers:

Yankee

Originally the *Loodschoener* 4, a Dutch pilot schooner, designed and built by the Netherland Government in 1897, the Yankee was 102 tons, 92 feet long. Very strongly put together, she spent two years with her oak frames seasoning before her planking was added. After 29 years on pilot station in the North Sea and English station, she was forced to retire when steam vessels took over her job. In 1926 she was purchased by Captain Claude Monson of Ipswich, England, becoming the British *Texel,* and then six years later Captain Irving Johnson bought, renaming her *Yankee.*

While refitting her in Hamburg, Capt. Johnson gave her a fore yard, originally the fore royal yard of the schoolship *Bremen* which was then being broken up. With Gloucester, Massachusetts as her home port, Captain Johnson took her on three world voyages, the first starting in 1933, the second in 1936 and the last in 1939. When Capt. Johnson re-joined the U.S. Navy in World War II, his schooner went to Admiral Billard Academy at New London as a training ship for the boys. In 1948 Captain Swift added her to his fleet, but being too deep for local waters, he sent her north. Finally, worn out, she was laid up in the Bra d'or Lake of Nova Scotia, eventually sinking to the bottom.

Yankee II

After the war Captain Johnson replaced his first *Yankee* with a second, once the steel *Duhnan,* built by the German Government in 1912 as a pilot schooner, and considered as one of their fastest. The R.A.F. had taken her to England as a prize of war; the captain had bought her from them. He gave her three yards on her fore mast, and staysails between masts, so technically she was a "staysail topsail schooner" but he preferred to call her a brigantine. Her two steel masts which were hollow acted as exhausts for her galley stove and auxiliary engines.

Yankee II was an exceptionally fine seaboat and very easy to handle. Once the captain took her through the Cape Cod Canal under sail alone when her engine would not run. His first world voyage in her started from Gloucester in November, 1947, and he completed his fourth and last in the spring of 1958. *Yankee II* would generally carry 19 men and 5 women who would pay their own expenses, better than $4500 each for the eighteen month cruises.

The two-master was later sold south, and carried on her cruises under new ownership from Miami. On July 22, 1964, *Yankee II* drifted ashore on a reef off Rarotonga in the South Seas; it was her end.

Albatross

Christopher Sheldon and Alice Strahan met aboard the *Yankee II* as crewmates on the 1957-58 voyage. They became engaged in Cape Town and were married soon after their return to the States. As they had so enjoyed the life at sea, they decided to follow in Irving Johnson's footsteps. The nearest vessel that they could find to the *Yankee II* was the *Albatross,* almost an exact sister ship. She had been built in Amsterdam as the *Alk* in 1921 for the pilot service, a steel schooner 92 feet long, 21 foot beam, and 11 foot draft.

In 1937 the German Government purchased her for use as a training ship, and during the early part of the war she worked with Nazi submarines in the North and South Atlantics. In 1949 she was bought by the Royal Rotterdamsche Lloyd as a training vessel for their future officers. Five years later Ernest Gann, author of "Twilight for the Gods", became her owner, sailing her to San

Francisco where he had her re-rigged as a brigantine. She later cruised the Pacific, and was used in the filming of his book.

The Sheldons took her over while she lay in Lisbon in 1959. Their first voyage led them down the Mediterranean, through the Suez Canal, around the Cape of Good Hope, and in time, to Mystic, Connecticut. They had formed "The Ocean Academy", a sea-going school for teen-agers, and now they set off with their students on what was scheduled to be a ten and a half month voyage.

On May 2, 1961, when the brigantine was in the Gulf of Mexico, bound from Yucatan towards Nassau, she was suddenly struck without warning by a white squall. Thrown on her beam ends, she quickly filled and sank, taking down with her six of her crew, including Mrs. Sheldon who had been below deck trying to get the boys topside. The thirteen survivors were picked up by a cargo ship, the *Gran Rio*, which landed them in Tampa.

CHAPTER VIII

The Fishermen

~~~~~~

ODAY practically all the Grand Bank fishing vessels are motor driven craft. Although it has been many years since either Gloucester or Boston has sent out an all-sail schooner to the Banks, a handful of windships continued to work out of Lunenburg, Nova Scotia, up until the outbreak of war in 1939. And in recent years, the type has not been completely extinct in New England waters for there have been several interesting examples on hand.

During the late 1930's a number of Newfoundland fishing vessels called in at Gloucester, ofttimes to bring south a load of salt fish, and to return north with a mixed cargo, perhaps salt in their holds and drums of kerosene on deck. Although the majority of these schooners had engines, and should be classed as auxiliaries, they still retained their windship features, and used their sails when at sea.

Bessie Marie

One such schooner was the *Bessie Marie* from St. John's. She differed from the Gloucester schooners in that, although she was a fisherman herself, she was a tern; her lines were very much like the usual two-masters', and if she had been given two sticks instead of three, she could have passed for an Essex-built craft. Launched from the yards of E. K. Mills at Burlington, Newfoundland, in 1929, she was 108 feet long. Her owners were Ashbournes Limited.

Then there was the schooner *Palitana,* also out of Newfoundland. And the schooner *Pasadena* which made several round trips to Gloucester. In the summer months she would go salt fishing on the Grand Banks, perhaps making three trips out a season. When the weather became too bad on the Atlantic, she would turn to freighting, carrying salt herring down to Cape Ann, going back to Lunenburg with coal.

There were quite a few other of these fishing schooners which differed only slightly from the Gloucesterman of the 1920's. The British vessels carried a bit more canvas still, and they had not all covered their wheels with houses. Even after World War II the New England fisherman was using some of his old schooner hulls, but they had been converted into motor vessels; if they did carry any canvas, it was no more than for steadying purposes.

There are a few schooners that deserve mention.

Bluenose

Of all the Grand Bank fishing schooners, the Nova Scotian *Bluenose* was certainly the most famous. For a quarter of a century she was the "Queen of the Banks", first winning the International Fishermen's Trophy Cup, symbol of the sailing championship of the fishing fleets, in 1921, and holding it until the end when sail had been replaced by power. She was an able vessel, built for speed but also to stand up to winter conditions on the North Atlantic when fishing. Most of her years she was purely a sailing ship, but towards the end, she had engines as well.

The first of the International Fishermen's Races took place in 1920 after the Canadians had challenged the Gloucestermen. The Yankee-built *Esperanto*, then fourteen years old, whipped the pride of Lunenburg, the *Delawanna* in her home waters. To avenge their defeat, the Nova Scotians called on William J. Roue of Halifax to design a winner; The *Bluenose* was the result. She was built by Smith and Ruhland of Lunenburg early in 1921. She was a big fisherman, one of the largest of her type, 143 feet overall, 112 feet on the waterline, 27 feet beam, and nearly 16 feet draft. Her frame was of oak and spruce, her bottom planked with birch, and rails and top of oak; her decks were pine. Her mainmast of Oregon pine towered 81 feet above her deck, and her main-topmast was another spar more than 53 feet in length. With all sail set, she spread some 10,000 square feet of canvas. She turned out to be exceptionally fast although other vessels built to her same lines never had her speed. Some fishermen have said that when she was launched the heel of her keel struck bottom so hard that she took a peculiar warp throughout her hull, that being the secret of her success. If that were so, no one was ever able to copy it.

After a summer of fishing, the *Bluenose* met the Gloucester schooner *Elsie* in October, 1921, for her first international race. With Captain Angus Walters at the wheel, the big Canadian schooner took two races from the much smaller *Elsie*. If the *Esperanto* had still been afloat it might have been a different story, but she had been lost some months before. A year later Gloucester challenged again for the cup, this time with the *Henry Ford*. The series was sailed off Gloucester. After the first race was declared "no contest," the *Ford* led the way home in the second race, but the Canadian found her stride in the next two to keep the cup. In 1923 Gloucester sent the great *Columbia* to Halifax. Many have considered her the fastest of all Gloucestermen; she is said to have made seventeen knots on occasion. The *Bluenose* won the first race, and was home first in the second, but a protest gave the race to the *Columbia*. Before the ensuing arguments had died down the *Bluenose* had gone back fishing, and the series were suspended; the two queens were never to meet again.

In 1929 the aging Lunenburg schooner went ashore on the rocks in Placentia Bay, Newfoundland, when feeling her way in for bait during a thick fog. For a time it seemed that she might be a total loss. Then, after four days of pounding, she was hauled clear. With her bottom partly stove in, it appeared that her racing days were over. Gloucester now felt that it could make one more challenge for the cup with the *Bluenose* out of the way. The *Gertrude L. Thebaud* was built, designed by Frank Paine, the noted yacht designer. A challenge was sent to Canada. The Nova Scotia fishermen felt there was only one defender, the *Bluenose*, but she was in poor shape for racing. However, Captain Walters agreed to bring her to Gloucester in 1930 for the Cape Ann tercentenary celebrations, but he would not put up his Trophy Cup for the masts and spars of the defender were not good, her sails were baggy, and her hull was badly strained. The late Sir Thomas Lipton put up a cup for the series.

The first race was a light weather affair with the *Gerty* slipping in an easy winner while the *Bluenose* slogged along through the slight swell. A few days later they started out again, this time in a 25-knot breeze, real fishermen weather. The *Thebaud* led across the starting line, but the mighty *Bluenose* came racing through the seas, her rail down in the boiling foam, her rigging singing in the gale as she picked up the speed of her former self; this was her day. By the first mark, the "Novy" was six minutes ahead. As the wind approached 40-knots with the gale building up the seas, the *Bluenose* gained another six minutes on the second leg. But that was all there was to the race as neither vessel was able to locate the third marker; the storm had swept it away. During the race the *Thebaud* very nearly lost two men. One was washed overboard by a passing comber; a second wave washed him back aboard. Another man, fouled in a line, was snapped over the rail, but the line had wrapped about him, so his shipmates were able to pull him safely out of the flashing foam.

The *Bluenose* lost the last race when Captain Walters, well in the lead, failed to cover the *Thebaud* as she tacked off shore. The smaller schooner found a breeze that gave her the edge and the Lipton Cup.

The following year Gloucester sent the *Thebaud* down to Halifax in an attempt to secure the International Cup as well, but this time the *Bluenose* was ready. She won the first race by more than a half hour over the 36-mile course, and the second one by some 12 minutes. In 1933 the *Bluenose* went out to the World's Fair in Chicago to be part of the "Century of Progress" Exposition, and the official Canadian representative there. In 1935 she crossed the Atlantic, Halifax to Plymouth, England, in 20 days to be present at the Jubilee Celebrations of King George V. On her return to Canada in the fall, she met very heavy weather off the south of Ireland receiving so much damage that she had to put back for repairs before going on.

The Bluenose and the *Thebaud* met in the last series of fishermen's races in the fall of 1938 off Gloucester. To say the least, the races were more a battle of words than good sailing. There was no proper racing weather, mostly light airs, hardly enough to fill the sails, on several of the days, and the vessels were not able to complete the course in the time allowed; not once did the wind suit.

The first race was held on October 9th with the *Thebaud* winning by almost three minutes, covering the 36-mile course in about five hours flat. The *Bluenose* evened the series by taking the second race, a 40-mile affair, in 4 hours, 39 minutes, leading her rival by almost 12 minutes. The "Novy" took the third race, also, by better than six minutes. The fourth race was sailed through heavy rain squalls which at times sent the vessels' lee rails under water for short spurts. The *Bluenose* covered the first leg, 9¼ miles, in just over 39 minutes, averaging over fourteen knots. However, the breeze did not hold, and the *Thebaud* was able to slip into the lead to cross the finish line first. The last and deciding race took place on October 26th, a day of calms and fitful breezes, perhaps perfect for yachts but certainly not for fishermen. The *Bluenose* crossed the starting line first, and she was never headed, covering the 36-mile course in seconds under four hours, some three minutes faster than the *Thebaud*.

The old champion had held onto the crown that had been hers for seventeen years. Never again will the fishermen race for their type has gone; the *Bluenose* will go into history as the last of the "Queens". She truly belonged to the era when sail was still to be seen on the Banks; she herself had fished there without power for many years. The *"Gerty"* was a newcomer, almost an afterthought, so perhaps it was justice that the Lunenburger had won.

After the *Bluenose* returned to her home port there was talk of turning her into a memorial to Canada's deep-sea fishermen, but the fund was never completed. When the war came she was converted into a freighter; her Grand Bank days were over. During the next few years she worked in the West Indies waters, often running between South and Central American ports and Tampa. Her end came late in January, 1946, when she struck a reef off the coast of Haiti, sinking a few hours later. Her crew of eight were rescued.

Although the *Bluenose* has gone, Canada has not completely forgotten her as her likeness appears on the Canadian ten cent piece and the fifty cent stamp.

Edward Trevoy

The schooner *Edward Trevoy* had one of the longest and most active lives of any of her contemporaries that were built along the Maine coast for fishing. Launched at Boothbay in 1883, she was 81 feet long, 22 feet beam, and 7 feet depth. Named after her captain, she soon became well-known in the Gloucester fishing fleet as she spent her earlier years on the Banks.

Eventually she turned to freighting, and for many years was a familiar figure in the sand trade, loading cargoes at Essex, Ipswich, and Newburyport for Greater Boston. During this period she had one serious accident. In late December, 1920, loaded with 150 tons of sand from Essex for Quincy, she drifted ashore the day after Christmas at King's Cove, North Weymouth. The outgoing tide left her stern on the mud flat, but her bow deep in the channel at such an angle that her sand shifted forward so that when the tide came in her bow was too heavy to lift. The little schooner was submerged almost completely at high water. However, a day or two later a floating derrick hoisted her back onto an even keel, and apart from a thorough soaking, she was little damaged.

Rail and road transportation was rapidly ousting the fleet of sailing coasters during the 1920's, and by 1926 the *Trevoy* was laid up for lack of business. In the spring of 1929, when she was purchased by George Smith of Liverpool, Nova Scotia, from Frank D. McCarthy of East Boston, she changed over to the British flag. She was now 46 years old. Six years later she again changed hands, this time going to Captain Reinhardt of Goldboro, Guysborough County, who kept her busy in the lumber trade.

The *Trevoy* made her last visit to her former home ports when she brought a load of timber south in the fall of 1939, going to both Gloucester and Boston. Not long after her return to Nova Scotia, she was laid up at Yarmouth until she was purchased by Ray M. Tanton, manager of the Percy Tanton Lumber Company, Summerside, Prince Edward Island. Mr. Tanton wrote of the *Trevoy*'s later events:

"She was placed on a slip and given a thorough overhauling following which she sailed for Summerside, P.E. Island. She was later registered at Charlottetown in my wife's name, and engaged in the carrying of lumber and coal from New Brunswick and Nova Scotia ports, Malagash salt to the Madalene Islands and produce to Sydney, Pictou, etc.

"In the spring of 1942 we joined the merchant marine and carried lumber and explosives for the United States and Free French Governments, also carried coal from Sydney to St. Pierre. On two occasions while on this run she was almost sent to the bottom during heavy fog by convoys on their way to England; the area we were sailing was a favorite stamping ground for the submarines.

"In 1942, she was struck and badly damaged by a destroyer in the Strait of Canso, and later sailed for her home port, Summerside, for rebuilding, but unfortunately same never materialized as she sank at the wharf in twenty-seven feet of water; proper equipment lacking due to war conditions, salvage operations were not successful. Thus, December, 1942, witnessed the passing of the grand old vessel.

"For your information, I might add that during her last years we also carried Diesel auxiliary power in order to maintain schedules. To my mind, one of the most pathetic sights one could witness was during a stay in Port of Newfoundland; an elderly gentleman came on board, and with tear-filled eyes stated that he was a member of the crew when she sailed on her maiden trip to the Grand Banks. He informed the Captain that she was then known as the 'Queen of the American Fishing Fleet.' I regret being unable to recall his name, but in 1942, he claimed he was then 79 years of age."

The *Edward Trevoy* was in her sixtieth year when she sank.

Gaultois

One day early in December, 1936, a 100-ton schooner came in from the open sea, sailing up Boston Harbor. She was the *Gaultois* with a cargo of Christmas trees that she had brought down from the port of Gaultois, Newfoundland. Lying at "T"-Wharf she might have come and gone almost unnoticed but her skipper, Captain George Francis, had trouble disposing of his load so that she made her name in the newspapers. However, few realized that she was one of the little Western Ocean schooners, one of the last trans-Atlantic traders of the days of wood and sail.

The *Gaultois* was not unlike the average Gloucester fishing schooners, about the same size and build, and the same rig. In fact, she had probably spent much time on the Banks herself. In the 1920's she went into the salt fish trade, taking dried fish from Newfoundland to Lisbon, Portugal or Oporto, Spain, returning with salt. When one considers that the North Atlantic can become ugly at all seasons, the *Gaultois* seemed very small for such a hard trade, but she was not unusual for there had been many others like her.

She was not a fast schooner, probably eleven or twelve knots being her top speed. Nonetheless, her passage time across the Atlantic was nearly always good. In 1925 she was 25 days on one of her eastward runs, and in 1926 she had an 18 day eastward trip, and a 19 day westward one. In 1927 she made at least two 18 day passages to Spain, and 29 and 22 day runs in returning. Below are several of her passages made in the 1930's:

1933—arrived Oporto April 24th; 19 days from St. Pierre, Miquelon.

arrived St. Pierre June 12th; 28 days from Lisbon.

arrived Oporto August 9th; 18 days from St. Pierre.

arrived Leixoes, Portugal, October 11th; 21 days from Gaultois.

arrived Gaultois November 30th; 33 days from Oporto.

1935—arrived Gaultois July 23rd; 20 days from Lisbon.
       arrived Oporto August 26th; 16 days from Gaultois.

Her run to Boston in December, 1936, had taken 11 days; she returned to Gaultois in six days, indeed excellent sailing for the small schooner.

In 1938 a dispatch from St. John's in November stated that the *Gaultois* had stranded at Dixon Point, Kent County, New Brunswick, and that her crew of five had been saved. However, it was not the end of the tough little vessel for she was back at sea again not so long after. A year or two later when she was at North Sydney she had an explosion on board which lifted her deck, but again she was repaired.

About this time her name was changed to *Fahe;* she was still active in the earlier part of the war.

Gertrude L. Thebaud

The last Gloucester schooner to be built to challenge for the International Fishermen's Race trophy was the handsome *Gertrude L. Thebaud,* and although she was not a pure sailing ship since she removed her engines only when racing, she will be remembered as the last "Queen of the Gloucester Fleet".

Her building was made possible through the generosity of a Mr. Louis A. Thebaud, a summer resident of Gloucester who had become interested in the local races of 1929. The new schooner, named after his wife, cost some $75,000. She was launched from the Arthur D. Story yard at Essex on March 17th, 1930. She had a beautiful, sleek hull which was designed by Frank C. Paine who had also drawn the plans of the famous "J" yacht *Yankee,* one of the leading contenders to represent the United States in the Americas Cup series. The *Thebaud* looked a yacht, too, but for all of that she was strongly constructed, and when on the Banks she was to show that she could take the worst that the mid-winter Atlantic had to offer. Her large, ample hold could stow a fare of 175,000 pounds of fish.

After launching, the *Thebaud* was towed to Gloucester where engines were installed. When she departed for the offshore Banks on April 20th for haddock, she was very under rigged, no topmasts, and only a riding sail on her mainmast. At the end of the summer fishing season, she returned to Gloucester to prepare for her first series of races with the *Bluenose.* The Gloucesterman had her engines removed, bent on a full suit of canvas, and by the end of September was ready to go out under sail alone. Her first trial, with more than 80 guests aboard, found her doing ten knots, leaving a clean wake. A day or two later she had an unofficial race with Mr. Frank Crowninshield's well-known yacht *Cleopatra's Barge,* considered one of the fastest schooners of her class in yachting circles. In light airs, the yacht led the fisherman over the 15-mile course by only four minutes.

Following the *Thebaud's* two victories over the *Bluenose* off Gloucester, the Gloucesterman put her fancy sails ashore, lowered her topmasts, took aboard her engines, and went back to the fishing grounds. A year later she became a sailer again when she prepared to try for the International Cup. To help her tune up for the races, the 21-year old *Elsie* also donned racing canvas. Much to the surprise of the waterfront, the old-timer put up a gallant struggle against the new racer, and in the first trial race of 18 miles, the *Thebaud* was only a little over three minutes ahead at the finish line; ten years before the *Bluenose* had beaten the *Elsie* by nine and eleven minutes in their races. In a second race with the *Elsie* the *"Gerty"* won by eight minutes.

On October 12th the *Thebaud* set out on one of her greatest runs. Following a noisy send-off by the townspeople who blew every available whistle and foghorn, the two-master set all her canvas as she sped down the harbor before a strong northwester. Rounding the Eastern Point breakwater at 11:30 in the forenoon, she made a marvelous picture with her white sails stiff against the blue, cold sky, her shining black hull throwing showers of sparkling spray across her decks. All afternoon Captain John T. Matheson drove her for all she was worth, but towards sundown, with the wind still rising, he ordered the kites taken in. The crew struggled with the topsails, staysails, and jib topsail. At first the Captain thought he would have the mainsail furled, too, but it was then decided that the wind would drop with the sun, so the sail was left set. However, after dark the breeze veered around to the north, approaching gale force. Too late to take in the big sail now, for fear of ripping it, the *Thebaud* tore through the night at thirteen, fourteen, and even, at times, fifteen knots. At 4 o'clock in the morning of the 13th, the light of Cape Sable was sighted, and shortly afterwards, with the dawn, all sail was set again as the wind dropped and the sea quietened. All day the *Thebaud* drove along at seldom less than thirteen knots as she raced up the Nova Scotian coast. As she dashed around Sambro and headed for Halifax Harbor, the wind shifted to the westward, allowing her to keep on the port tack. She had not tacked once since leaving Gloucester.

The clock was close to six as the racing schooner slid by Chebucto Head and on into the inner harbor. The *Thebaud* had covered the 400 miles in the record time of 30½ hours, 100 of those miles in seven hours, averaging better than 13 knots from Gloucester to Halifax. The great *Esperanto* had taken 52 hours for the trip in 1920, and the *Columbia* was 38 hours in 1923; the *Bluenose* had gone to Gloucester from Lunenburg in 35 hours. None of these passages touched the *Thebaud*'s fast trip.

However, for all her speed, the Gloucesterman failed to defeat the old *Bluenose* for the cup, and she came home in a half gale, taking 34 hours from Sambro Head to Thatcher's. Owner-Captain Ben Pine had ballasted his vessel for heavy weather. On the run east he had got the weather he had expected, but the race days had brought light breezes. The racing rules prevented him from removing the ballast once the series had begun. As soon as the races were completed, the strong winds returned, but they were too late for the *"Gerty"*.

The *Thebaud* went back to fishing with her engines doing most of the work. In September, 1932, her young skipper, Captain Jimmy Abbott, wished he had a little more canvas when th/ schooner was caught off Cape Cod in a heavy gale. Raging seas that battered her hull had opened the seams, and the driving wind had thrashed her jumbo and foresail to ribbons. At the height of the storm, as the engines were churning to keep her off the beach, a monster sea, foam crested, crashed across her rails, sweeping everything before it. The men at the pumps hung on for their lives, but as the decks had cleared of the water it was found that Austin Snow and Edward Zinck had vanished. For an hour Captain Abbott searched the stormtossed area for his two men, but they were never seen again.

In April, 1933, the *Thebaud* with Captain Pine and a crew of fishing captains from other vessels went to Washington, sailing up the Potomac to the Navy Yard where they were greeted by the President of the United States and the Prime Minister of England who was with President Roosevelt at the time. The fishermen were seeking federal aid for their industry, and spent several days visiting various senators drumming up sympathy.

After the *Thebaud* returned to Gloucester, she was transformed into a floating museum with countless booths to display various products of Massachusetts manufacture at the Century of Progress Exposition in Chicago. In order to pass safely throught the St. Lawrence Locks, it was necessary to cut two feet from her deep keel. She was completely rigged aloft, but she kept her engines as well. Following the greatest send-off ever given any vessel out of Gloucester, the *Thebaud* departed under all sail on July 28th. After a stop at Portland, she put into Halifax for engine repairs, and then on through the Gut of Canso into the Gulf of St. Lawrence, and so to Chicago.

The *Bluenose,* which had arrived at the Fair some time before the Gloucester schooner, was making money by taking out passengers for day cruises on Lake Michigan. She still had no engine, relying on her canvas alone. Captain Pine thought that his vessel, too, could pay her expenses, especially as she had the power to take her in and out of port on time. However, he was told that his engines made his vessel a "steamboat", and as such, he came under steamboat regulations. The way the *Thebaud* was fitted out made it impossible for her to fulfill the rules. In the end, Captain Pine received special permission from President Roosevelt to carry passengers for profit.

At the end of the summer, she returned to Gloucester to resume her fishing again, and the next few years found her busy in her trade. Once in awhile she found herself in trouble. One winter when she was trapped off Nova Scotia by an approaching storm, she tried to make Yarmouth for shelter, but a blinding blizzard forced her to heave to and ride it out. Within a few hours the wind was shrieking through her rigging at eighty to ninety miles an hour, piling up huge seas around her. Those not on watch stayed below while those on duty hung on inside the wheel house. Suddenly, without warning, a monster wave came bearing down on the laboring vessel. Those not at the wheel dove through the hatch below to the after cabin. With a shuddering crash the water struck. All fourteen dories were nearly carried away as their cradles were ripped from the deck. Hoops to the riding sail were torn loose. The windows to the pilothouse gave before the onslaught, tons of water pouring in. The *Thebaud* struggled to free herself, shaking off the extra load from her decks. That was the worst of the storm, but when it was over she was forced to make port for repairs.

On another occasion the fisherman had engine trouble somewhere off Sable. Sad to relate, she did not have sufficient canvas to work her own way back to port, and it was necessary to call the Coast Guard on the radio-telephone for a tow back home. By now she was little more than a motor vessel.

The *Thebaud* raced once again in 1938 when the *Bluenose* came to Gloucester. Although the larger Lunenburger took the series, there was no doubt but that the *Thebaud* was one of the fastest of the great racing schooners. With the right breeze, she was capable of 16½ knots. Perhaps only the *Columbia* and the *Mayflower* of the more recent Gloucester schooners were faster.

The *Thebaud* went back fishing in the late fall of 1938, remaining a Banker until the war days. In 1942 she joined the United States Coast Guard Corsair fleet for duty on submarine patrol offshore. When the enemy menace was over, she returned to civilian duty, but not as a fisherman. She went to the West Indies to become a freighter in the island trade.

Her end came in 1948. Then owned by William H. Hoeffer of New York, she was at a wharf in La Guaira harbor, Venezuela, on February 6th during a severe storm. Another vessel, drifting down on her, set her adrift herself in the harbor; she was wrecked on the rocks at the breakwater. In April she was finally abandoned as too costly to salvage.

Robert Max

The *Robert Max* was a fishing schooner which was built by the McKay Shipbuilding Company at Shelburne, Nova Scotia, in 1920; she was launched as the *Clara B. Creaser*. A good sized vessel of 172 gross tons and 127 feet long, she was owned for many years by H. Creaser of La Have.

In 1930 she was purchased by J. Thornhill of St. John's becoming the *Robert Max*. In her later years she turned to cargo carrying, making an occasional passage to U.S. ports. In midwinter, 1939, she made a quick run from New York to Grand Bank, covering the stormy 1000 miles in eight days. She came to Boston in April, 1941. The Germans sank her on August 4th in the North Atlantic.

Thomas S. Gorton

The very last of the all-sail, engineless Gloucester fishing schooners was the *Thomas S. Gorton,* built by Tarr and James in their Essex yards in 1905 for Captain William H. (Billy) Thomas. A typical fisherman of 140 tons and 106 feet long, she was a two-master with her mainmast and topmast rising 135 feet above her deck; her main boom was all of 75 feet long, and her bowsprit jutted 30 feet beyond her stem. During the winter months, when the topmasts were left ashore, she sailed under her four lowers, the mainsail, foresail, jumbo and jib; in the summer months, with top-masts aloft, she added fore and main-topsails, balloon-jib and fish-ermen's staysail.

The *Gorton* departed on her first trip to the Banks on August 30th, 1905, in search of haddock. Two weeks later she arrived at the Boston fishing wharves with 70,000 pounds of fish packed away in ice. She was what was known as a dory-fisherman, her crew of some twenty-five men fishing from ten or twelve dories that she carried in two nests on deck on either side of her fore-boom. On the Banks, the dories would put out with generally two men each to set trawl, a line with over 1500 hooks; when ten dories were out at once, 15,000 baited hooks would be near the bottom. After several hours, the dorymen would haul in their lines, often filling their dories with freshly caught fish.

The *Gorton* made a great name for herself in the haddock business, and when Captain William H. Thomas was her master, she set several records for catches. For twenty years she was an active fishing schooner, in good weather and bad. Many a winter gale she rode out on the shallow banks, tossing and pitching and rolling in the angry seas that snarled all about her, when snow and spray and spume seemed almost solid as they drove before the bitter winds, lashing her rigging until it was white and large with ice. She was a strong, able schooner. Once, in February, 1918, she went ashore off Boston, and when she was pulled clear after two days of bumping, she was not even leaking. She was one of the fastest schooners of her period; her sister schooner *Esperanto* was the first winner of the International Fishermen's Races.

By 1925 powerful engines were rapidly replacing canvas on the Grand Banks, and those craft which still relied on sails alone were finding it increasingly difficult to compete with the more modern types. Her owners, by then the Gorton Pew Company retired the *Gorton* from fishing, and put her in the hard, salt-her-ring trade between Gloucester and northern ports. This meant taking bulk salt, a heavy dead weight cargo, far down east to Newfoundland ports, and returning with her hold filled with her-ring packed in salt. Many an old Gloucester schooner ended her days in this laborious business, and only the best of them were able to keep at it long without showing signs of wear and age.

[171]

In January, 1929, the *Thomas Gorton* had a very close call with disaster. Captain Wallace Parsons, one of the best known mariners out of Gloucester, was in command of the two-master when she sailed from Bay Island, Newfoundland, with a half cargo of 300 barrels of herring for Gloucester. She was hardly a day out before she ran into a terrific gale with huge seas which had been built up by the 75-mile an hour winds. The schooner struggled to survive. A monster wave thundered across her railing, burying her deck under tons of swirling water. Her two dories, which were all she now carried as a freighter, were smashed to kindling. Her jib and foresail went to ribbons with a roar, and her fore boom snapped in two. The hull, now badly strained, began leaking. Led by their captain, the crew pumped for their lives, doing 2500 strokes an hour on the hand pump to stay afloat. They stuffed their mattresses, quilts, and clothing into the leaks to try and cut them down. For a whole week they worked, and when *H.M.S. Dauntless* sighted them on January 27th, the men were completely exhausted; they could not have lasted another day. The Navy vessel called for aid, and a tug came out from Halifax to tow the *Gorton* in for repairs.

That summer the schooner sent aloft her topmasts and bent on a full suit of sails for the last time. The port of Gloucester, to determine its fastest sailing schooner, arranged a series of races open to all. Only four vessels came to the starting line, but they probably represented the pick of the fleet. Th smallest and youngest was the *Progress,* built in 1913, and 96 feet long. Next in size was the famous old *Elsie,* built in 1910, and 106 feet long. Always considered a very fast sailer, she has been called the highest development of the New England fishing schooner. The third vessel was the *Arthur D. Story,* built in 1912, and 113 feet long. The last schooner was the *Thomas S. Gorton,* by far the oldest.

The Race Committee had planned to have three races, but the first two starts were in very light airs so that none of the vessels were able to finish in the given time. The day of the third race found conditions slightly better with something of a breeze stirring the water, but it was far from ideal race weather. The heavy *Gorton* never had a chance. Perhaps if there had been a gale of wind she might have done better, but as it was, it was a stern chase for her nearly all the way. The *Progress* slid away from her sisters, covering the 37½ mile course in 5 hours, 30 minutes, 53 seconds. The *Story* followed her across the line 11 minutes later. Then came the once-fast *Elsie* 3 minutes behind the *Story,* and yet another 7 minutes passed before the *Gorton* came home. The old schooner had sailed her last race, but she was to long outlive her three rivals.

Less than a year later, the *Progress,* when fishing off Cape Cod, caught fire while her crew were with their trawls in the dories. She sank amid a sea of flame while her men watched helplessly from their small boats. In 1934 the *Elsie* was sold to Newfoundland interests. Shortly afterwards she opened up at sea, sinking after her men had been forced to abandon her. The *Story* was the next to go. Like the *Gorton,* she had entered the herring trade, but unlike the *Gorton,* she had been given engines to supplement her canvas. Deep laden with salted fish, she sailed from Bellaoran on March 3rd, 1935. The next day a very heavy gale swept the entire area; the *Story* and her crew of eight were never seen again. Only the *Gorton* remained.

The aging schooner continued to operate between Gloucester and the north, now the very last of her breed. Most of her runs were uneventful, but sometimes she would get caught in a blow. In June, 1934, she departed from Gloucester with an unsually large cargo of salt, some 800 hogsheads or 240 tons, that had her so deep in the water that the wash from a passing harbor tug splashed through her scuppers and across her decks. Her skipper, Captain Donald McCuish, said that she was carrying too much, but with a summer voyage in prospect, there would be little chance of bad weather. However, the *Gorton* was only a couple of days out when a fresh, spring gale struck. The crew fought to take in the mainsail and jibs as the storm came on. Throughout the night, like a rock awash, the *Gorton* lay hove to with only her foresail and jumbo set. One monster sea, larger than the rest, caught her off balance, crashing aboard amidships, leaving the dory smashed in its wake of green foam. Dawn brought the end of the storm, and the *Gorton* was able to proceed. The next few days were wet with fog, but Dan McCuish, typical of the captains of Gloucester, seemed to smell his way north. On the ninth day out, she slid into Canso Harbor where part of the salt was put ashore. Then she went on further north for her herring, not returning to Gloucester until late in the summer.

In spite of her age, the *Gorton* was a very dry ship; the pumps had to be used only once a day, and then for only a few strokes. Until 1933 she had been very tight but then she had an unusual accident at the Magdalen Islands in the Gulf of St. Lawrence. While loading herring there, she had been forced to put to sea during a blow. When the weather had cleared, the *Gorton* returned to her anchorage, and picked up her buoyed cable in the middle of the night. After the shackle had been made fast, all hands turned in. When morning came, they were amazed to find their ship aground. It was then discovered that there was only a fathom of chain hanging from her hawsehole. Apparently, when they had slipped their cable, the chain had snapped, but the short fathom length was sufficiently heavy to hold the buoy in place. When they hauled the end of the cable aboard, there was nothing to stop them from drifting, and it was luck that had kept her off a rocky shore, putting her into mud instead. There had been very little damage, but the slight strain on her hull had started the tiny leak.

The last voyage that the *Gorton* made under the American flag was one of the hardest she ever had. In the late fall of 1934, she went back north for another cargo. After loading at the Bay of Islands, Newfoundland, she had sailed five days before Christmas with her hold full and a big deck load. She had not been underway long when she ran into a bad winter gale that gave her a terrific beating. Her dories were swept away by the seas. Ice formed in her rigging and on her decks and railings, weighing her down so that her men thought she would surely founder. At the height of the storm, an extra large wave dashed across her bulwarks. The mate jumped for the rigging, but one of the crew, Henry Tobin, was a little late, and before he could get a secure grasp, he was swept away from the vessel. And then a blasting squall struck the *Gorton,* dipping her down until her leeward rail was under the seas, and sending her slithering sideways. When she righted herself, she scooped Henry Tobin back aboard, little the worse for wear.

Those in Gloucester doubted very much that they would ever see the schooner again; they felt that the storm would swallow her as other storms had taken so many other windships. Word came down the coast of the terrible storms offshore, but never a sign of of the two-master. She was not seen, she was not reported. All hope had about given up when she suddenly appeared through the snow squalls off Gloucester breakwater on New Year's Day, still under sail, and all well. She had taken twelve days for the run, most of which had been through storms and gales and blizzards.

Not long after this passage, the Gorton Pew Company sold their old schooner to Captain Arthur Earle of Carbonear, Newfoundland. In the early spring of 1935, the last all-sail Gloucesterman departed for the last time; an era had passed. The *Gorton* loaded a cargo of 450 barrels of fuel, range, and lubricating oil from the Fauci Oil Company in Boston, and then set her head northward. Captain Lawrence Colford was in command.

The schooner now began a new life. Mr. Frederick G. Earle wrote of her next few years:

"My father A. M. Earle purchased this schooner in 1935, running her two years without power in the local and foreign trade. Being a sturdy ship and with the power age approaching, we installed a 60 HP engine, but finding this unsuitable, we removed this engine in the fall, and installed a 120 HP D.C. Glennifer, taking off her main boom, jibboom, and leaving her with foresail and riding sail.

"In the following years and up until the war started she had been remodeled with spars shortened and spiked, wheelhouse built on her stern, and stem altered to that of a knockabout.

"Through the war years, the *Gorton* traded from the Caribbean Sea to northern Labrador, carrying provisions, ammunitions and other war materials to outposts.

"Last spring we had her repaired, examined and remodeled in Snyders shipbuilding plant at Dayspring, Nova Scotia. The carpenters said 'she's still A-1 and as good as a new one built today.'

"We can not describe the changes made but the *Thomas S. Gorton* of today is quite different from the *Thomas S. Gorton* which sailed the New England coast a few years back."

Everything seems to have gone well with the old-timer until October, 1947. On the 6th, while battling a violent storm near Bonne Bay, Newfoundland, the auxiliary schooner smashed on the Whaleback ridge of rocks. Within a few minutes water was knee-deep in the engine room. Captain Clifford Abbott and his crew took to their dory as it did not seem possible for the hull to withstand the frightful battering that she was getting from the rocks and the seas. With great difficulty, Captain Abbott managed to make a landing on the jagged coast, but discovered to his dismay that they had come ashore on an uninhabited section. They did locate a shack with a little food, and after spending the night there, they hiked for miles to St. Paul's where they borrowed a horse to help them carry what they had saved from the wreck to the village of Sally's Cove.

The *Gorton*, in the meantime, left on her own, her sails still set, backed off the rocks, floating on her lumber cargo. Several days later she was picked up by fishermen who found her jogging along by herself. They sailed her into a bay, anchoring her in shoal water, not realizing her draft. At low tide the schooner took further punishment to her bottom, but before she began to breakup, her owners had her towed to St. Anthony's where they ran into insurance problems. The schooner was insured for "total loss" only. The owners claimed that as they had saved their vessel from total loss, thus saving the insurance company a big bill, they felt that the company should pay the bills for the smaller repairs. And on top of that, the fishermen were claiming salvage. However, the owners said that the fishermen had done more harm than good by putting her in shallow water.

Perhaps the most extraordinary part of this latest accident was the fact that the *Gorton* had drifted around near the Straits of Belle Isle for over a week without going ashore in the stormy month of October. No doubt, after nearly a half century of voyaging, she knew her own way around.

Still, sooner or later, all things come to an end. In 1956, in her fifty-second year, when bound for Labrador with a cargo of supplies, the *Gorton* ran into an iceberg, sinking within ten minutes.

One Gloucesterman, after an absence of nearly thirty years from New England waters, returned to become a museum piece:

L. A. Dunton

One of the last all-sail racing fishermen to be launched, the *L. A. Dunton,* named after a noted Boothbay, Maine, sailmaker, came from the yards Arthur D. Story in Essex in 1921. Designed by Thomas F. McManus, one of the most famous of all the fishermen designers, her lines were supposedly an improvement on his speedy *Elsie;* she was 133 tons and 104 feet long, 25 foot beam, and 11½ foot draft. However, speed-wise, the *Dunton* was a disappointment, never coming up to expectations, but she was a fine sea boat, powerful and strong.

She had been built at the same time as the controversial *Mayflower*, perhaps the fastest of all Essex-built schooners. Both vessels, ready for sea at the same time, rendezvoused off Gloucester, then set their courses for Nova Scotia. Captain J. Henry Larkin drove the *Mayflower* to windward, racing through the grey seas, while Captain Felix Hogan aboard the *Dunton* did his best to keep up. From Gloucester to Shelburne is 230 miles. For most of the way the two schooners had thick fog, head winds and hard squalls. The *Mayflower* was in seven hours before her rival.

They next raced from Shelburne to Canso. There were moderate northerly winds. The *Mayflower* took 38 hours; the *Dunton* came in 9 hours later even though she had started a half hour earlier. Now Hogan changed the trim of the *Dunton* to see if he could get her moving, but it was no use. When they raced from Canso to Grindstone in the Magdalen Islands the *Dunton* trailed in ten miles astern. Now the vessels took on bait, and went off fishing.

In October, 1922, the *Dunton* tried racing once again, this time in a series off Gloucester to select a rival for the Canadian *Bluenose*. There were four schooners, the *Henry Ford, Elizabeth Howard, Yankee* and the *L. A. Dunton,* and two races. The *Ford* won both, the *Dunton* brought up the rear (in the first race the *Howard* lost her main topmast, and did not finish). In the first race the *Ford* covered the forty mile course 37 minutes faster than the *Dunton,* and 39 minutes faster in the second race. The *Dunton* never raced again; her owners stuck an engine in her.

From now on the *Dunton* was a successful auxiliary fisherman. In 1934 she was sold 'east' to Newfoundland interests who not only had her fishing but freighting as well, even sending her across the Atlantic to Portugal for a cargo of salt. The war came and went, and still the *Dunton* carried on although by now her rig was considerably reduced, and she relied almost entirely on her engine.

In 1958 Edmund Francis Moran of East Boston formed a group called the *"L. A. Dunton* Associates" whose aim was to "save" the *Dunton,* to bring her back into New England waters to be set up as a fishing museum or memorial to the days of the Grand Bankers. Gloucester would have been the logical spot for her, but there was no interest there, no funds forthcoming. Finally, however, in 1963, with financial assistance from the Du Pont family, the *Dunton* was taken up by the Marine Historical Association at Mystic.

Today, fully rigged, fitted out as a dory schooner of old, the *L. A. Dunton* is one of the museum's outstanding exhibits.

CHAPTER IX

CHAPTER IX

The Square-Riggers

~~~~~~

THE FASTEST square-riggers ever built came from the New England yards, and the records made by Donald Mc-Kay's clippers that were launched in East Boston stand to this day. These were followed by the 'Down Easters' which came before the turn of the present century. They sacrificed speed for cargo capacity, having lines that were full and box-like. However, requiring large crews to handle their canvas, they were unable to compete with steam or with the fore-and-afters. By the end of the first World War, the square-rigger had very nearly passed from the New England scene, only a small handful remaining, mostly foreigners.

Therefore, it is quite surprising to find that a number of sailing ships still crossing yards have made their appearances in local waters at various times during the half-dozen years proceeding the second World War. A few were cargo vessels, others training ships, some were museums or historical craft, and three or four were yachts, but all of this group were square-rigged in one form or another. Like the schooners already mentioned, they bring to a close an era in this part of the world.

Abraham Rydberg

When the four-mast bark *Abraham Rydberg* entered Boston Harbor in the early days of the recent war, she was the first of her type in almost 22 years to come into New England waters. A steel vessel of 2345 tons and 270 feet overall, she still carried her original name, *Hawaiian Isles,* on her bell on the forecastle head.

Built in 1892 by Charles Connell & Company of Glasgow, her first owner was Andrew Nelson of Honolulu. Under the command of Captain Kustel, she set off on her maiden voyage from Swansea bound for San Francisco by way of Cape Horn. All went well down the Atlantic, but off the Horn she met head winds blowing with gale force, winds that had been gathering momentum in their race across the south Pacific, winds filled with sleet, snow and hail, and bitterness from the frozen Antarctic. Monstrous seas flung themselves at the new ship, battering her from stem to stern, flinging spray masthead high, sending green boiling waters across her decks. Day after day Captain Kustel drove his ship to round the corner, but the weather never abated, never gave him a chance to get a slant, so finally in desperation, he put about and ran before the storm. Passing far south of the Cape of Good Hope, she crossed the south Indian Ocean and so into the Pacific, arriving at 'Frisco 188 days out.

When the Hawaiian Islands became an American territory in 1898, all vessels which had been owned there by Americans or Hawaiians came under the Stars and Stripes. Amongst this fleet of 24 foreign-built vessels, which totaled more than 25,000 tons, was the *Hawaiian Isles*. She was a lovely looking ship at this time with her bronze-green topsides, brownish deckhouses, and buff masts and spars. She carried double topsails on the fore, main and mizzen, single topgallants, royals and skysails, a total of eighteen square-sails in addition to the dozen and more fore-and-aft sails that she could carry.

In 1900, the *Hawaiian Isles* was bought by Welch & Company of San Francisco who put her in a general tramping trade under Captain Walter W. Mallett. Leaving Honolulu in 1901, she crossed the Pacific in ballast to British Columbia where she loaded lumber for Port Pirie, South Australia. From there she again was in ballast, this time to Newcastle, New South Wales, to take on coal for San Francisco. Next, she went out to the Hawaiian Islands to load sugar for New York by way of Cape Horn. She carried a mixed cargo from New York to Melbourne and Sydney, her holds filled with furniture, harnesses, medicines, paper, bath tubs, and the like. She once more picked up coal at Newcastle, and then back to the Islands for another sugar run to New York.

In 1907, the *Hawaiian Isles* was one of 130 vessels that were laid up for many months at Newcastle while the Australian miners settled a strike. The following year saw the Welch fleet selling out to Captain William Matson who had founded the Matson Navigation Company. Captain Mallett remained with the ship, and early in 1909 made two good passages with her, 108 days from the Islands to Philadelphia, and returning to Honolulu in 128 days from the Delaware Breakwater.

In December, 1909, the four-mast bark was sold to the Alaska Packers Association for $60,000, some $40,000 higher than the usual market price of a 2000 ton windjammer at that time. Captain P. H. Peterson now took over command; he remained with her for sixteen years. Renamed *Star of Greenland,* she annually voyaged north with the Packers' fleet, acting as a floating barracks for the hundred and more cannery workers, mostly Chinese and Mexican, who packed away the freshly caught salmon during the season.

When the wind was right, the bark could still move along with the best of them. In 1921 she had bad luck with her weather, and took 35 days from the Golden Gate to Unalaska, a distance of about 2400 miles. The next year she had led the fleet of fifteen vessels home with a run of 16 days. In 1924 she tied with the *Star of Russia* going north; she returned in 12 days. Through the year her runs north averaged 19 days, south 15½ days.

The *Star of Greenland* made her last Packers' run in 1926, the same year that her owners first used a power vessel for the trade. She again led the fleet, taking 10 days; the *Star of Alaska* and the *Star of England* both took another day. The *Greenland* was now laid up at Alameda with a number of other square-riggers which had retired from the seas, but she was not to remain there long. In 1929 she was taken over by the Abraham Rydberg Society of Stockholm, Sweden, to become a training-cargo ship. Renamed *Abraham Rydberg,* and under Captain Sune Tamm, she took aboard 3100 tons of barley for Dublin, Ireland, the first windjammer to take wheat from the Golden Gate to Europe in seven years. Once it had been a prosperous trade for the windships, and one of the last occupations left open to them.

The *Rydberg* made a smart passage around the Horn, arriving at Dublin only 124 days out. The last 'Frisco Grain Race had taken place in 1921 when ten square-riggers had raced around the Horn on their way to England. The best passage had been made by the French three-mast bark *General De Sonis* which took 131 days; the slowest run had been done by the three-mast bark *Pierre Antonin,* all of 183 days. In 1922 only the German ship *Tamara XII* loaded wheat for Europe; she was 149 days to Falmouth. In comparison with these passages, the *Rydberg's* was excellent for a modern windjammer. Of course, in the days of the clippers 100-day passages were possible. The Boston-built four-mast bark *Great Republic* took a cargo of grain to Liverpool in 96 days. The "last of the wooden clippers", the *Glory of the Seas,* another Boston-built sailer, made her fastest grain passage in 1876, 103 days 'Frisco to Liverpool. The *Rydberg* will probably go down in history as the last sailing ship to load grain at the Californian port for the United Kindom.

After discharging at Dublin, she took 12 days to sail around to her new home port, Gothenburg, where she was completely refitted, getting new decks, a longer poop, and a full width midship house for forty cadets. The rigging was gone over, and all other necessary repairs completed. When she was ready for sea, she was in first class shape.

The Abraham Rydberg Society was founded by a Swedish shipowner of that name who lived from 1780 to 1845. At the time of his death, he left a considerable sum to start a nautical college to train seamen and officers for the Merchant Marine. In 1850 a small brig called *Carl Johann* after the King of Sweden was obtained for use in conjunction with the shore base. As she proved too small, a wooden ship was built in 1870; this was the first *Abraham Rydberg*. After 42 years she was replaced by a small steel ship which was later to become the American yacht *Seven Seas*. In 1929, the trustees of the fund felt that a cargo vessel would give the cadets a better training than they were getting, and, at the same time, help defray the expenses of the society. The purchase of the *Star of Greenland* was the result.

The cadets had to be between 16 and 20 years of age, and suitable for the life at sea. Each cadet paid a premium of $200 for the privilege of sailing aboard the bark, as well as supplying his own bedding and duffel. The cadets sailed the ship themselves, there being no other sailors aboard, only the Captain, the mates, the bos'un, the sailmaker, and the carpenter. The year spent aboard the bark would take them to Australia and back, during which time they would learn seamanship, navigation, and the ways of the sea, and what was more important, they would get character, learn to depend on themselves, learn the value of unity. They might leave Europe as boys, but they returned as men.

The *Rydberg*'s first outward passage with cadets was in the early fall of 1931, taking 96 days from Gothenburg to Wallaroo on the Spencer Gulf, South Australia. With 3500 tons of wheat stored away below, she returned to London in 123 days. Her next outward run was 108 days, and again 123 returning. She made one of her best homeward trips in 1934 when she was only 107 days to Falmouth. During this run she was struck by a terrific squall when south of the Azores, the force of the wind ripping her sails to shreds, and snapping off her fore-topgallant and fore-royal yards. Later in the voyage she met the old *Mauretania* which had held the Blue Ribbon of the Atlantic longer than any other steam vessel. Setting more sail, the *Rydberg* made a race of it with the great liner, the two shops plowing through the grey seas of the North Atlantic side by side. A strong following wind gave the bark her top speed, but the Cunarder slowly eased ahead, leaving astern the windjammer in all her glory, her sails taut before the gale.

In 1935 the *Rydberg* and the beautiful Finnish four-mast bark *Herzogin Cecilie* compared speeds. The Rydberg sailed from Wallaroo on January 7th; the *Herzogin* sailed from Port Lincoln on the 21st. The Swede took the road to the west as Captain Tamm felt that better weather was likely to be found that way, making conditions safer for his cadets although apt to make a longer passage. The Finn bark took the east road for stormy Cape Horn, rounding the point on February 25. Both vessels were greeted by light airs as they approached the Line, and their daily runs were not much more than 50 or 60 miles a day. The *Rydberg* drifted into the North Atlantic in the first day or two of April, crossing the Equator about 22 degrees West; the *Herzogin* followed on the 11th, at 30 degrees West.

On May 1st, when the *Rydberg* was still more than 700 miles from Land's End, England, one of the cadets sighted sails on the horizon. As the two vessels drew together signal flags were hoisted; the *Herzogin* had caught up with the *Rydberg*. Both ships, bound from the same Gulf to the same Channel, sailing opposite ways around the world, had crossed tacks at a spot in the North Atlantic only minutes apart after traveling thousands of miles in different directions.

The *Herzogin*, pride of the Grain Fleet, soon left the *Rydberg* astern. The Finn arrived at Falmouth on May 18th, 117 days out. The Swedish vessel crept along her course for another week, and then yet another week, not anchoring off Gravesend until June 3rd, all of 147 days from Wallaroo. The *Herzogin* had beaten her soundly, but the Finn was beaten by the German four-mast bark *Priwall* which had left Port Victoria on February 14th, and had arrived at Queenstown in 91 days. The German had had the best run of the 19 square-riggers in the race; the *Rydberg* had had the slowest.

[182]

Captain Tamm gave the ship up in 1935 to become the Marine Superintendent of the Society, and he was succeeded by Captain Hallstrom who had her for a year. In 1936 the bark was in a collision with the *S.S. Koranton* during a thick fog off the Devon coast, causing the main-topgallant mast to crash down, and considerable damage to her forecastle head. In 1937 the first mate, Oscar Malmberg was given the ship although he was only 25 years old at the time, and he sailed her for the rest of her days under the Swedish flag. He was an excellent sailor, and just the man to command the cadet ship, getting the best out of her. In 1938 he brought her the last 2200 miles to England in ten days, showing that the aging vessel had not lost her speed with the years.

The second World War was declared two or three days after the *Rydberg* had sailed from Sweden for the grain ports. After being looked over by Swedish and British cruisers, she carried on southward, finally putting into Buenos Aires for orders. There she loaded beancake for Sweden. On the way north she heard of German activity in the Baltic so put into Barbados in the Indies. After receiving further orders, she set out once more, but had to return to port with rudder troubles. Following repairs, she got as far as the north of Scotland when her owners decided that she would be safer away from the area of conflict, and she was sent back to New York, arriving there on May 5th, 1940.

She next went to Norfolk, loading coal for South America. At Santos, Brazil, she took on cotton seed meal for Boston, sailing on December 5th. As she neared the New England waters a winter westerly set in, the bitter head winds holding her 75 miles off shore until they abated. On February 12th the tug *Jupiter* picked her up some five miles beyond the Boston Lightship, towing her into harbor 69 days from Brazil. During this trip she had used her triangular courses, a rather unusual type of lower sail for a vessel of this sort, but very handy if not as efficient as the regular four-sided sail. The *Rydberg* generally used this canvas when in stormy waters as it was easy for the cadets to handle.

The towering spars of the windship caused a stir along the waterfront as she was taken up the harbor to a berth in the Mystic docks, just across from where Donald McKay had had his ship yards, many, many years before. Captain Malmberg and his British wife who sailed with him showed visitors about their vessel while the cadets explored Boston. The press made the most of the bark's visit, writing reams of the old sailing days.

With sand ballast, the *Rydberg* sailed on March 10th, again bound for Santos. She returned to Boston in July, this time taking only 49 days for the run north. Later she went on to Portland. By this time she was down to a crew of 14 as most of the Swedish cadets had joined Swedish power craft or worked their ways homeward. A few Americans filled some of the gaps.

She was eventually laid up at Baltimore on March 15th, 1942. With no sign of the war coming to an end and the price of ships at top levels, the Society decided that it was best to sell the *Rydberg*, and it was reported that the Portuguese payed $265,000 for her. She still had her "100 a-1" classification with Lloyds, and was in perfect condition. Renamed *Foz Do Douro,* she entered trade between Portugal and the Americas.

In March, 1945, she was given two diesels while in Philadelphia, and it can be said that these brought to a close her days as a sailing ship. Not long after this, her upper yards were removed, her bowsprit cut down to a stub, and her canvas put away for good; she was a motor ship. For awhile she was active between Lisbon and ports along the Gulf of Mexico, but eventually was broken up in Italy in 1959.

Aloha

The yacht *Aloha* deserves mention if only because she was one of the very few bark-rigged yachts to have ever been in commission. Built by the Fore River Shipbuilding Corporation of Quincy, Mass. in 1910, she was 659 gross tons and 180 feet long. With a sail area of 15,000 square feet of canvas, she had double topsails, single topgallant, and royals. Although a handsome vessel, her looks were somewhat marred by a funnel amidships, an engine room exhaust. The figurehead of a woman on her bows was a fine bit of carving.

During the first World War the *Aloha* was rigged down for duty with the Navy. When peace returned, she donned her canvas again to make a world cruise. Sailing from Newport, Rhode Island, on September 15th, 1921, she passed through Panama Canal, and then on to the Hawaiian Islands, Japan, China, India, Arabia, and back via the Suez Canal and the Mediterranean. She returned to Newport on June 1st, 1922, after a 22 day run from Marseille.

For many years she was a familiar sight along the East Coast. However, in later years she left her yards ashore, just setting stay-

sails in order to cut down the work of her crew. When her owner
Arthur Curtis James passed away in the late 1930's, the aging
bark went to the ship-breakers at Fall River as he had wished.

Bear

One vessel that will long be remembered in the history of
exploration is the venerable old *Bear,* veteran of the Arctic and
the Antarctic polar seas. Built at Greenock, Scotland, in 1873, she
was designed for the Arctic seal fisheries, and consequently was
strongly put together with oak planks six inches thick; many parts
of her 198 foot hull were 30 inches thick while in the bows were
bracing timbers 18 inches square. She was rigged as a three-mast
barkentine. Below decks she had a steam engine which gave her
up to seven knots in a calm; under steam and sail with the right
conditions she sometimes got up to twelve and fourteen knots.

When she set off on her first sealing voyage from St. John's
Newfoundland, in March, 1874, she was the outstanding vessel
of the fleet of 300 sail that ranged from small schooners to good
sized barks. Heading north, her bows plowed the blue waters
until she reached the soft ice off Labrador. When the seals were
sighted, her men dropped over the sides to cross the bergs to the
schools, returning soon with the valuable pelts, and before long
the stench of blood and grease rose from her decks as the dead
animals were cured.

After ten annual trips to the sealing grounds, the *Bear* returned to Greenock for a complete overhaul, much needed after
the years of battering the ice and battling the bitter gales of the
northern seas. She returned to St. John's in 1884, but before she
had a chance to depart on another sealing expedition, she was purchased by the United States Government for $100,000 to be used
for the rescue of the Greely Expedition which was trapped in Lady
Franklin Bay in Northern Greenland. In 1881, an expedition
under Lieutenant A. W. Greely had set up a camp to study the
winter conditions of the north. Their relief ship in 1882 had
failed to break through to them, and the relief in 1883 had had no
better luck, ice blocking the passage. The *Bear* was the last hope,
being selected as the most suitable vessel for the attempt. She was
rushed to New York where she was further strengthened and fitted out for the arduous voyage before her, and at the same time,
she was fully commissioned in the United States Navy.

Leaving New York on April 25th, 1884, she proceeded to St.

John's for final supplies. Then, with the U. S. cutter *Thetis* as flagship, she was on her way again on May 4th. Head winds greeted her, but there was no waiting as she had a long way to go in the few weeks of summer before the winter freeze-up began again. Belching black smoke, she batterd her way on, first past icebergs, and later pan ice, ice fields from two to four inches thick, through which she had to grind her way. Ever north she went, with the temperature hovering at 15 degrees. Lookouts kept a constant search for Greely's men, never knowing just where they would find them.

When Greely had found there was no relief in 1883, he had started south in early August with his men, traveling in four small launches, hoping that they would meet their rescuers. Heavy gales had damaged their craft, and only after constant work had they managed to get their remaining supplies and scientific records across the ice to shore. With the long Arctic winter closing down on them in October, they had set up a new camp at Cape Sabine. For months storms lashed at them, blizzards and gales for days on end. Even with their food rationed, their supplies gradually gave out, and before spring some of the men had died from starvation. As the weather warmed, the survivors searched the horizon for signs of help.

Not until June 22nd did the *Bear* and the *Thetis* arrive. Only Lieutenant Greely and six men remained alive. The seven were placed aboard the *Bear* which raced southward with them to Portsmouth, New Hampshire, where they received complete medical attention. If the *Bear* had never sailed again, she would always be remembered for that gallant dash to the north and back again, but there were many seas before her yet.

The Navy was now through with the barkentine; as far as they were concerned, she was obsolete, and it was even hinted that she might be broken up. Decommissioned, she was laid up in New York to await her fate. She had not been there long when the Revenue Cutter Service looked her over. They required a vessel for patroling the icy waters of the Bering Sea; The *Bear* was just what they wanted. Again refitted, and now suitably armed, she left New York on November 9th, 1885, heading south. After refueling at Rio, she steamed through the Straits of Magellen, stopping for further supplies at Valparaiso. She made San Francisco on February 23rd, 1886, 87 days sailing time from New York.

With Captain M. A. Healey in command the *Bear* began a

duty that was to last more than forty years. As each spring came, the barkentine would leave the States, bound north, carrying mail and supplies to the pioneers and settlers along the Alaskan coast. She took doctors with her, and medical equipment. She was the one contact with the outside world. She was the law of the north, protecting the seals from poachers, judging cases on shore, settling disputes. As the ice thawed, she would stick her nose through the Bering Strait into the Arctic Ocean above the Arctic Circle. Her puff of black smoke from her tall stack attracted the inhabitants to the landings for their yearly news of the world. The *Bear* remained all summer far in the north but as the winter nights set in, she would turn south again, heading back for San Francisco to lay up for the winter months.

She had a close call with destruction in 1894 when she went aground at Sitka Harbor in Alaska. Reports drifted down the coast that she was a total loss after her crew had been removed as she was battered to bits by the heavy seas. However, the word was exaggerated, and some weeks later she came back home not too seriously damaged after her grounding.

On her homeward trip in 1897, the *Bear* put into Seattle where it was learned that eight whaling ships with 265 men were trapped by the ice off Point Barrow, the most northern point of Alaska. President McKinley in Washington asked if the little ship would try a rescue dash although never before had a vessel sailed north at that time of year. With a volunteer crew, many of them regular men, under the command of Captain Tuttle, she left Seattle on November 27th, only three weeks after her arrival there.

Driving northward, she bucked through dark, cold seas, fighting the early winter weather that lashed at her. Flying spray iced her rigging so the crew had to chop it away to work her lines. With engines and sails, she smashed forward, plowing onward, so small in so vast and lonely an area. By the time she arrived at the Bering Sea, she was surrounded by ice, and as each day passed, there was more and more chance of her getting caught herself. Finally, she halted at Cape Vancouver, Nelson Island, but the whalers were still 1200 miles to the northward, across fields of frozen wastes.

Three of her officers, Lieutenants Jarvis and Bertholf, and Surgeon Call left the Bear to start a long hike through the snow towards the whalers. At Cape Prince of Wales they rounded up a herd of reindeer which they drove before them for 800 miles; the animals were to be food for the stranded men. The journey was full of hardships under terrible conditions. Seldom able to make more than ten miles a day, they were 120 days before they reached their goal. They were only just in time for by then the whalers, out of food, were eating their walrus boots.

In the spring, the *Bear* came on, but it was not until July that she appeared. Ice had remained heavy that year, and at one time, after she had joined the whalers, drifting ice had suddenly packed around her before she could get clear. As the pressure increased, the decks in the engine room bulged while the ice around the stern threatened to snap her rudder. All hands went over the side with axes and ice cutters; after a long fight they saved their ship from being crushed.

Some of the busiest years of the Bear's life were in 1899 and 1900 when the great Alaska gold rush was on, and every available craft was setting out for the Yukon district. Many a vessel that began the long passage was hardly harborworthy. Some foundered before they had gone far, and the *Bear* was credited with numerous rescues. Amongst the rabble in the scramble north were gun-toting individuals who knew neither law nor order; the officers of the *Bear* took care of them in many courts.

In 1904 a lumber schooner rammed the barkentine, the force of the crash carrying away the foremast with the yards. When she was rerigged at Oakland, a bridge between the funnel and the foremast was added, greatly aiding the piloting but taking away from her looks.

The Revenue Cutter Service became part of the Coast Guard in 1915, the *Bear* going under the C. G. flag with the rest of the fleet. This was the first year since she had taken up the Bering Sea patrol that there were no whalers to watch over; the era of the windjammer whalers was over. In 1917, when the United States entered the war, the *Bear* gave up her white paint for a coat of grey, coming under the orders of the U.S. Navy, but with the return of peace, she went back to her duties.

By 1921 the Coast Guard felt that the *Bear* was geting old. Examined by the Navy, she was found to be still fit, but she was condemned as obsolete, just as she had been condemned 35 years before. However, there was no vessel to replace her at the time, so she was sent north again. Before she returned to port she rode out one of the fiercest hurricanes to ever strike the area, the whining winds attaining a force of 150 miles an hour at the height of the storm. The little ship again proved her worth; she came through the blow unscathed.

The year 1924 was a bad one for the *Bear*. First she got caught in the ice, the pack forming tightly around her, and damaging her propeller. Later she went ashore off Cape Prince of Wales where a heavy surf dashed her against the rocks. This time it looked like the end for her, but again her hull withstood the pounding, and she was successfully refloated.

In 1926 the three-master made her last voyage to the Bering Sea. She had gone north 35 times, getting through the ice on all but four occasions. She had become an institution on the West Coast, and there were only a few who did not know of her by name. She was more than just a ship, she was a symbol. She represented the Stars and Stripes, law and order, the guardian of the northern settlers. When she had first started her patrols, Alaska was a land of wilderness; she had seen it develop through the years, and watched its towns grow as the population multiplied. The *Bear* had lived through an epoch.

Once more it seemed that she was destined for the junk yard, but a group in Oakland, California, banded together to save her, and she became a marine museum of the City of Oakland. She had not been long in her new role when Admiral Byrd looked her over during his search for a vessel to replace his *City of New York* for his next expedition to the South Pole. As the *Bear* came up to his strict requirements, Admiral Byrd asked the City of Oakland if they would part with her. The authorities agreed to put her up for public auction. All would have gone well but a junkman un-expectedly bid a $1000 for her. However, after he understood why Admiral Byrd wanted the ship, he bid no further, and the *Bear* went to the Admiral for $1050. Renamed the *Bear of Oakland* by the Admiral as a token of gratitude to the City, she was given a temporary refit before departing for the East Coast. Before passing through the Panama Canal, she paused at the Mexican port of Salina Crux to refill her coal bunkers. The Mexicans, noting the guns that she still carried from her Coast Guard days, thought that she had arrived to stir up a revolution, and they held her for two days before they could be persuaded that she was on a peaceful mission. A month after leaving San Francisco, the *Bear* entered Boston Harbor, arriving on August 10th, 1932.

Although the expedition was to have started as soon as the *Bear* was ready, it was postponed for a year when Admiral Byrd was elected chairman of the National Economy League. However, during this period, preparations were carried out, supplies located, and the ship made fit for the long voyage. A steamer, the *Jacob Ruppert,* was to go along also, and she was to carry part of the *Bear's* steaming coal.

The barkentine eventually headed out from Boston on September 25th, 1933, bound for New Zealand. After passing Cape Hatteras, she ran into a nasty gale off Diamond Shoals, and loaded deeply as she was, she had to fight for her life to stay afloat. Huge seas swept aboard the tiny vessel, and before long water was getting below faster than the pumps could take care of it. The engines had to be stopped as the flooded conditions worsened, and the *Bear* was hove to under sail while all hands spent the night bailing water from the bilges. She came through the ordeal safely, but she was strained, so had to put back to Newport News for drydocking. She was on her way again on November 1st.

After passing through the Canal, the *Bear* started across the Pacific on November 17th. A month later she stopped at Tahiti to coal. She arrived at Wellington on January 6th, 1934, but not before she had weathered another severe storm, almost a hurricane, which drove her to shelter in Hicks Bay of the North Island, New Zealand. In Wellington further supplies were loaded, including a heavy tractor that went on deck. Some New Zealanders doubted that the old ship would survive the trip to the ice fields, thinking that she was too old and worn, but they did not know the *Bear.*

After putting into Dunedin for a few final items, she departed on January 19th, bound south. The winds were fair, and the waters free of ice, so that 12 days out she entered the Bay of Whales at Little America. The ship of the north which for sixty odd years had bucked the floes of the Arctic was now deep in the Antarctic, a world away from her former haunts.

Supplies were unloaded onto the ice, the dog teams and tractors lugging them inland. Before the *Bear* returned to New Zealand for the winter, Admiral Byrd took her on a cruise of exploration, poking her bowsprit into the near-by ice fields while making many scientific observations. During all of the ship's runs, she made a continuous series of sonic soundings, adding greatly to the then meagre knowledge of the ocean depths in that part of the world. She then made a dash out of the Bay of Whales to meet the British exploration vessel *Discovery II* which was bringing a doctor for them, and also some additional supplies. The return to

Little America was nip and tuck all the way as ice was ever increasing about them. At times it did not seem as if she could fight her way through. Those on the *Bear* realized how imperative it was that they leave the doctor with the ice party during the winter months, and they also knew that many of the men still on the ice had to be taken aboard as there were not enough supplies for all; the *Bear* had to get back to Little America. Somehow she managed it, after beating and fighting her way through the pack.

On February 26th, eight hours after arriving at the Base, she was off again, bound north. In the South Pacific terrific gales smote the windjammer, worse than anything she had known up north. Blowing as much as 100 miles an hour at times, the wind lashed through her rigging, and at one time she was sailing four knots under bare poles, her engines stopped. Huge seas bore down on her, sometimes crashing aboard with a thunderous roar. Here and there about them floated mountains of ice, any of which could have smashed her sides to kindling, and sent her to the bottom if she had had the misfortune to ram one. Rolling onward, 50 degrees roll on each side, once or twice almost on her beam's end, the *Bear* struggled through the gales which seldom let up. For seventy percent of her trip the wind was blowing over 60 miles an hour. She finally made Dunedin on March 12th.

During the winter months the barkentine was overhauled and given new rigging and some new spars. By the springtime she was ready to return to Little America, and on January 1st, 1935, she set out once more. She was so deeply laden with supplies and stores she only had 20 inches freeboard. With Lieutenant Robert A. J. English in command, the *Bear* did not take a direct route to the Bay of Whales, but along the rim of the Ross Barrier so that further surveys and observations could be taken. She arrived at Little America on January 19th, royally welcomed by the men on the ice who were awaiting their mail from home.

The next two weeks were a mad scramble to evacuate Little America, the men working the clock around to get supplies aboard the ships. With the crumbling ice of the barrier making it impossible to safely bring the *Ruppert* alongside to take on stores, the *Bear* had to act as a shuttle, running between the ice shelf and the steamer with her cargo. Once an edge of the ice gave way, crashing against the wooden ship, but she merely shuddered, rolled with the blow, and came to no harm; if the *Ruppert* had been in her place, the steel sides would have been ripped open.

On February 5th, the *Bear* departed from the base, bound for home by way of New Zealand and the Panama Canal. Weeks later she arrived back in Boston, weather beaten and salty, and apparently at the end of her adventures. As she was getting old now, no one expected that she would put to sea again.

For several years she lay almost forgotten at a wharf, soot collecting on her decks and rigging, her paint chipping. Then President Roosevelt commissioned Admiral Byrd to head a government financed voyage to Little America to lay claim to vast areas of the frozen south lands to prevent aggressor nations from moving in there for an attack on the Americas. Once more the *Bear* was chosen to make the trip, and she became the flagship. Joining her was the *Northstar*, the vessel that had relieved her in the Bering Sea patrol in 1928. Much work was done on the *Bear*. Her old steam engines were replaced with modern diesels, making much more cargo space. She was fitted aloft with a set of the finest Oregon pine spars, her foreyard being 60 feet in length and 16 inches in diameter. She was given a new bear figurehead as her old one had gone to a museum.

On November 22nd, 1939, she left Boston during a heavy blizzard with a crew of 39 men. She carried 78 sled dogs and 18 months of supplies. Lieutenant Commander Richard Cruzen was her master. After picking up an airplane at Norfolk, she went through the Canal, and on the last day of the year she arrived at the base at the edge of the ice. During the next few weeks she made Antarctic history by pushing through the ice further eastward than any other ship had done in that latitude. With the help of the 'plane her men were able to locate leads and open water which otherwise they might have missed, and thus they were able to discover more than a score of capes, bays and islands.

Before the *Bear* was through, she had one of the closest calls in her long history when she was trapped by ice, and only luck saved her from being crushed between the mighty bergs. Her 'plane was able to spot an avenue of escape at the last moment, and she only just got to clear water in time.

Again the *Bear* wintered in New Zealand, returning to pick up the expedition in late December, 1940. Before leaving the frozen lands, the barkentine followed around the edge of the ice pack, checking on the coast line. When she was finished, 900 miles of coast had been discovered, 14 new islands sighted, six mountain ranges plotted, as well as two long peninsulas and many bays. The expedition had been a great success.

By the time the *Bear* arrived back in Boston, the Battle of the Atlantic was on. As many United States warships had been given to Britain, there was a shortagt of patrol craft so the *Bear,* now 67 years old, became a cutter again, but her sails were removed and her top-hamper cut down; her bowsprit was sawed off.

Her new orders took her back to the waters she had first known, back north to Greenland. She slipped out of Boston Harbor unnoticed for war censorship covered all ship movements. Then, weeks later, on October 14th, 1941, she was back again with the German ship *Busko* that she had captured in the act of setting up a radio spy station to help the Nazi submarines. The *Bear* had made the first U.S. Naval capture of the war.

Again she went back to sea, carrying on until more modern ships could be built to take her place. Without her sails she rolled heavily, and she was hard on her crews, but she served her purpose. In time she came back to Boston, and was finally laid up.

After the war she was offered for sale, and was eventually bought by Frank M. Shaw of Montreal for $5199.00. In the late spring of 1948 he had her towed north to Canada where she was to be reconverted back into a sealer, as she had been 75 years before, but instead of refitting she found herself in a mud berth across the river from Halifax. In 1962 she was purchased by an American who planned on taking her to Philadelphia, there to be turned into a restaurant and nautical exhibit. After expensive alterations, she departed in tow from Halifax. A few days out a gale struck and the tow line parted. Next, her fore top hamper collapsed, a yard arm stabbing a hole in her hull beneath the waterline. Slowly she filled, and on March 19, 1963, sometime in the night, she slipped beneath the seas, going down some 260 miles east of Boston.

Benjamin F. Packard

The last of the wooden down east full-rigged ships to be in New England waters was the mighty 2076 ton *Benjamin F. Packard,* built by Goss, Sawyer & Packard of Bath, Maine, in 1883. Named after the partner in the firm, the *Packard* was a typical square-rigger of the type that followed the clippers, a heavy ship with full lines and good cargo capacity, sails' last hope in the competition with steam. She was certainly not a fast ship, and her earlier voyages were generally lengthy ones. Records show that her runs between New York or Baltimore and San Francisco averaged 148 days, her slowest passage taking 172 days, while her two best runs were 130 days. Returning to the East Coast she was apt to make better time on account of the prevailing Westerlies in the southern latitudes, but even then there is only one outstanding passage, that of 94 days, completed when she arrived at New York on July 18th, 1892, with a general cargo. She had raced the *A. G. Ropes,* another Bath-built ship. Both had sailed the same day, but the *Ropes* not only came in a day ahead of the *Packard,* but she had stopped to take the crew off a sinking ship near the Horn, and had landed them at Pernambuco. On one occasion in her earlier days, the *Packard* loaded in Liverpool, England, and had taken 153 days to get to Port Moody in British Columbia.

About the turn of the century she was employed in carrying coal from Norfolk to Honolulu, returning with sugar. Her last Cape Horn passages were done in 1907 and 1908, eastward with lumber to New York, and returning to Puget Sound in May. Apart from a few years just after her launching, the *Packard* had been owned by the great windship company of Arthur Sewall in Bath until this time. Now she changed hands the Northwestern Fisheries Company of Seattle putting her into the salmon cannery trade, sending her north each year to Alaska. Many of the down easters ended their days on this run, but the *Packard* did not seem to wear out. Her waterline had been girdled with iron to withstand the sharp ice floes that she might meet on her passages. In later years the Booth Fisheries operated her on the same run, but by the time she returned south in 1924, she found that steam had finally ousted the wooden sailers from the trade, and she reverted to lumber carrying, her owners then being Hanson, Heider & Company of Seattle. However, she loaded only once again, setting off for New York with some 2,000,000 feet of lumber aboard. Her owners thought that she would make better time on the end of a tow line, so she did not sail with a full crew. However, when she finally did come into port, having passed through the Panama Canal, it was said that when the wind had been right, the *Packard* had set a sail or two, and then it was all the tug could do to keep up.

Following her arrival in New York, she received a good deal of publicity in the newspapers, and was frequently called the "last of the clippers". On October 21st, 1925, her flag was hauled down by her skipper, Captain D. J. Martin, thus ending her days as a commercial vessel. A few old salts from Sailors Snug Harbor came over to witness the ceremony, and before they left the ship, they sang some of the old sea shanties, bringing back memories of the days when she was a proud Cape Horner.

For a time it seemed that the Packard would become a barge, but Theodore Roosevelt Pell, a wealthy New York yachtsman, purchased her for less than $10,000, and plans were made to turn her into a marine museum. The scheme seems to have fallen through for soon after this she was used by the Junior Naval Reserve as a training ship. After that she lay aground in Manhasset Bay, Long Island. In December, 1929, an antique firm bought her for $1000. A few months later she had a new owner who moved her across the Sound to Playland at Rye Beach, New York, where she became a show boat and dance hall. Sometimes she set a jib as she lay at her wharf, the jib advertising a fireworks display that could be seen from her decks. A steep gangway ran up her mainstay so that the fun-loving city folk could walk aloft to her huge main yard to get a view of Playland below them. At nighttime dances were held aboard her, and she was a gay spot although very few guests ever thought of the grey seas that had once poured across her decks, or of the wind in the rigging while the crew fought their way aloft to furl sail in the days when she was a younger ship.

With little upkeep the *Packard* slowly disintegrated with the passing years, and by 1939 she was in such poor condition that the proprietors of Playland decided it best to do away with her before a falling spar hit a guest. However, it was not an easy matter. Needing close to 26 feet of water to float in, the *Packard* was hard aground, and was hemmed in by a sand bar that had formed since she had moved to the wharf. The wrecking firm of Merritt, Chapman & Scott completely stripped her where she lay, removing all her spars excepting her bowsprit. In later years her yards found their way to the Marine Museum at Mystic where they are to this day. With a great deal of hauling, the *Packard* was dragged from her berth, and at last floated in deep water; pumps had to be kept going to keep her dry.

The tug *Bouker No. 7* took her in tow out into the Sound, back into New England waters to a dumping ground off Stamford, Connecticut, and it was here, in the early evening of May 19th, 1939, that the *Packard* went into 190 feet of water when the plugs were knocked out of her bottom.

Little interest was taken at the old ship's passing although it can well be written that it was the end of the era of the wooden square-riggers in New England waters. However, the *Packard* was not the last survivor of the wooden ships, that honor falling to an almost forgotten vessel, the *Grandee,* built at Portsmouth, New Hampshire, in 1873. Like the *Packard,* she was a typical Cape Horner, a powerful ship heavily rigged, setting a main skysail in hear earlier days. She must have been unusually rugged for one dark night in January, 1877, when well south of Cape Horn she ran full tilt into an iceberg, yet getting clear without too much damage. The *Grandee* became a barge when her deep water days were over, and from 1910 on she was owned by the Dominion Coal Company who used her to haul coal from Sydney and Louisburg to Montreal, Halifax and St. John. After 1937 she remained in Halifax Harbor as a coal barge, and during the recent war was used for bunkering convoys. As she was being broken up in the summer of 1946, she caught fire, being completely destroyed. Her figurehead has been in the Peabody Musum in Salem, Massachusetts, for the past thirty years.

A few other contemporaries of the *Packard* lasted until recent years on the West Coast. The one time ship *Emily F. Whitney,* built by Abiel Gove in his East Boston yards in 1880, not far from the site of Donald McKay's waves, was with the *Packard* in the Alaska trade during their declining years. She almost became a permanent museum, but the plans fell through. For a few years she was used as a summer home by her owner, and later still the Sea Scouts used her rigging for their practices. Finally, on December 2nd, 1940, when she lay off Alameda, California, some small boys set her on fire. As she was then classed as a menace to navigation, no attempt was made to put out the flames, so she burned right down to her waterline.

Yet another New England ship to end her days on the West Coast was the *St. Paul,* built at Bath in 1874 by Chapman and Flint. At one period she was well known as a "hell ship", and in the 1880's seamen so shied away from her that her master and mates were forced to rely on the dockside crimps to shanghai men aboard her for crew. The tale is told that on one occasion a Baptist minister was dumped into the forecastle one sailing day in 'Frisco. He did not regain consciousness until the ship was well on her way, leaving him no alternative but to turn to with the men to work the ship around the Horn to Liverpool.

After the turn of the century she became a salmon packer in the Alaska run, her final trip under sail being in 1924. In the early

1930's she became an aquarium, but as she was not receiving the necessary upkeep, she gradually aged. By 1939 her upper rigging was lowered because of the danger of falling spars. Although there were hopes of preserving her, her end came in the war years when she was towed north to become a breakwater.

The ship *Santa Clara,* built at Bath in 1876, also came to her end on the West Coast. By the turn of the century she had already joined the salmon fleet, and when that work was done, she became part of the movie fleet owned by the Hollywood studios. Her end came in 1950 when her dying hulk was blasted out of Cerritos Channel, Los Angeles Harbor.

And lastly, two other Bath square-riggers, both built of steel, should be mentioned. One was the four-mast bark *Erskine M. Phelps* that Sewall built in 1898. She was a fast vessel, making a great name for herself in her wanderings that took her all around the world. On several occasions she topped the 300-mile a day mark, and once, when racing the mighty German five-mast bark *Potosi,* the *Phelps* logged 359 miles from noon to noon. After the first World War, she became an oil barge at San Francisco, remaining there on the West Coast in that capacity between the wars. She went back to sea during the second World War, but still as a barge on a towline, first to the Russell Islands, and later to Finchaven, New Guinea, where she bunkered the various naval craft. She had been well armed with anti-aircraft guns, and it is said that her U.S. Navy gunners brought down more than one Jap plane with their fire. Well kept, she was in fine condition at the end of the war, but in December, 1945, the U.S. Navy sank her at Manus Island in the Pacific.

The other steel vessel of the *Packard's* era was the three-mast bark *Kaiulani* which Sewall built in Bath in 1899. The first ten years of her life were spent in running between the Hawaiian Islands and the West Coast in the sugar trade. She then entered the salmon business, changing her name to *Star of Finland* when taken over by the Alaska Packers Association of San Francisco in 1910. She was always a very fast ship, one of her best runs being from Alitak, Alaska, to 'Frisco in nine days in 1914. When the Packers sold out their fleet of windships, they clung to the *Star of Finland* although they did not send her north after 1927. Ten years later she went back to sea briefly to help make the movie "Souls at Sea"; then she was tied up again. However, her sailing days were not over yet for in 1941 she was overhauled at Alameda.

Now owned by the Hammond Lumber Company and under the Panamanian flag, she was once more *Kaiulani*. With Captain H. G. Wigsten in command, she sailed from Port Aberdeen, Washington, with 1,173,000 feet of lumber as cargo on September 5th, 1941. After a stop at Pitcairn Island, she rounded the Horn in moderate weather on December 17th. When 126 days out, she arrived at Durban, Africa, on January 29th, 1942. She was having crew troubles now, notwithstanding the high seagoing wages that were then prevalent. Her last run under canvas took her through the Roaring Forties to Hobart, Tasmania, where she arrived June 19th, 1942, 44 days from Africa.

Once more there were crew troubles, and this time Captain Wigsten could get no new men. The owners sold their ship. The buyers had her towed to Sydney, Australia, where her towering rig was cut off, and an engine was installed in her hold. She spent the remainder of the war coaling Dutch steamers in the South Pacific. In 1948 she was sold by the Maritime Commission to Vincente Madrigal for $18,250.

Sixteen years later the Philippine people presented the aged hulk to the people of the United States, President Johnson accepting the gift during ceremonies at the White House on October 5, 1964. The Maritime Historical Society of the District of Columbia is now making plans to re-rig the bark, then sail her back around the Cape to the States, to set her up as a maritime museum in the Capital. It is said that she is the sole survivor of some 17,000 U.S. merchant square riggers.

Charles W. Morgan

Last of a long line of New Bedford whalers is the ship *Charles W. Morgan* which was built at that port in 1841 by Jethro and Zachariah Hillman for Charles W. Morgan, a well-known whaleship owner after whom she was named. A bluff bowed vessel, she was constructed of live oak with copper fastenings, and her rig was that of a full-rigged ship, single topsails, single topgallants and royals. She was not large, being only just over 105 feet long and 314 gross tons.

She sailed on her first whaling voyage on September 6th, 1841, with Captain Thomas A. Norton in command, bound out for the distant Pacific Ocean. Sailing through lonely seas with her masthead men clinging to their hoops high above her decks ever on the lookout for the spout of a whale, she passed through unchartered waters as the hunt went on. The cry "Thar she blows!" would always bring a frenzy of activity to the decks of the whaler as the crew rushed to their stations. The boats would be lowered in a rush for the men to be after their quarry. When the whale had been harpooned, and eventually killed, it would be towed back to the ship where the blubber could be stripped off in chunks for the try-pots that boiled out the oil.

The *Morgan* returned to New Bedford on January 1st, 1845, having been out for three years and almost four months. Stored below in her hold were 1600 barrels of sperm oil, 800 barrels of whale oil, and 10,000 pounds of whalebone, a goodly catch bringing her owners $69,591.; she had made a profitable start in what was to be a long, active life.

Her first twelve voyages took the *Morgan* to the whaling grounds of both the North and South Pacific Ocean, the Indian Ocean, and the Atlantics, always returning to New Bedford every three to five years. In 1849 she was bought by Edward M. Robinson who had her for one voyage, and in 1853 she was taken over by the I. Howland Jr. & Company who sent her out on three voyages. J. & W. R. Wing next owned her, purchasing her in 1863, and operating her for 52 years. In 1867 they cut down her rig to that of a bark, stripping the yards off her mizzen mast.

The thirteenth voyage of the *Morgan* saw her depart from New Bedford on October 6th, 1886, bound for the North Pacific. On November 4th, 1887, she arrived at San Francisco with 275 barrels of sperm oil and 1050 barrels of whale oil. During the next nineteen years, the Wings sailed her out of 'Frisco, sending her to hunt in the waters off Japan. Each voyage took about a year, with a month in port between trips.

On her thirtieth voyage, she left San Francisco on November 25th, 1904, to fish the South Pacific grounds. Later she rounded the Horn, arriving back at her birth place on June 12th, 1906, with 1570 barrels of sperm oil. After 27 cruises for the Wings, she was sold in 1916 to Captain Benjamin D. Cleveland, an old-time whalemen who took her to the Antarctic for a year, returning with 200 barrels of sperm oil and 1018 barrels of sea elephant oil from the Kerguelen Islands.

In 1918 she was bought by John A. Cook Company who changed her homeport to Provincetown on the tip of Cape Cod. After almost fourteen months at sea in the Atlantic, she came back with 1200 barrels of sperm oil. Her next voyage was a short one as she had to return to port when her captain became sick. Her last whaling voyage began on September 9th, 1920, with Captain Gonsalves in command. Her days as an active whaler came to a close on her return to port on May 28th, 1921, with 700 barrels of sperm oil.

In 1922 the bark went back to sea to help make one of the greatest sea pictures ever filmed, "Down to the Sea in Ships". Later in the year she was in another film, "Java Head"; in this she portrayed a merchantman; the locale was Salem.

The *Morgan* was now laid up at Fairhaven. She was very nearly lost on June 30th, 1924, when a burning steamer drifted across the harbor from New Bedford, and set her on fire, but the prompt work of the city firemen saved her. Two months later the whaler *Wanderer* put out to sea, passing the *Morgan* on her way. Not many hours later the *Wanderer* was a complete wreck on the sharp rocks of Cuttyhunk Island, thus leaving the *Morgan* as the last surviving square-rigged whaler under the American flag.

The *Morgan* herself might have rotted away if Mr. Harry Neyland, a nationally known marine artist, had not taken an interest in her. At first he tried to get the Whalemen's Club of New Bedford to use her as a club house, and when they turned him down, he approached the City of New Bedford, offering to give her to the City if they would install the ship at Marine Park as a museum. When this plan was rejected, Colonel E. H. R. Green came to the rescue by having the *Morgan* berthed in a cofferdam on the edge of his estate at Round Hill, turning her into a permanent exhibition for the public.

From 1925 to 1936 the whaler was kept in perfect condition. During the summer months she was fitted out as if she were about to start on a whaling voyage, even the sails bent, and occasionally set when the breezes were light. She had been given her original ship rig back. Owned by a group known as "Whaling Enshrined, Inc.", her commander at this time was Captain George Fred Tilton who had spent many years in sail and whaling; he was an ideal guide for the many thousands of visitors who flocked to see the exhibit.

Troubles came in 1936 when Col. Green passed away, leaving no provision for the whaler in his will. When the heirs closed the estate, she was cut off from the public, and very soon began to show her years. The hurricane of 1938 struck her with all its force, and if her hold had not been filled with rock ballast, she would probably have been swept from her berth onto the near-by airport. However, damage was done, and by 1939 disintegration was setting in so rapidly that it was obvious that the ship would not last much longer if nothing was done to save her. When the City of New Bedford again rejected a plan to preserve the whaler, the Marine Historical Association of Mystic, Connecticut, offered to take her over.

On October 31st, 1941, after several weeks of preparations, the *Morgan* was floated clear of the berth that had held her for sixteen years. In tow of a Coast Guard cutter, she came back to New Bedford for the last time, making fast to Union Wharf at Fairhaven where she was made ready for the longer trip to Mystic. On November 5th she sailed on what can be considerd her 39th, and last voyage, outward bound, never to return. William H. Tripp, the curator of the Old Dartmouth Historical Society's Whaling Museum in New Bedford, was her last commander for the run. She seemed a little reluctant to leave her home waters for she grounded in the harbor on a sand bar, remaining there for two hours until the incoming tide floated her.

Passing down Buzzards Bay, she stole past the flashing light of Hen & Chickens in the darkness, and later the lights of Brenton Reef and Watch Hill. Dawn found her off Fishers Island, not far from the Mystic River. As Army dredging operations were still going on, the *Morgan* was unable to enter the river, her 14 foot draft being too much to clear the bottom. She was taken on to New London, docking at the Coast Guard base. On Saturday, November 8th, the whaler came to her last berth. The skies were cloudless as she was towed up the narrow, winding river, through the highway bridge, to a point off the museum wharf.

Today she is again in a cofferdam, berthed in a bed of sand. During the war years she was rather neglected on account of more important work that had to be done, but since then she has been getting a thorough overhaul. Her rigging was in very bad shape, and had to be completely renewed, even new masts and spars. When her rotten foremast was lifted out of her, the marks of an ancient penny could be seen on its base; the penny had been placed there for good luck when the mast had been stepped in 1841. Unfortunately, the penny dropped off the mast while it was being moved, and it was never found.

The Morgan has been a lucky ship. It has been estimated that during her career she earned close to $2,000,000 for her owners.

Although she sailed further than any other of her contemporaries, she was seldom in trouble. She had grounded a few times on distant reefs, lightning had struck her, and once she had been on fire. She had ridden out two hurricanes at sea, being nearly wrecked in one of them off the Crozets in the Roaring Forties belt in the South Indian Ocean. Sometimes she had had crew troubles, but so did all other ships in her day. Her complement as a whaler had been between 35 and 38 men, but through the years she must have had some 2000 men serve aboard her at one time or another.

There is no doubt that she was the greatest of the whalers.

CHAPTER X

More   Square - Riggers

~~~~~~

THE OLDEST surviving vessel of the United States Navy is the frigate *Constellation* which was built by Samuel and Joseph Starrett in their Baltimore shipyard. A 36-gun ship of 1278 tons and 176 feet long, she first took to the water on September 7th, 1797.

Sailing from Baltimore on November 10th, her first cruise took her to the West Indies station to keep peace among the islands, and to halt the privateers who had been seizing merchant ships along the traffic lanes. After taking several small prizes, she met the French frigate *Insurgent* of 36 guns and 450 men near St. Kitts, and after a sharp battle caused her to surrender. Actually it was not a clear victory for the Americans as the French commanding officer later wrote that if he had realized the state of affairs between the two nations, he would never have allowed the American to come up with him since he could have held her off with his two long 18-pound stern chasers.

After putting into Norfolk, the *Constellation* went north to New York, doing the run in the smart time of three days. She was always a fast ship, and was aptly named "The Yankee Race Horse" on account of her speed. The larger 44-gun frigates, such as the Constitution, had one fault, lack of speed, but the smaller frigates seemed to be exceptionally fast in both light airs and strong breezes.

The second cruise of the *Constellation* again took her southward. She had been at sea for thirty days again when she was hit by a very bad gale which built up huge seas before winds of hurricane force. At the height of the storm one mighty comber caught the frigate under her stern, wrenching off one of her quarter galleries, and flooding the after cabins as well as twisting the rudder head. She had to work her way into Norfolk for repairs.

Some weeks later, she fought the French 45-gun frigate *La*

[203]

Vengeance in a great battle in the West Indies. The Frenchman managed to knock away the Constellation's mainmast, the wreckage coming down in a heap on deck. However, before the firing was over, the *La Vengeance* was reduced to almost a floating wreck with her colors hauled down. Nonetheless, after dark, she managed to escape from the American ship which could not follow her owing to her own torn rigging. The Frenchman put into Curacoa with 200 killed and 60 wounded; the American limped into Jamaica for repairs.

Her next cruise, from 1802 to 1805, took her to the Mediterranean where she was in action against the Barbary pirates along the North African coast. She put into many ports which were to know American sailors in a war a century and a half later. She helped restore peace, and opened up sea lanes that the pirates had closed. Following the two year blockade of Tripoli, and the peace treaty, she returned to the States, to be laid up at the Washington Navy Yard for the next five years.

She was rebuilt in 1812, but found herself bottled up in Norfolk by the British during most of the War of 1812. Her crew beat off a Red Coat land attack to destroy her, and that was about all the action that she saw. After the war she returned to the Mediterranean, and then went to the West Indies and Brazil. She was laid up during a refit in 1823 and 1824, but went overseas again until 1844 when she was placed out of commission. Ten years later she was rebuilt in Norfolk before crossing to the African coast looking for slavers. During the Civil War, she searched the seas for Confederate vessels in European waters. Between 1865 and 1868 the *Constellation* was a receiving ship at Norfolk first, and later Philadelphia. Washington used her as a gunnery ship for a year, and from 1873 to 1892 she was part of the Naval Academy at Annapolis. After her last annual summer cruise with midshipmen, she was moved to Newport, Rhode Island, in 1893 where she was connected with the Naval Station there. During a part of World War I her name was changed to *Old Constellation* while a modern battle cruiser carried her name. However, when the newer ship was sent to the junk yards, the frigate reverted to her original name.

As time passed, the old ship became very run down, the Navy taking little care of her, just keeping her afloat at the wharf. On August 24th, 1940, she was recommissioned. At this time she was providing living quarters for 150 enlisted men. By the end of the war, it was obvious that she would not last much longer if something were not done to preserve her. The Navy finally had her towed to Boston in October, 1946, very nearly losing her en route when a six inch leak developed from the pounding of head seas in Cape Cod Bay. After her auxiliary power pump broke down, her crew of 18 manned hand buckets in the light of battle lanterns to bail her out in an attempt to keep the water down. By the time she made port, there was four feet of water in the hold.

The Navy estimated that it would take at least three years to repair her rotted timbers and rigging, but the vessel had only been in Boston a few months, when it was announced that she was to be taken back to Newport. She was due to leave Boston on February 7th, 1947, but the Navy suddenly decided that she was not sufficiently seaworthy to tackle the winter seas. She did start out on July 19th, but had to return to Boston when a summer breeze sprang up.

In 1955, after she had been placed in a floating drydock, she was carried to Baltimore. Today, again afloat, she is being slowly reconditioned as funds come to hand.

Constitution

Certainly the most famous ship in the United States Navy is the frigate Constitution, perhaps equally well-known as *"Old Ironsides"*. Today she is permanently moored to a berth in the Charlestown Navy Yard, Boston, just across from the spot from which she was launched in 1797.

Designed by Joshua Humphreys, the *Constitution*'s keel was laid in November, 1794, in Hart's Shipyard, and she was ready for sea almost three years later, on September 20th. However, she stuck on the ways. Two days later a second attempt was made to put her over, again ending in failure. However, on October 21st, she finally took to the harbor waters, the finest frigate of her day. A 44-gun ship of 1444 gross tons, she was 175 feet long, 44 feet wide, and 23 feet deep.

The *Constitution* departed on her first cruise on July 22nd, 1798, in search of British privateers who were harassing shipping off the American coast. On September 9th she made her first capture by taking the 24-gun ship *Niger* with a crew of seventy. After leaving her prize at Norfolk, the American frigate carried on south to the West Indies to patrol those waters. In January, 1799, she recaptured the British ship *Spencer* from the French frigate *Insur-*

gent. Five months later she returned to Boston for a quick refit; in July she was back at the San Domingo station with 400 men and officers. Some months later her crew had taken the British ship *Sandwich.*

After spending a year in her home port, the *Constitution* crossed to the Mediterranean in 1803 as Commodore Edward Preble's flagship in the war against the Barbary pirates. After capturing the large Moorish frigate *Maimona,* the Boston frigate took part in the siege of Tripoli, smashing at the shore batteries with her cannon while her small boat crews attacked the corsairs. The peace treaty was signed on June 3rd, 1805, a great victory for the young American Navy. No longer would American ship masters have to pay tribute to the Moors, and all American seamen who had been held captive were freed. The *Constitution* returned to Boston in October, 1807.

During the next few years she remained on the Home Station, and was laid up for a time. In 1811 she took the American minister to France. The beginning of the War of 1812 found her at Washington, but within a week she put to sea in search of the enemy. While bound for New York to join Captain Roger's squadron, she fell in with five sail in the light mists off shore, and it was not for some hours that Captain Isaac Hull realized he was with British men-of-war. For a time it seemed that the American would be captured, but with some smart seamanship Captain Hull managed to get away by having his boat crews take out the kedge anchors ahead of the ship, thus hauling her clear of danger. However, his men had to work for two days without cease before the English lost them.

In the next two months, the *Constitution* was to make a great name for herself. Sailing from Boston on August 2nd, she cruised along the Nova Scotian shore, taking several small British craft. She was off the Gulf of St. Lawrence on August 19th when she met the British frigate *Guerriere* which had a short crew of 282 men to fight her 30 long eighteen pounders, 2 long twelve pounders, and 18 carronades. The *Constitution* had 456 men aboard at this time, and although she was called a 44-gun ship, she was armed with 32 long twenty-four pounders and 22 thirty-two pound carronades. The action lasted only 25 minutes, but in that time the Britisher was turned into a blazing hulk with 79 men killed or wounded while the Yankee ship only had 14 killed or wounded. Several of the *Guerriere*'s men, impressed American seamen, had refused to fight, so had been permitted to remain below during the battle. It was during this fight that the *Constitution* got her nickname *"Old Ironsides"* for the enemy's cannon balls bounced off her sides as if they were built of iron.

After a short refit in Boston, the *Constitution* put to sea again, this time destroying the British 38-gun frigate *Java*. A year later the American frigate was chased into Marblehead by two British frigates, the *Juno* and the *Tenedos*. Later she sneaked into Boston harbor where she was blockaded for nearly nine months. However, she slipped out in December, 1814, to carry on her work. Her last battle of the war was against the British frigate *Cyane* and the sloop *Levant* which she met on February 12th, 1815, off Madeira, capturing the two of them by superior maneuvering and seamanship.

Following the war, the now-famous frigate spent five years laid up at New York. Then she went back to the Mediterranean in 1824, crossing the Atlantic to Gibraltar in 24 days. She made many courtesy calls at the various ports during the next few months, showing the American flag and acting as a symbol of friendship. However, she was getting older all the time, and when she eventually came back to the States, her timbers were found to be in such poor shape that she was condemned to be broken up. At this time Oliver Wendell Holmes wrote his famous poem "Old Ironsides", thus saving her from the scrap heap.

In 1835 the *Constitution* made a voyage to France, and later in the year called at various European ports in the Mediterranean; she also visited Syria and Egypt. Many distinguished guests came aboard, including King Otto of Greece when at the Port of Athens, Mahomet Ali and the Viceroy of Egypt at Alexandria, and later the ambassadors of Belgium, Denmark, England, and France when at Lisbon. The frigate returned to the States in July, 1838.

From 1839 to 1841 she sailed in Pacific waters, in the West Indies in 1842, and then in 1844, after another complete overhaul, she departed from Norfolk on April 7th on her longest voyage of all. After a hard ten day run to New York, she took on final supplies before leaving Sandy Hook on May 29th, passing out to sea under full sail. On June 16th she anchored at Fayal, then on to Madeira and Teneriffe. She was 32 days in the run to Rio de Janeiro where she remained for a month. On September 25th, *"Old Ironsides"* passed Tristan da Cunha in a Roaring Forties' gale, much too rough to make a landing there. Another storm struck at her south of the Cape of Good Hope on October 3rd, snapping her crossjack in three places. After a stop at Madagascar she went on to Mozambique and Zanzibar, and across the Indian Ocean to Sumatra, Singapore, Borneo, and to Cochin China. She next stopped at Manila and Honolulu before crossing the rest of the Pacific to Monterey, California. From there she sailed south, rounding Cape Horn in a blizzard on July 4th, 1846. Again stopping at Rio, she picked up a fleet of sixteen coffee vessels, escorting them north to the Delaware Breakwater on account of the war with Mexico. She arrived home in Boston on September 28th, 1846, having sailed 52,279 miles around the world in a little less than two and a half years.

After laying up for three years during another overhaul, she became the Mediterranean flagship until 1851. Finally, in 1853, she departed on her last voyage of active service under sail. Following a 21 day trip from New York to Gibraltar, she worked with the African Squadron stopping slavery along the coast. However, by now steam was taking the place of sail, and in 1855 she was laid up at Portsmouth, New Hampshire. Later, for a short period, she acted as a training ship at Newport and Annapolis. In 1878 she was sent across the Atlantic carrying the American exhibit to the Universal Exposition at Paris. She left France for the last time on January 16th, 1879.

When she had spent two more years cruising with cadets along the East Coast from Halifax to the Indies, she furled her sails for the last time in 1881. During the next few years she was used as a receiving ship at Portsmouth, New Hampshire, but in 1897 she was towed to Boston for her centennial celebrations. After this, she became a historical exhibit in Boston Navy Yard. Having fallen into very poor shape, she was partly restored in 1905, but it was not for another twenty years that she was given a complete refit, being rebuilt from keel to truck. The expense was borne by the American people who wanted to save the frigate from rot and ruin. Today very little, if any, of the original *Constitution* remains as she has been rebuilt so many times. However, she is little changed from the days when she fought the Barbary pirates. Once she had carried on her stem a figurehead of Hercules; this was destroyed in the wars off Tripoli. Later she had a figurehead of Andrew Jackson, but the figure was sawed off one dark night when the ship was in Boston harbor. Today the *Constitution* has no figurehead, only a roll of carved scroll. Her present rigging plan is taken from her old plans that were in the Navy archives. In her earlier days she set a skysail on occasion, the skysail mast being rigged abaft the royal mast, but it was only a fair weather kite, and not very often used.

The frigate last put to sea in 1931 when, after recommissioning, she toured the coastal ports of the United States, but she never moved under sail, only a the end of a tow line. Before her return to Boston in May, 1934, she was visited by some 4,600,000 people who wanted to tread the decks of such a famous vessel. Since that time, she has been in the Navy Yard at Boston. Until the recent war, she was considered "in service, not commission", but in August, 1940, President Roosevelt ordered her to be put on a full commission status, taking her place with the rest of the Navy. The Admiral's flag of the Navy Yard flew from her mizzen truck.

Today *"Old Ironsides"* is still a mecca for tourists. She is a perfect example of a ship of the United States Navy in the days of sail, and it is to be hoped that she will be preserved for future generations to see and admire.

Daniel M. Munroe

On several occasions during the World War II years, an old grey barge named *Daniel M. Munroe* passed through the Cape Cod Canal in tow as she worked between Nova Scotia and ports west of Buzzards Bay. Although mastless, there was something about her which indicated that once she had been a windship, her fair lines and upsweeping bow.

Lloyds Register shows that she was built as the steel bark *Olivia* by the famous A. McMillan & Son Shipbuilders of Dumbarton, Scotland, in 1892. She was a good sized vessel of 1216 gross tons and 220 feet long. By the turn of the century she was under the Norwegian flag, registered at Xiansand. During the first World War she became an auxiliary barge with power, owned by the Gypsum Packet Company of Windsor, Nova Scotia. She was now the *Daniel M. Munroe*. In later years her engines were removed, and she became a towing barge.

Danmark

One of the smartest square-riggers seen in New England waters in the last days of sail was the small full-rigged ship *Danmark*. Built at Nakskov in 1932 as a training ship for the Danish Merchant Marine, she is 188 feet long and 777 tons; she replaced the *Georg Stage* which later became the *Joseph Conrad*.

Manned by some 120 cadets, she was a familiar vessel on the Atlantic in the years before the war as she made her training cruises. Although she has a 250 horsepower diesel, the engines are seldom used, and once in deep water, they are practically shut down. A typical cruise was as follows:

1935—sailed Falmouth, England, October 3rd.
    arrived Teneriffe in 9 days.
    sailed Teneriffe October 16th.
    arrived Buenos Aires in 43 days.
    sailed Montevideo December 15th.
    arrived St. Helena in 28 days.
1936—sailed St. Helena, and arrived Azores in 35 days.
    sailed St. Michael's March 2nd.
    arrived Copenhagen in 25 days.

The *Danmark* was in the West Indian waters when the Nazis swept into Denmark in 1940, so instead of returning to her country overrun by the enemy, she put into Jacksonville, Florida. There she lay for almost two years. Following Pearl Harbor, her commanding officer, Captain Knud L. Hansen, offered her to the United States Coast Guard. In January, 1942, she arrived at New London to join the ships at the Academy there, hoisting the Stars and Stripes to her gaff instead of the Danish flag. Her captain and several of his Danish officers remained with the ship; most of the 120 Danish cadets had already gone off to war in British and American steamers.

Throughout the war years the *Danmark* played an important part in training future Coast Guard officers. She became a common sight along the Sound, and she was a visitor to most of the harbors there. The September, 1944, hurricane found her anchored off City Island, New York. Getting under way at 8 o'clock in the morning, she sailed up the Sound, but at noon, when off Bridgeport, she turned back after her radioman reported the approaching storm; it was too late to stand out to sea to weather the blow. Captain Hansen looked for a good anchorage. Plotting the course of the hurricane, he noted that the center would hit near New London, so he made for the westward, finally anchoring behind City Island.

With the wind getting stronger as the minutes passed, the barometer steadily dropped. The Coast Guard cadets, making their first trip in a vessel, prepared for the worst. All sails with the exception of the topsails were unbent and stowed below. Everything moveable was either lashed down or put where the wind could not get at it. Both anchors were dropped, 85 fathoms of chain to port, 65 fathoms of chain to starboard. The yards were braced around as near as possible to fore-and-aft to cut down windage aloft. Captain Hansen saw that if he did drag ashore, his ship would strike a mud bottom and would not be damaged.

The hurricane reached its peak in the late afternoon with the wind blowing at nearly 100 miles an hour. The *Danmark's* small engine was kept going ahead to take some of the strain from the anchors. The ship never budged from her anchorage, and no damage was done although the driving rain washed most of the tar out of her rigging.

Perhaps the great success of the *Danmark* as a training ship is due in great part to Captain Hansen who has had her from the day that she was launched. He knows his vessel, and he can handle her in an amazing fashion. On one occasion when the *Danmark* was returning to New London the engine broke down. As the ship came up the harbor under full sail, the crew expected that they would heave to near the bridge to await a tow through the draw up to the Academy wharf, but that was not Hansen's plan. He blew the whistle for the bridge to open. Then, without taking in a sail, he sent his vessel through the narrow opening with only inches to spare on either side of the yardarms. Passing under the high auto bridge, the *Danmark* moved majestically on. At this point, Hansen passed the word to clew up sail. As she came opposite her dock, the anchor was dropped, stopping the bow of the ship but allowing the way to carry the stern around. Seconds later Hansen called for the boys to haul on the braces. The sails, now hanging in great folds from the yards, caught aback, sending the ship stern-first as the mate payed out the anchor chain. Her small boat carried a line to the wharf, and in a few minutes the *Danmark* was snuggly at her berth, bow outward. The whole maneuver had been done under canvas alone.

Hansen could take a handful of youngsters who had never set foot on a ship before, and in a few hours he would have them aloft handling sails and lines. Joining the yacht cruise of the Cruising Club of America in 1945, the *Danmark* followed the small craft to Block Island. Off the entrance to New Harbor, Hansen had the boys tack ship to stand out to sea; this was the first time his group cadets had ever tacked the square-rigger. An hour later they were heading back, and not long after they swept up the narrow channel even though the wind was forward the beam. The small harbor was full of yachts; it did not seem possible that the full-rigger could avoid hitting at least one, especially as she was still under sail traveling at a good speed. However, Hansen, picking his anchorage, suddenly brought his ship up into the wind, almost stopping her in her tracks. The anchor roared down as the boys raced aloft to put on a harbor furl.

The first time Captain Hansen took the *Danmark* down the East River at New York, the wind was ahead with not enough room to tack. With the tide behind him, he put the *Danmark* on the tack that would gain the most ground. Then, as he came to the far side of the river, he would back his sails into the wind, traveling backwards across the channel to the other side where he would again fill his sails, and so down the river.

He told about the first time that he passed under the old Brooklyn Bridge. According to the tables that he had aboard, there were some five feet of clearance for his 130-foot mainmast under the span. However, as they approached the bridge, it did not seem possible that the mast would not hit. One of the boys climbed to the truck just to see how close it would be Even he thought that they would hit. It was too late to turn back now for the tide was sweeping the *Danmark* on. All eyes watched as the bridge and the mast came together. When they were under the lowest part, the boy aloft put his thumb on the truck; his litle finger touched the bridge. Hansen passed off the incident with a shrug as he said: "She's an old bridge; she must have sagged!"

The end of the war with Japan found the *Danmark* starting out on what was to be her last full cruise under the American flag, taking the Coast Guard cadets as far as New York City with various stops along the Sound. After that, she started one more cruise but it was never completed. Her Danish officers were anxious to get home; they had been away for five years. The *Danmark* had done her work well, training some 4500 Coast Guard cadets. She had never been in trouble, and had certainly earned her keep. On September 26th, 1945, while at the Academy, the Stars and Stripes were lowered, and the Danish flag hoisted once more. As the full-rigger departed for New York, the Coast Guard band played "Auld Lang Syne."

The *Danmark* took on supplies in New York, and not long

The four-mast bark Abraham Rydberg off Boston Harbor early in World War II.

The Benjamin F. Packard was the last of her type in New England waters.

The whaler Charles W. Morgan at sea.

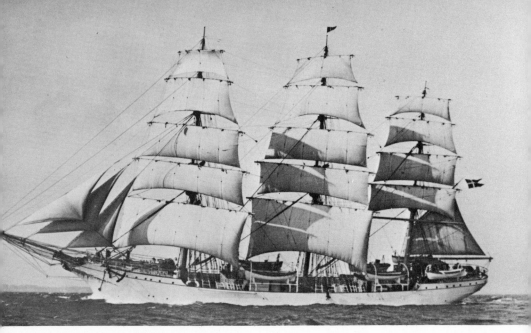

The full-rigged ship Danmark.

The Bear, below, a few hours before she sank. Note her broken fore-rigging smashing the hull below the waterline.

The U.S. Coast Guard bark Eagle in a breeze of wind.

The Tusitala, the last full-rigged ship to carry a cargo under the Stars and Stripes, on her last voyage in 1932.

The barkentine Nantucket with her stun'sails set.

The ships Joseph Conrad and Seven Seas at Newport, in 1937.

Deck view of the Brava Packet schooner Maria Sony — fitting out at Fairhaven in 1959.

A view looking aft from the bowsprit of the Frank Brainerd.

A deck view aboard the Frank Brainerd during heavy weather.

The Coriolanus, once Queen of the Jute Clippers, in her last sailing days was a Brava Packet.

The Capitana at New Bedford as a Brava Packet in 1940.

The Annie B. Mitchell becalmed.

The Cape Verde packet brigantine Madalan awaiting passengers at Providence.

The Lucy Evelyn at sea.

Deck view aboard the five-mast schooner Cora F. Cressy.

The Lucy Evelyn in 1963 as a store at Beach Haven, New Jersey.

The high bows of the Cora Cressy — when she was a dance hall in Boston.

The four-mast schooner Edna M. McKnight just after her launching at Camden, Maine, in 1918 and, below, the end of her at Boothbay Harbor. Part of the hulk is still there.

left: The Zebedee E. Cliff and the
Courtney C. Houck in the mud of Boothbay Harbor in the late 1930's.

The four-mast schooners Hesper and Luther Little ending their days at Wiscasset, Maine.

The Luther Little out in a breeze.

The Maud M. Morey, left, and the four-mast schooner Freeman, both at Boothbay Harbor in 1939.

*The five-mast schooner Jennie Flood Kreger at East Boston;
the four-mast schooner Horace A. Stone in the background.*

afterwards she was on her way across the Atlantic. In late 1946 she took out her first group of post-war Danish cadets on a long cruise that was to take them through the Panama Canal, and north to Seattle. Homeward bound, she put in at Jacksonville, making fast to the same dock where she had spent the earlier years of the war. Later on, she stopped in at New London for a few days. She sailed on March 5th, 1947. She passed Dover, England, 20 days out, and after a stop at Frederikshaven she arrived at Copenhagen on April 5th.

This lovely full-rigged ship will long be remembered in New England waters. She made a quick return visit in the summer of 1964 as part of "Operation Sail" when a group of foreign training ships came to New York.

Eagle

The Germans, firm believers in sailing ship training for their apprentice seamen, built three fine barks in the years before the recent war for that one purpose. The first, the *Gorch Fock,* launched in 1935, had accomodation for 262 men; the second, the *Horst Wessel,* which was delivered five months after the keel was laid down in 1936, had room for 289 men, and the last, the *Albert Leo Schlageter,* launched in 1937, was a sister to the *Wessel.* They were all handsome craft, painted white with superstructures dark cream, and masts ochre. Although they had diesels, these were seldom used.

At the end of the war, when the German vessels were being distributed amongst the Allies, the *Horst Wessel* was handed over to the United States Coast Guard. As she had always carried a giant eagle on her stem as a figurehead, she was renamed *Eagle.* Under the eagle there had been a badge with a Nazi swastika; this was replaced with the Coast Guard shield. In the fall of 1946 the bark was sailed across the Atlantic to New London to be prepared for her American cadets. Although numerous changes were made, many of the German signs and notices were left in place.

The *Eagle* is a large training ship, some 1700 tons and 194 feet long. With double topsails and single topgallants, she sets a total of 21,300 square feet of canvas. Her engines can give her a speed of ten knots in calm weather.

In June, 1947, the *Eagle* departed from New London with 17 officers, 102 cadets, and 58 enlisted men on a cruise that was to take them to Bermuda and the West Indies before returning north

[213]

to New York. In the fall she visited Gloucester and Boston. She then was layed up at New London for the winter. In July, 1948, the *Eagle* arrived at London, England, by way of the Azores. On this voyage she carried eight tons of foodstuffs as a gift for the people of old London from the people of New London.

She is the only actively sailing three-mast bark under the Stars and Stripes today.

Emery Rice

In the days when the United States Naval vessels still carried sails, the auxiliary bark *Ranger No. 4,* a 12-gun boat, was launched from the yards of Harlan and Hollingsworth at Wilmington, Delaware, in 1876. She was 199 feet long and 1261 gross tons.

Commissioned on November 27th at the Philadelphia Navy Yard, she was first on the North Atlantic Station; she went out to the Asiatic Station in 1877. During 1880, she was laid up on the West Coast, but a year later she departed on a tour of survey duty, first on the west coasts of Mexico and Central America, later moving up into the North Pacific. She worked along the coast of Lower California between 1886 and 1889. During the next six years she was active from Central America to the Bering Sea surveying and patroling. Laid up at Mare Island Navy Yard, California, from 1896 to 1899, she was completely overhauled before returning to sea. Her rig was cut down to that of a barkentine, and her well deck was closed in.

After further duty on survey work along the Mexican coast, she crossed the Pacific to the Philippine Islands where she acted as mother ship to the destroyers in those waters. In 1908 she came back to the States, arriving at Boston in the end of November. The next year she left the Navy to become a schoolship for the State of Massachusetts, being renamed *Nantucket*. For a short spell in the first World War she was called *Rockport* as a new battle cruiser was to be named *Nantucket*. However, in 1918 the barkentine was again *Nantucket*.

Nearly every spring, the school ship set off on a 10,000 mile cruise which would take her and her 118 odd cadets to new lands, often across the Atlantic, sometimes to the Mediterranean. Other summers she would go to the West Indies. Returning to Boston each fall, she would remain at the Charlestown Navy Yard throughout the winter months acting as the base school.

In early 1932, she was re-rigged as a bark in order to give

more competition to the watches aboard her, each watch taking a mast. She always attracted great attention with her yards for she was one of the last square-riggers to carry stunsails, her stunsail yards always being aloft. She was possibly the last sailing ship to carry a spritsail course, a squaresail set from a yard beneath her bowsprit. She had single topsails but carried nothing above her single topgllants, so seemed rather squat.

The engine of the *Nantucket* was quite interesting for it was a horizontal, compound, back-acting, coal burner which could develop some 500 horsepower. It was once said that there was only one other engine like it, that one being in the Science Museum in London, and that the Smithsonian Institute had requested the Nantucket's engine when she was through with it. When she was on her long cruises, the engines would be shut down for about a third of the time, just proceeding under canvas alone. She was not fast, and considered anything over 220 miles a day as good.

She was a fair sea boat although on one occasion shortly before the war she came very close to foundering in heavy weather. However, the experience was a great lesson for the cadets, something that they could not get in books ashore.

In 1941 the Maritime Commission sent out instructions that all state training ships should bear the state's name, and so the *Nantucket* became the *Bay State,* the nickname for Massachusetts. The war disrupted the cruises of the bark, taking her cadets from her. As there was no room for her at the Charlestown Navy Yard, she was moved down to New York, joining the fleet of training vessels at the United States Merchant Marine Academy at Kings Point in July, 1942. Her name was changed again, now to *Emery Rice.* Until October, 1943, she cruised in Long Island Sound with a complement of about 100 cadets or midshipmen. Toward the end of the war she served as a station ship, berthing a part of the Academy's greatly increased war-time complement.

At the end of the war she became a museum ship, her spar deck being housed over to cover a display of many excellent models and other articles of nautical interest. Under the charge of Rear Admiral Richard R. McNulty, Supervisor of the U.S. Merchant Marine Cadet Corps, himself a graduate of the Massachusetts Maritime Academy in the days when the *Rice* was the *Nantucket,* the old gun was an interesting exhibit, but in March, 1958, she was sold to a Baltimore shipbreaker.

[215]

Florence C. Robinson

One of the strangest craft to come into Gloucester harbor in the last decade was the brigantine or hermaphrodite brig *Florence C. Robinson* which had been built in Jaffna, Ceylon, in the late 1920's as the *Annapooranvam*. The waters around India are one of the last strongholds of sail, and even recently many rigs which have long been extinct on the American coast still were to be found there. A small number of brigs continued to operate between the Maldive Islands and Colombo. Wooden barks, similar to the old East Indiamen of the early 19th century, traded across the Bay of Bengal to Burma. Brigantines, some with the old-time fashion of painted ports along their sides, could be found in many of these out-of-the-way ports. The *Annapooranvam* was one of these latter vessels.

After trading for eight years, she was bought by the well-known yachtsman William Robinson who renamed the vessel after his wife. With Captain Donald A. MacCuish, once skipper of Gloucester's last all-sail fisherman, in command, the brigantine with a crew of five Hindus set out on the long voyage to the States by way of the Suez Canal. On May 3rd, 1938, they left Candia astern; 31 days later they put into Gibraltar. With provisions for a thirty day Atlantic crossing, the brigantine left the Straits on June 8th, bound for Gloucester. Winds were light, the going was slow. Although an engine was below deck, it was of no help as it had broken down long before this. One week passed another, and the little sailing ship wallowed on. Food and water began to run low. The Hindus had to stop anointing their heads with fresh water, part of their daily religious rites, having to use salt water instead. When Captain MacCuish realized that they could not make Gloucester with their supplies, he set course for Bermuda, arriving at Hamilton after 31 days at sea. With fresh provisions stored below (there was never a lack of rice for the Hindus), they set off again on July 23rd.

Crossing the Gulf Stream, the *Robinson* entered the fog belts which rather puzzled the dusky crew who had never seen it quite so thick before; they felt that they were going into another world in the clouds. The chill in the air was something new to them, too, though they did not complain but carried on with their ship's work, still dressed in their cottons. On August 1st, 80 days out from Crete, the brigantine rounded Eastern Point, and came up Gloucester harbor. Although the voyage had been a lengthy one,

Captain MacCuish said that it had been due entirely to their bad luck with the winds for the *Robinson* had a good turn of speed when the breeze was right. On the last lap, as she crossed Massachusetts Bay, she had a race with the schooner-yacht *Blue Dolphin,* leaving the powered craft in her wake.

After spending the remainder of the summer in Gloucester, the *Robinson* set off for Tahiti on November 28th, this time with a white crew and Sterling Hayden in command. Sailing as a merchant vessel the brigantine could not use her repaired engine as there was no engineer aboard; the propeller had to be removed to satisfy the law.

All went well until they were in the Gulf Stream where a winter gale struck at them, the stronger gusts of wind reaching 70 miles an hour. The fore-topsail ripped from her gaskets, and in seconds had lashed herself to ribbons. The foresail started to go next, but Hayden and one of the crew, Arthur Hansen, fought their way aloft to secure the canvas. An extra strong blast caught them unawares, and both were blown backwards on the footropes, only saving themselves by grabbing for the backstays. Great seas were running, towering at times over the small vessel, but she was an able craft, seldom taking any solid water over the rails. Later on a fire broke out when the galley stove acted up, but quick action prevented much damage.

Once the brigantine got into the Trades, she knocked off 218 miles in 24 hours, an average of over nine knots for the day. After a short stop at Jamaica, the *Robinson* carried on to Panama, arriving there in mid-December. Here the propeller was put on to give a push for the remainder of the voyage. In the Pacific, they stopped at the Galapagoes to deliver a grist mill to one of the residents. On February 16th the brigantine sailed into Papeete, Tahiti.

The *Robinson* remained in those waters, now belonging to a copra trader. With her yards removed, she was reduced to a bald-headed schooner rig, with her once silent engine doing most of the work these days. Her run was mostly in the Tuamotus although she did sail to Hawaii and the other groups once or twice.

Intrepid

New England shipbuilders showed that they had not forgotten their art when George Lawley & Son launched the steel auxiliary barkentine-yacht *Intrepid* in 1930. Built at a cost estimated to have been $650,000, she was 205 feet long overall, 152 feet on the waterline, with a draft of 16 feet. She could set 19,131 square feet of sail from her three masts. On her foremast she had above her foreyard double topsail yards, a single topgallant, and a royal.

Owned by Walter P. Murphy of Chicago, the *Intrepid's* first voyage was across the Atlantic to Europe. On her return to the States in the fall, her engine tail shaft broke, forcing her to carry on under sail alone to Halifax. In 1938 she again was in trouble when her propeller dropped off while on a cruise in Canadian waters, having to be towed from Murray Bay to Quebec for repairs.

Early in the war years the *Intrepid* was taken into the United States Navy. Her towering rig was cut off, and she became a motor vessel renamed the *U.S.S. Sylph*. She survived the war, but was in very poor condition when peace came.

Jadran

The *Jadran* was a smart Yugoslavian training vessel that came into Boston in July, 1938, with 150 cadets. Although technically a three-mast barkentine, she had more the appearance of a three-mast topsail schooner as her fore-lowermast was the same height as her main and mizzen lower masts. Built in 1932, she was 720 tons displacement, 190 feet long, and she had a 375 horsepower diesel which gave her an eight knot speed in calm seas. Aloft she was able to set 8600 feet of canvas.

The name *Jadran* means Adriatic.

Joseph Conrad

One of the smallest full-rigged ships to sail deep water was the *Georg Stage,* a frigate of some 212 gross tons only just over 100 feet on the waterline. Launched from the yard of Burmeister and Wain in Copenhagen, Denmark, in 1882, she had been rebuilt as a school-ship to the order of Frederik Stage, a Danish shipowner whose son Georg Stage had died from tuberculosis. Annually, she took 80 Danish cadets ranging in age from fifteen to eighteen on cruises about the Baltic and the North Sea. She was a smart little vessel, strongly built of Swedish iron. Her decks were teak topside, the houses of steel. Aloft she carried the old-time single topsail rig, typical of the frigate of a century earlier. Her fore and main lower masts were of iron, the jibboom of larch, and the rest of her spars of pitchpine. Her longest yard, the main, was only 50 feet from tip to tip, and her shortest, her mizzen royal, a mere 19 feet in length. She could set 10,000 square feet of canvas.

In 1905 *George Stage* met with her first serious accident when she was run down by a steamer near Copenhagen, sinking with a loss of 26 of her boys. When she was later raised and repaired, she was given a series of watertight bulkheads. Although she had a small diesel engine (from 1906 to 1916 she had no power at all), it was seldom used, only in cases of emergencies.

In 1934 plans were made to replace her with a larger vessel, and she was sold to Mr. Alan Villiers who was already noted for his books about the large Australian grain windjammers. The ship changed hands in August when the Danish flag was hauled down, and replaced by the Red Duster of England. Her new name was *Joseph Conrad.*

On September 3rd she departed from Copenhagen, arriving at Harwich, England, ten days later. After taking aboard supplies, she set out for the States on October 22nd with 32 hands aboard, of which eight were cadets. Head winds held her up in the Channel, and she beat across to France eleven times before she crawled clear. After crossing the Bay of Biscay, her jibboom carried away in a squall, but repairs were made at sea, and she rolled onward. This was the first time the *Conrad* had left her home waters; the deep waters were new to her although to her liking.

She paused at Madeira when 19 days out. Another 35 days passed before she poked her nose into Nassau harbor where she stayed for three days. On December 19th she sailed north, saw Christmas at sea, and came into New York on December 30th, 69 days from Harwich, having sailed 6766 miles.

On January 2nd, 1935, the *Conrad* had the second serious accident of her career when her anchor chain snapped during a wintery squall. She drifted across the harbor to smash on the rocks of Bay Ridge. Although she was badly holed, Merritt-Chapman Company successfully refloated her and after a period in dry dock, she came out completely repaired, ready for her longest voyage.

January 31st saw her setting sail as a tug towed her by the Statue of Liberty, bound from the icy harbor for the warmth of Rio de Janeiro. Before she crossed the Line, she had to battle for her life in a Gulf Stream gale. One terrific squall caught her aback, blowing some of her sails to ribbons with its savage strength. The ship crossed the Equator 36 days out, creeping through the calms with intermittent rain squalls and blue skies. On March 30th the anchor went down in Rio bay.

From there the ship took 31 days to Cape Town, and another 49 days to Bali across the Indian Ocean via the West Winds. She romped along often doing ten knots, sometimes twelve, knocking of 1200 miles in a week. She was good sea boat, riding the wild crests like an albatross. Here she was dry-docked for painting. After six months supplies were stowed away, she sailed on July 31st for Sydney by way of China and Sulu Seas with stops here and there along the route. Winds were light much of the time, sometimes not even enough air to stir the stunsails that were set from her fore yards. On September 28th, the *Conrad* was hove down in the lagoon of Nissan Island so that her bottom could be cleaned and scraped free of the marine growth which had rapidly grown in the warm waters. Heaving down close to the beach, with the tackles fast to the trees ashore, was an art once practiced by the New Bedford whalers, but a custom almost forgotten in this modern age.

Less than a week later the *Conrad* was on her way again, pausing in the Solomons and at Guadalcanal. As they crept through the Coral Sea, malaria fever broke out, weakening the crew but not causing any serious harm. The frigate arrived at Sydney on December 9th, 131 days from Singapore, a distance of 7800 miles. Once more supplies were stowed away before putting to sea on the 18th. The *Conrad* was hardly in deep water when a series of gales struck her, and for the first time on the voyage, she had to heave to to ride the mad seas. She needed 13 days to run down the coast to Melbourne. On the last day of January, 1936, the ship departed for Auckland, taking 23 days for the passage.

She now retraced her course, passing again through the Coral Sea to leave a gold expedition at Samarai. From there she headed for Tahiti. Head winds and calms greeted her at first, and on April 3rd, she drifted ashore on the sharp coral of Wari Reef. Her stout iron hull prevented her from breaking up. With the aid of the bower anchor, she was able to pull herself free to continue on her way. A stop was made at Lord Howe Island, New Zealand was sighted again, and on June 18th she came to Papeete, 79 days from Samarai.

After two weeks in port during which time preparations were made for the long passage to New York, the *Conrad* set out on July 2nd. Heading southward for the strong west winds, she made good time, reeling off the knots. Once she had to heave to for a day while an icy gale lashed at them, causing minor damage to the tiny ship. The fore-topgallant mast was sprung, having to be sent down for the remainder of the voyage. She rounded Cape Horn 37 days out, turning north into the Atlantics. Another gale stopped her in the South Atlantic for a few hours as the huge seas were making it dangerous for her to carry on, but as soon as the weather moderated, she went back to her course. On September 15th the Equator was crossed again, and a month and a day later she arrived in New York, 106 days for the 13,000 miles from Tahiti. The entire voyage had covered 57,800 miles; she had been at sea for 555 days.

On November 10th, 1936, the *Conrad* changed hands and flags when she was purchased by Mr. Huntington Hartford of New York. She now became a yacht. In August, 1937, she raced the ship-yacht *Seven Seas* from Newport, Rhode Island, to Bermuda. Both ships began the race with sails furled and crews below decks. To give more room to maneuver, the ships started a half hour apart, the *Seven Seas* getting under way first. There was very little air, the breeze not filling the sails. The conditions were better for the smaller, lighter *Conrad* so she easily took the starting honors. The 750-mile race was not much more than a drifting match which the *Conrad* won by a single minute using her 24-hour handicap; she had taken ten days. The return race to Newport was taken by the *Seven Seas* with a seven day run; the *Conrad* was two days behind her.

In 1939 Mr. Hartford turned the frigate over to the United States Maritime Commission with whom she resumed her role as a training ship. In December she was sailed from New York to St. Petersburg, meeting very bad weather off the Florida keys, and she had her canvas ripped and rigging damaged. Working out of St. Petersburg, the *Conrad* took cadets on short cruises in local waters. In March, 1940, she was in the race to Havana, coming in last astern of the fleet of racing yachts. By early 1946 the rigging of the ship was in such poor condition that it was thought best to lay her up. Furhermore, the Commission felt that the little ship would be of no further use to them. There was an indication that now she would be broken up, but a special act of Congress gave her to the Marine Historical Association of Mystic, Connecticut.

As vandals had destroyed her engines, and as her rigging was so badly worn, the *Conrad* had to be towed north. On August 4th, 1947, she passed through New York's Narrows astern of the tug

Christine Moran. The next day she came to her new home port, berthing at the same wharf as the whaler *Charles Morgan.*

She is now used as a base for Sea Scouts and Girl Mariners where they can take up courses in maritime subjects. Her 65 year old hull is a little aged now, but it is still a tribute to her Danish shipbuilders.

Marsala

One of the largest sailing ships to be under canvas in the New England waters during the last days of sail was the bulky 5-mast barkentine Marsala, a massive vessel of 2422 tons and 284 feet long. One of a fleet of eleven built to the order of H. Piaggio of Orange, Texas, she was launched from the yards of the International Shipbuilding Company at Pascagoula, Mississippi, in 1919. First called *City of Vicksburg,* she was originally fitted with oil engines and twin screws. It had been hoped that with her large carrying capacity, for she was hardly more than a box with its ends brought together, that she would be a big money earner in the war boom which was still on when she was laid down. However, the bubble had burst by the time she was ready for sea. In 1920 she was sold, taking on the name *Marsala* at that time.

When she arrived in Boston in May, 1922, with 3500 tons of bituminous coal from Norfolk, it was said that she was the first of her type to have entered the port. Not long after, Pendleton Brothers of New York took her over, removing her engines, and sending her to sea as a pure barkentine. Not being a very easy ship to handle under sail, she was laid up a good deal of the time, and for a while it seemed that she might end her days on the mud flats with other dying vessels. In 1932 she was taken over by the American Nautical Academy in Washington, D.C., to become a training ship, certainly a poor choice when there were so many other windjammers available at that time which would have been a great deal more suitable for the purpose. She was a hard ship to work, and even the best master with a large crew of cadets could not have been expected to get very much out of her.

She was frequently in trouble. In 1937 the Coast Guard had to tow her into New York with her steering gear broken down. A year later she was at New London when the hurricane in September struck. Caught by the wind, the huge ship swung around, smashing into the wharf. Her bowsprit broke off as it swept a dockside building. Some newspapers at the time reported that as this shed collapsed, a fire started which eventually burned out a large section of that part of the town. The *Marsala* herself, apart from the bowsprit, was little damaged. Not long after, she put back to sea.

On November 24th, 1938, the big barkentine was bound south from New London when she ran into the path of a heavy storm off the Virginia Capes. As the barometer dropped, Captain Oliver C. Bohld ordered all the fore-and-aft sail furled, leaving only his fore topsails set. His crew of 12 and the 22 cadets could do nothing more but wait. Then the wind struck with a hissing roar, staggering the five-master with its strength. Suddenly one of her masts snapped, crashing over the side amidst splinters and tangled lines. A moment later a second mast went, then the third and fourth. The foremast snapped off just above the lower cap, leaving only the foreyard aloft. The stout hull rose to the mounting seas, pitching and tossing and rolling in the flying foam and spray. She was sighted by the steamer *City of Savannah* on the 25th, and not long after, the Coast Guard cutter *Mendota* came out to tow her into Norfolk. The *Marsala*'s sailing days were over.

Early in World War II, the *Marsala* found new work. With her fore-lower mast still standing, she was anchored off Little Creek, near Norfolk. On her bows was her new name, *YAG 17*. Boarding nets were hung on both sides of her hull. Day after day army assault craft loaded with armed troops circled the one-time windjammer. One after another they would rapidly come alongside, long enough for the soldiers to scramble up the nets. As the troops raced across her decks and down the far side, the assault craft would swing under her bows, and be ready to pick them up again. After weeks of this practice, the troops would be ready for the larger invasion craft off Africa and in the Pacific.

One day some LSTs tried to use the *YAG 17* to train their boot-officers in docking ships. The first LST approached at speed. At the last moment a puff of breeze suddenly swung the hulk slightly, and the LST crashed into her stern with a splintering of wood. The second LST fouled along her side, and some of her railing carried away. Yet another LST fouled her bows. Finally the *YAG*'s Commanding Officer had to call a halt to the experiment "before one of us sinks the other".

And so the *Marsala* was left to the small assault craft and the curses of the troops who had to fumble around the rope ladders in fair weather and foul as they prepared for war. Later she was wrecked on a nearby beach.

Sagres

Rickmers of Bremerhaven, Germany, were builders of several of the last survivors of the square-rigger days. Their beautiful *Herzogin Cecilie* was Queen of the Grain Fleet for more than a decade, their huge *R. C. Rickmers* of 5548 tons was sail's last effort against steam, their *L'Avenir* was a handsome Belgian training ship, and their smaller barks *Penang* ex-*Albert Rickmers* and *Winterhude* ex-*Mabel Rickmers* were members of the Grain Fleet in the 1930's.

Another of their numerous vessels was the ship *Rickmer Rickmers* which they launched in 1896. Like the majority of their designs, she was a good looking vessel, well proportioned, and a good sailer. Not a large ship, she was 1980 gross tons and 263 feet long. During her first year she was operated by her builders who sent her wherever cargoes were to be had. In 1900 she loaded wheat at Astoria for Europe, meeting the crack ships of the day in the long race around the Horn. The *Cedarbank* had the best passage, 103 days, but the *Rickmers* was second with 108 days. The noted *Clackmannanshire* followed her by two days, and the well-known British-built Canadian-owned flyer *Muskoka* took 111 days. The rest of the fleet trailed in behind them.

In 1905 the *Rickmers* was cut down to a bark in order to reduce the number of men required to handle her. Before the outbreak of the first World War she changed hands with her new owner, C. Krabbenhoft of Hamburg, renaming her *Max*. Unable to get back to Germany in 1914, she put into Lisbon where she was requisitioned by the Portuguese Government, and again renamed, becoming *Flores*.

Between 1924 and 1927 she was made over into a Portuguese Naval training ship, returning to sea as the *Sagres*. In the following years she frequently crossed the Atlantic with her cadets, visiting South American ports. In 1931 she was given a 700 horsepower engine to help her in and out of ports; it is rarely used when at sea.

In late May, 1948, the *Sagres* with a complement of 307 men set out on her annual summer cruise, this time bound for the United States. First she eased south from Lisbon, putting into Funchal. From there she carried on to St. Vincent in the Cape Verdes. Her next passage covered 3000 miles to Boston which was done under sail alone. When she was nearing Cape Cod a nasty summer gale swept up the Atlantic, forcing the bark to ride out the storm under her "lateen" sail (mizzen staysail) before carrying on. She came up Boston harbor on July 10th, 27 days from the Islands. Later she went around to New Bedford and Providence where the Portuguese-Americans feted the crew and cadets, giving parties and entertainments for them. A proposed stop at Fall River had to be abandoned when it was learned that the Mount Hope bridge was only 135 feet above the water. The bark's maintruck was 140 feet from her waterline. Before returning home she visited New York.

As a training ship the *Sagres* was beautifully kept up. Although a sailing vessel, she was moderately equipped, even airconditioning in the Ward Room. Her decks were spotless, and her lines flaked down by the pin rails form intricate designs on the deck. The Portuguese have not forgotten their King Henry the Navigator for his likeness forms the bark's figurehead; her name *Sagres* was taken from the port where he founded a navigation school in the 15th century. In 1961, retired from sea-going duty, she was renamed *Santo-Andre,* used as a harbor depot-ship.

Sea Cloud

The last four-mast bark ever built was the mighty yacht *Hussar* which was launched from the yards of Fried Krupp Germanawerft at Keil, Germany, in 1931. Designed by the New York firm of Cox & Stevens, she was 2323 gross tons and her overall length was 316 feet; her waterline was 254 feet while her beam was 49 feet, and her depth almost 25 feet. She was the only vessel of her type to carry a main skysail in many years. She also had royals, single topgallants, and double topsail, her total sail area being some 26,000 square feet of canvas.

Although she had a lovely rig, her beauty was spoiled by a series of ugly deck houses, an athwartship bridge just after of the foremast, and a short but noticeable funnel. However, she was fitted out in a most luxurious style below decks. Her cost is said to have been well over $1,000,000, and was perhaps three times that figure. Few vessels were as lavishly decorated as the *Hussar.* Apart from the quarters of the owner's family, there were accomodations for 14 guests, and in addition to that, she had space for 75 hands. The cabins were like bedrooms in the best hotels ashore. The bathrooms had marble tiles, and the washbasins were gold plated. In the smoking room stuffed heads of animals, rhinoceros, antelopes, and the like, adorned the walls. Her diesel engines could push her along at fourteen knots.

This huge windship has cruised extensively. Some years before the war, her name was changed to *Sea Cloud*. When her owner, Mr. Joseph E. Davies was the American Ambassador to Russia, he kept her anchored in Leningrad harbor; it is not on record what the individual communist thought of this magnificent floating palace. Her last run before the war brought Mr. Davies back from Antwerp where he had been Ambassador to Belgium. She was then laid up at Jacksonville partly rigged down.

In 1942, Mr. Davies turned the *Sea Cloud* over to the U.S. Coast Guard, charging them $1.00 a year for her use. With her rig still further reduced, she was used as a patrol craft, and at one time it is said that she had an all-Negro crew aboard her.

An amusing tale is told in conjunction with the *Sea Cloud* at the end of the war. When the training ship *Danmark* was about to start back for Denmark, her commanding officer looked about for another suit of sails. Someone in the Coast Guard suggested that she take the *Sea Cloud*'s canvas; with cutting down, it would have been suitable. Everything had been arranged when someone thought of asking Mr. Davies if he expected his yacht back. The answer was yes, and furthermore, he wanted her back fully rigged. The sails were saved, but it was too late to get many of the spars back for they had been shipped out for use all over the world as derricks with the fighting forces. The story closed by saying that it took nearly another $1,000,000 to put the *Sea Cloud* back into first class shape.

Again a yacht, she visited New England waters in the years right after World War II. Later she was owned by Gen. Rafael Trujillo Jr., of the Dominican Republic. In 1963, when she was put up for sale, the asking price was two million dollars. In 1965 there was talk of sending her back to sea as a cruise ship with a two week trip that would cost each passenger between two and four thousand dollars.

Seven Seas

Launched as the *Abraham Rydberg* in 1912, this small full-rigged ship set royals over single topgallants and double topsails. Her length overall was 168 feet, but she was only 138 feet on the waterline. Fitted out as a training ship for the Abraham Rydberg

Society, she was built by Bergsund M. V. Atkieb of Stockholm, Sweden.

In her earlier days, she had space for 120 boys who slung their hammocks in a large open space amidship below decks. Aft she had her captain's quarters as well as those of the senior officers; the petty officers were berthed up forward. The cooking was done in a small deck house.

In 1929, when the*Abraham Rydberg* was replaced with the four-mast bark *Star of Greenland,* she was sold to become an American yacht; she was renamed *Seven Seas.* Her passage across the Atlantic, a slow one as she met much heavy weather, took all of 50 days from Cowes to New York. Later she was taken to the Norfolk Shipbuilding and Dry Dock Corporation in Virginia where she was thoroughly overhauled. A saloon the full width of the ship and 13 feet long was done in oak with bookcases and sofas built in, as well as a coal-burning fireplace. Forward of that was a four room suite with two bathrooms for the owner and his family. Aft of the saloon were two cabins and a bathroom for guests, and still further aft was a smoking room, pantry, three small cabins, and another bathroom. The chart room was in the stern.

The galley was made larger and modernized and a dining saloon 24 feet by 10 feet was built abaft the mainmast. The officers and crew lived forward, the forecastle having accomodations for ten men. Every comfort was built into the ship, hot and cold running water in the bathrooms (she could carry 7500 gallons of fresh water), over 225 electric outlets for her 110 volt circuit, cold storage boxes and freezers. Her engines could give her a speed of ten knots.

Owned by Mr. Inglis M. Uppercu of New York City, she made her first cruise as a yacht to the West Indies, and later visited the St. Lawrence River, going as far as Montreal. After that she was seen in many waters, often being the outstanding vessel at yachting regattas. She was an ideal vessel for cruises, being very comfortable. With only a 13 foot, 5 inch draft, she could get into most of the smaller harbors without trouble.

When she raced the *Joseph Conrad* to Bermuda in 1937, she was owned by Mr. Walter Gubelmann of Charleston, South Carolina. She generally spent her winters near Palm Beach, and her summers in New England waters.

The war years found her in service but as a motor vessel. When peace returned, she was offered for sale, the asking price being $50,000 as she lay in Miami without her rigging in place.

It is said that she went under the Mexican flag, used as a motor freighter in the banana trade.

Tusitala

One of the last commercial full-riggers on the Seven Seas was the lovely iron ship *Tusitala,* the last ship to have been built by Robert Steele & Company at Greenock on the Clyde. Steele had launched a long line of famous tea clippers that had made great names for themselves in the China trade. They had all been well constructed, with the very best materials, and the *Tusitala* was no exception. Christened the *Inveruglas* in 1883, she had been a medium sized ship of 1748 tons and 260 feet long. She carried a fair rig, double topsails, single topgallants, and royals; her mainmast was 153 feet high. Her main yard was 89 feet from tip to tip, the main royal 50 feet.

After a voyage to Australia, she was bought by the firm of Thompson, Anderson and Company of Liverpool who had a fleet of snow-white sailers, the names of which all began with "Sierra"; the *Inveruglas* became the *Sierra Lucena.* During the next few years she regularly traded between the United Kingdom and India, loading salt, jute, rice and timber. One of her best outward trips was from Penarth, Wales, to Mauritius in the Indian Ocean in 67 days in 1900.

In 1904 she changed flags and name when she became the Norwegian *Sophie,* and for the next nineteen years she plodded the oceans taking cargoes when and where she could find them. During the first World War she payed her owners well. Under Captain Hans M. Mikkelsen, she freighted Argentine wheat to Europe. When she was in the River Plate she was in a collision with a steamer, stoving in her bows and smashing her bowsprit. Repairs were made in hurried war-time fashion, and she lost some of the good looks that Steele had built into her. Her new spike bowsprit was not pretty; it was a length of tapered mast.

At another period in the war, she was chartered by American interests to carry food across the Atlantic. Although still owned in Norway, she carried Swiss colors at this time, and had the word "Schweiz" painted amidships on both her sides. Following the war she took a load or two of coal from Norfolk to the Baltic, but soon after, the slump came along, and the *Sophie* was laid up at Hampton Roads.

In 1923, when there was a chance that the ship would go to the shipbreakers, she was purchased by a group called "The Three Hours for Lunch Club" who were mostly writers and artists. They had great plans for her. An elaborate ceremony was held on board the day the Stars and Stripes were broken out aloft. She was renamed *Tusitala*, which means "Teller of Tales" in Samoan, after Robert Louis Stevenson. A letter from Joseph Conrad was read by Christopher Morley to climax the rites. However, the plans fell through, and again the ship changed hands. She made two voyages from New York to Rio de Janeiro, outward with coal, and returning north with manganese ore.

Mr. James A. Farrell, president of the U. S. Steel Corporation, took over the ship now, operating her under the house flag of the Argonaut Line. Her first voyage for her new owner took her through the Panama Canal to Hawaii, and back across the Pacific to Seattle. She returned to New York on November 4th, 1924. With Captain James P. Barker in command, she sailed down the Hudson River without tugs early in 1925, and it was said that she was the first full-rigger to leave New York unassisted in 53 years. Again she passed through the Canal to the Pacific, going to Seattle. She returned to Baltimore in 112 days; she had taken 71 days to go from Seattle to Colon. Her next run from Seattle was much better, only 80 days.

In 1928, after passing through the Canal on her homeward run, the ship went through a rather strange experience. In the late afternoon when there was little breeze, a dark cloud was suddenly sighted coming up over the horizon. All hands rushed to shorten sail before they realized that it was not wind but a cloud of swallows that was approaching. The birds covered the ship, perching on the rails, the deck, the yards and the bowsprit. They got into the cabins and the forecastle, anywhere that there was an opening. Thousands of them died before dawn; the remainder took off when the breeze came in from the southwest. Just where they had come from was hard to say, no one knew where they were going; they were part of the mysteries of the sea.

Later in the voyage, the *Tusitala* was caught in a raging midwinter gale off the ever stormy Cape Hatteras where towering, ugly seas were running, foam crested and flying spume, driven by a frenzied wind. After several sails had blown to rags, the old ship settled down to ride out the blast under a goosewinged topsail, coming through the blow unharmed although the steamer *Vestris* foundered not many miles away from her. Bound in for Baltimore, she refused the tug off Cape Charles, sailing half way up the Chesapeake before she was halted by a blinding snow storm.

In 1929 the *Tusitala* was 100 days out to Honolulu from New York, returning to Baltimore in 106. As a rule her cargo west would be some 2600 tons of sulphate of ammonia for use as fertilizer on the sugar and pineapple plantations in the Hawaiian Islands. She would return with sugar. Her last run under sail brought her into New York in 1932, again 196 days from Honolulu via the Canal. Then she was laid up near the George Washington Bridge on Riverside Drive where she remained for five years, her tall spars rising above the traffic that scurried past almost under her bowsprit.

James Farrell had been operating the *Tusitala* for sentimental reasons. He had been running her constantly at a loss, but he had been keeping the American flag flying from the gaff of a square-rigger, the last full-rigged commercial ship operating under the Stars and Stripes. Expenses had been soaring upward, and by 1937 he realized that she would not go to sea again. At first he offered her to the United States Maritime Commission for use as a training ship, but Congress could not see its way to vote funds for her upkeep. There was nothing left to do but to send her to the ship breakers.

Late in the summer of 1938, the *Tusitala* was towed away from New York to the yards of the Marine Liquidating Corporation in Fall River, Massachusetts. Just when the end seemed in sight, she was saved when the Maritime Commission discovered that they could use the ship after all. Towed back to Staten Island, a considerable amount of money was spent on refitting her as a training ship. Her old deck houses were burned off, and new, enlarged rooms were built. Double-decked bunks for 120 seamen and 30 petty officers were added to the 'tween decks. Showers and basins with hot and cold water were installed, and a modern galley with oil stove was so arranged that all hands could eat at one setting, cafeteria style. All ports were covered with copper screening, and in the rigging red lights were placed to warn off airplanes. Electric outlets were put in for those who used electric razors. A few of her aged iron plates needed renewing; these were replaced with steel ones when iron was not forthcoming. Her rigging was patched up, but her royals were left off.

In May, 1940, the *Tusitala* was towed away from Staten Island, going south to St. Petersburg in Florida, where she became a barracks ship for the cadets of the Commission. There she remained until the end of the war. As there was no further need for her, she was towed to Mobile, Alabama, to be layed up with a number of steamers. However, in late 1947 a tug moved her across to a dry dock, and there she was broken up; by 1948 hardly her keel remained.

CHAPTER XI

The Cape Verde Packets

～～～～～～～～～～～～～～～～～～～～～～～～

THE LAST deep-water sailing ships to operate out of the
United States are the packet vessels that run between New
Bedford and Providence and the Cape Verde Islands off the African
coast. Ever since the islanders first came to New England nearly a
century ago, to join the ships of the whaling fleet, a spasmodic service with windships has been carried on between their homeland
and Massachusetts and Rhode Island. When the whaling business
died, the islanders found other employment in the mills and the
cranberry bogs. In time they developed a large colony along the
shores of Buzzards Bay.

Inasmuch as the trade was not sufficiently lucrative for power
vessels, the islanders were forced to rely on aged windjammers
which they were able to buy at low prices. In the early days, many
of their craft were ex-whalers. The last whaler in the service was
the schooner *John R. Manta.* She, with the schooners *Winnepesaukee* and *Trenton,* sailed from New Bedford in November, 1934.
Neither the *Manta* with 32 persons aboard nor the *Winnepesaukee*
with 13 were ever seen again; the *Trenton* made Brava safely, but
was wrecked a few months after. In later years the islanders used
ex-merchantment and even aging yachts. Being born sailors, the
Cape Verdians were able to take these old crocks to sea, although
it is amazing that more of them were not lost.

Perhaps their most interesting vessel in recent times was a
former clipper ship.

Coriolanus
The beautiful full-rigged ship *Coriolanus* was built for the
China tea trade but she never carried a cargo of tea as she came
too late, steam and the Suez Canal driving wind ships from that
particular run. Launched from the yard of A. McMillan of Dumbarton on the Clyde in 1876, she was 1053 gross tons and 217 feet

long. It has been said that she was one of the loveliest iron ships ever built; at the Shipwright's Exhibition in London in 1877 her model won the Gold Medal, the highest award, for her fine lines.

Her first owners, J. Patton & Company of London, sent her out to Calcutta with a general cargo on her first voyage, and she proved herself to be a true clipper by signalling the Hooghly pilots 68 days out, anchoring off Calcutta 69 days from the Channel, setting a record that has never been beaten by sailing craft. As all of her runs in this India jute trade were above average, she soon earned the title "Queen of the Jute Clippers", making a name for herself as an exceptionally fast ship.

In 1886 she was purchased by the well-known London shipping company of John Stewart, one of the last firms to operate sailing ships under the British flag, who put her in general trade. In the spring of 1890, the *Coriolanus* very nearly met her end when she was in a collision with the steamship *Claymore*. The clipper at the time was approaching the English Channel with a load of nitrate from Chile for Hamburg. Apparently those on the steamer had not realized the speed of the windship, never dreaming that there was any possibility of an accident. At the moment of the crash, the steamer's captain and officer of the watch were in the chart room, leaving only a Chinese helmsman watching the compass at the wheel. With a crunching of plates, the sharp stem of the clipper plowed into the midship section of the *Claymore,* splitting her wide open as part of the windship's tophamper came smashing down on deck. In a very few minutes the steamer foundered, her crew only just getting away in their boats.

With her bows stove in, the *Coriolanus* just managed to stay afloat, but it did not seem that she would last long. That evening a steamer came up to the wreck, taking aboard both crews, and leaving the windship to her fate. For all of two weeks the clipper drifted on her own. Now and then a vessel would sight her, but none believed her worth salvaging. At length the steamer *Bostonian* put a line aboard her as her master felt he could get the hulk to port.

The long 600-mile tow was a matter of touch and go the entire way for if the clipper's collision bulkhead had given, the deeply laden vessel would have gone down like a rock. However, luck smiled on them, and the clipper was taken safely into Passage West where the cargo was discharged until repairs had been completed. She then reloaded, proceeding to Hamburg after a lengthy delay.

[233]

On her last voyage under the British flag, she had Captain John W. Steel for master. Leaving the Channel, she set her course for Brisbane, Australia. At first the winds were ahead, but as the gale swung favorable, she really picked up her heels as of old, knocking off 17 knots as she raced through the seas. Later, as the wind still freshened and the combers grew, canvas was reduced to upper topsails. She still danced along at almost 15 knots with her decks dry, and only a dash of spray across her bows from time to time. Once during the run a heavy squall struck her when she had most of her sails set. With the wheel put down, she ran off before the wind at her very top speed; her mate said later that he believed she had been doing over 20 knots for a short time.

Three days before Christmas, 1890, the *Coriolanus* arrived off Brisbane 90 days out. Wishing to give his men shore leave for the holiday, Captain Steel asked the pilot to get him a tug to take them up the narrow two-mile channel beyond the bar leading into the inner bay. The pilot replied that there was only one tug, and she was booked for another ship, the *Salamanca*, which had arrived just ahead of the *Coriolanus;* they would have to wait until the holidays were over. But Captain Steel did not see it that way. Early the following morning, as the tug took hold of the *Salamanca*, the former jute-clipper set her sails as her anchor came up. Off the bar buoy the *Coriolanus* was up with the *Salamanca*. There was not much room for them both in the channel yet neither could stop for fear of drifting down on the lee bank. With her yards braced around as far as they would go, her weather braces free, the clipper felt the freshening breeze, almost seeming to leap forth. Giving her a full sail for a moment to gain speed, Captain Steel jammed his ship into the wind as he came opposite the *Salamanca*, shooting her past her and her tug. She then drove on up the channel and into the bay at 14 knots. They were in for Christmas.

The clipper next loaded at Lyttelton, New Zealand, with 1350 tons of grain for England. She made a fast run to the Horn, 17½ days for the 4600 miles; her best day's work was 340 miles noon to noon. It was unusual weather for not once did she have to furl her main skysail. She met nasty weather in the South Atlantic, and some of the ships that she passed were shortened down to upper topsails while she still set everything as she bowled along at a steady 14 knots. She was 73 days out when her anchor dropped in Falmouth harbor, an excellent passage.

As she was a small carrier, the Stewart Company sold her

at this time to the Germans for some $40,000, and for the next few years she was back in the jute trade; her home port was now Bremen. In 1896, while outward bound to Rangoon in ballast, the crew of the *Coriolanus* found that the dunnage in her after hold was afire. For a time it was feared that she might have to be abandoned. The American ship *Sterling,* bound from New York to San Francisco, stopped to help fight the flames, and although the fire was not completely extinguished, it was at least held down so that the clipper could proceed to Bahia, Brazil. The damage had been severe, but after repairs she was able to return to sea.

Six years later found her at anchor in the roadstead at Algoa Bay with 17 other square-riggers when a terrific gale struck from the open sea. Before the storm had abated every ship present had been driven ashore. Of the 17 ships, only five survived to sail again; the *Coriolanus* was one of these.

She had not been too successful under the German flag, and this was the crowning blow. She now went to Norwegian owners who rerigged her as a three-mast bark. For a short time in 1903 and 1904 she returned to the Red Duster of the British merchant marine, owned in East London, Africa, but in 1905, she belonged to Norway again with her homeport at Xiansand.

For the next fifteen years she sailed the seas, plodding the trade routes of the world with little fuss, safely weathering the first World War. As the Norwegians turned to steam, they sold off their windjammers, getting rid of the clipper about 1921 when she became the *Tiburon* under the flag of Panama. Within a year she was in trouble. In June, 1921, she lost her main royal mast when passing under Brooklyn Bridge. A week or two later she arrived in Boston, supposedly to finish loading a lumber cargo for Africa, but she apparently also had alcohol aboard, and in July she was seized by the Government for smuggling liquor ashore. In September she was sold for $7525.

Renamed *Eugenia Emilia* in 1922, she entered the Cape Verde packet trade, arriving at St. Vincent on July 17th, 42 days out from New Bedford. She was sold in 1923, and by 1924 was under the Portuguese flag. A year later her name had been changed to *Lina,* hailing from the Cape Verde Islands. A new owner, who had picked her up for $1000, gave her back her original name; she was kept in the packet trade.

During her last years, the old ship still had speed, being able to do 300 miles a day, and on one occasion clipping off 16 knots all one night. Towards the end, she made a record passage from New Bedford to San Antone, Cape Verde Islands in 17½ days in spite of being becalmed for three days in the doldrums. On the return trip she was struck by a black squall which brought down some of her upper rigging in a tangled heap on deck. Her crew fought to save her, cutting away the broken spars as raging seas swept across her rails. The ex-clipper was still seaworthy, and she limped on a sad sight under shortened canvas. When she made fast to the wharf at New Bedford on September 11th, 1930, her sailing days were over. Her last passage had taken 35 days from Fogo with eight passengers and a crew of 38 men.

Her owner could not afford to rerig her, and when he could not pay off his crew, the clipper was sold at auction for only $690. For awhile she lay at New Bedford until a scheme was hatched to send her back to sea again. A tug took her to Boston; for months she lay at a wharf there. On June 1st, 1932, she was towed to Bath for overhauling, but expenses proved far too much for the owners so she was just left there rusting away.

Finally in August, 1936, she moved for the last time, now in tow for Fall River to the General Iron Smelting Company to be broken up. By January, 1937, the rigging and decks were gone, and torches were burning off her old iron plates. In a few months only a section of the keel of the Queen of the Jute Clippers remained in the mud; the last of the clippers was but a memory.

Frank Brainerd

The three-mast schooner *Frank Brainerd* was another windship to end her days in the packet trade. She was a typical down east schooner, having been built by Cobb, Butler & Company of Rockland in 1908. She was not a large vessel, only 244 gross tons and 121 feet long. She had a depth of 8½ feet which permitted her to enter the shallowest harbors, but to add depth to improve her sailing qualities, she carried a centerboard amidships which caused her mainmast to be stepped to the side.

For many years the tern was engaged in the local coasting trade, generally freighting lumber and pulp with an occasional coal charter. In 1923, when owned by Captain Stevens of Wells, Maine, the *Brainerd* was wrecked off West Gouldsborough, Maine. Although she was declared a total loss, her captain worked on the hulk, and before summer was done, she was back at sea again. She carried her A-1 classification until 1935, for some 27 years.

In 1930, Captain Charles V. Griffin, who had once sailed the huge six-mast schooner *Wyomind,* was in charge of the *Brainerd.* At this time she was busy in the pulpwood trade to Bangor. Three years later she was mixed up with a cadetship scheme known as the "West Africa Trading Corporation". The plan had been to sail to Africa on a voyage of barter. The original vessel that was to have been used was the *Coriolanus,* but when she could not be fitted out, the Corporation turned to the barkentine *Reine Marie Stewart;* she, too, proved to be too much. As a last hope, the *Frank Brainerd* was chartered. The schooner took aboard a number of cadets in Boston. However, with the funds gone, the plans came to an end. The tern went back to work shortly, loading anthracite at New York for Maine.

In 1936 the schooner was sold to Captain Benjamin Costa and a group of his associates for the Cape Verde trade. After she had been given a refit at Fairhaven, the *Brainerd* took aboard a general cargo and six passengers, amongst them a mother and her two small children. She had a ten man crew. On November 17th, the three-master cleared New Bedford, passed down the Bay, out by Hen and Chickens, and bore away across the Atlantic. Nine days later, when she was 450 miles northeast of Bermuda, a howling gale struck at her. At first, she rode the seas comfortably, but without warning one of her masts, perhaps eaten by hidden rot, let go, crashing over the side, and taking with it the other two masts. A litter of wreckage clung to the vessel, threatening to batter in her sides while the crew struggled to chop it away with axes.

For two days the *Brainerd* wallowed in the still raging seas. Although she took a little water in, she was buoyant and seaworthy when the oil tanker *Bancolite* appeared on the scene. Nevertheless, Captain Costa was unable to persuade any of his crew to stand by the hulk to make an attempt to sail her to port under jury rig. She was abandoned on November 29th in Latitude 38 degress 10″ North, Longitude 41 degrees 20″ West.

Although the *Brainerd's* loss was recorded in the 1937 issue of the "Merchant Vessels of the United States", she re-appeared again as active in the 1941 copy. This, however, was a mistake, and was corrected in the 1942 restricted issue.

Dorothy G. Snow

Many of the Cape Verde packets have been ex-fishing vessels which had long since seen their best days when they began this trans-Atlantic run. One of the last of these was a small Canadian schooner, the *Dorothy G. Snow,* which had been built at Shelbourne, Nova Scotia, in 1911.

A typical Grand Banker, she was 98 gross tons and 98 feet long. In June, 1939, she changed hands and was thoroughly overhauled. On August 7th she arrived at Providence, seven days from Yarmouth. Although she was due to sail for the islands, she was delayed by the usual red tape involved in shifting from British to Portuguese registry during war time.

She eventually departed on April 25th, 1940, bound to the eastward. She was not seen again in New England waters until 1959 when she came into Providence, 40 days out from the islands with two passengers. Her name was now *Maria Sony.* Her passage home was a long, grim one. After a storm which forced her into Bermuda, she spent ten months licking her wounds, making repairs before pushing on. She has not been back in New England waters since that time.

Corona

The *Corona* was built as a handsome steel sloop yacht by N. G. Herreshoff at his Bristol yards in Rhode Island back in 1893. She was a large vessel for a single master as she was 136 gross tons and 123 feet overall. She was first named *Colonia,* but in 1896 when she was altered to a centerboard schooner, she became *Corona.*

In 1905 she was owned by Arthur F. Luke of New York. Twenty years later she was owned by Cleveland H. Dodge, also of New York, and in 1935 she was owned by John L. Souza of New Bedford. In 1936 she went under the Portuguese flag.

The *Corona* made several round trips to the islands during the next few years. She last departed from the whaling port on November 16th, 1940, with 110 tons of mixed cargo and eight passengers. She carried a crew of 18 men, enough for a full-rigged ship. As she passed down the bay in the dusk, she sighted the *Capitana* inward bound, a strange scene in a modern world.

She has not returned to the States since the war.

Capitana

The three-mast steel barkentine *Capitana* was originally launched in 1927 as a two-mast schooner yacht from the yards of J. S. White & Company at East Cowes, England. She carried several names in her earlier years, *Xarifa, Radiant, L'oiseau* and *Georg-*

ette; she became *Capitana* in 1939 when she was purchased for the Harvard Columbus Expedition that was to retrace the courses sailed by Christopher Columbus. She was named after the ship that carried Columbus on his third voyage of exploration. A good sized vessel of 190 gross tons and 142 feet long overall, she donned her barkentine rig in 1939.

On August 28th, she departed from Oyster Bay, flying the Harvard University pennant from her main truck. Three weeks later she had arrived at the Azores, and on October 16th dropped anchor in Lisbon harbor. Early in November she cleared Cadiz for Madeira in the wake of the *Santa Maria,* and then on to the Canaries, across to Trinidad, and along the shores of Central America. For 10,000 miles the expedition followed courses and identified landfalls which were mentioned in the logs and notes of the great explorer. They proved that Columbus had given very accurate records, and that his navigation had been a good deal more than merely primitive.

A few months after the *Capitana's* arrival at Miami in March, 1940, she was sold. Not long afterwards, she arrived at New Bedford to fit out for the packet trade. She made one run during the summer, returning to New England in November with a 36 day crossing. She had 11 passengers, and 45 tons of goatskins for cargo.

In 1941 she was sold to Iceland for the fish trade, and in 1964 it was reported she was *Xarifa* again, under the Greek flag.

Lucy Evelyn

The last commercial three-mast schooner in New England waters to be active was the Yankee tern *Lucy Evelyn* which had been built in 1917 by Frye, Flynn & Company of Harrington, Maine, at a cost of $60,000. She was a pretty little soft wood vessel of 374 gross tons and just under 140 feet in length. Her first owner, E. C. Lindsay of Machias, Maine, kept an interest in her until well into the second World War.

The *Lucy Evelyn* did well in her earlier years, at a time when schooners were making big earnings. In February, 1919, she was chartered to load lumber at Gulfports for Las Palmas in the Canary Islands at $60.00 per thousand feet; she could carry well over a quarter million feet of lumber. She was no clipper, and was perhaps a little slower than some of her sisters, but she was steady and reliable. She was well built, and was able to take a great deal of punishment through the years, yet remaining in service after her contemporaries had gone.

In mid-October, 1925, she was bound from Machias to New Haven with 300,000 feet of lumber when she was caught in a heavy northwest gale some 75 miles southeast of Highland Light. As her sails were torn to shreds, and seas opened her seams, a call for help was hoisted in her rigging. A passing vessel called the Coast Guard cutter *Tampa* which raced 200 miles to give aid to the tern. By this time the *Evelyn* was in sinking condition, only floating on her cargo. Her crew, headed by 72 year old Captain J. H. Jasper, were living on a platform that they had constructed on the after cabin. Much of the time the entire forward section was right under water. Half of her deck load, some 90,000 feet of wood, was washed away by two foam-crested combers which had swept right over the helpless schooner. An ocean liner had passed close to the floating wreck, but had not paused to help. After taking the schooner's crew aboard, the *Tampa* towed the waterlogged tern to Boston where she was pumped dry. Less than a week later, she was towed to the Cape Cod Canal to proceed on her way.

One of the *Lucy Evelyn's* most protracted passages took place in 1933 when she set out on February 19th from Lubec, Maine, for New York with a mixed cargo of potatoes, dried fish, and lumber. After weathering at Searsport, she put to sea in late February only to be hit by a northwest blizzard off Cape Cod. This was followed by strong westerlies that drove her across the Atlantic, very nearly to the Azores. As she had not been sighted for two weeks, radio instructions were sent out on March 10th to all Coast Guard vessels patrolling the waters between the Canadian border and New York to make a search for her. On March 17th, with the help of the Trade Winds, the tern arrived at San Juan Puerto Rico, for supplies. She set out again for New York, only to meet more westerlies; on April 6th she crawled into Barbados by which time her crew had thrown overboard the rotting potatoes. Several weeks later she made New York, but by then any hope of profit on the voyage had gone.

Captain John Mitchell of Harrington, Maine, had the *Evelyn* this hard trip. He seems to have had bad luck on more than one occasion. In 1921 he had taken the tern schooner *Spendrift* on her maiden voyage which should have been from Machias to Halifax, but a northwest gale drove him 2000 miles off his course, and he made Nassau, 47 days out.

The *Lucy Evelyn* kept busy during the 1930's working for the most part out of Machias in the general cargo trade. She frequently loaded coal from New York for Maine ports. Other times she took scrap metal, and also made a few granite runs. Now and then she was in minor trouble. In 1935, she got ashore off Boothbay Harbor, losing her rudder. In May of that same year she went up on the Virginia coast, coming off without harm. In March, 1936, she was a week overdue at New York when she was sighted still off Cape Cod, by Highland Light, just fighting headwinds. In July, 1940, when becalmed in a thick fog 30 miles east of Mt. Desert Rock, she was struck by the *S. S. Yarmouth* which did considerable damage to her stern. The steamer called for the Coast Guard who towed the tern into Machiasport where she was repaired. A year later she got stuck across the Machias River, blocking all traffic until the next tide floated her clear.

The *Lucy Evelyn* had kept busy through the years, and with the war and the great demand for tonnage, she had all that she could handle. For many years Captain John T. Irons had commanded her most successfully. When he retired in 1941, Captain Alvin Wasson, who had been mate of the *Rebecca R. Douglas,* took her over, and on several occasions showed that she was not quite the slow poke that she was reputed to be. Hiram Higgins, who sailed before her mast, wrote from Vineyard Haven on April 12th, 1942: "Left City Island, NY yesterday noon. Got here around 10 o'clock this morning. The *Lillian Kerr* and the *Rebecca Douglas* and the old *Lucy Evelyn* left City Island together. The *Douglas* beat us about thirty minutes, and we came in with the *Kerr* about a mile astern. The whole three of us are anchored here now." Another time he wrote that the *Evelyn* and the *Douglas* had been off Highland Light together, and added: "Believe it or not, we beat her home to Jonesport. Don't let anyone tell you the old *Lucy* won't sail. I know she will". And other time: "We are in Vinal Haven, Maine, now. We come down here in 69 hours from Sandy Hook. They say this thing won't sail; I bet she will beat the *Theoline* with fair wind any day of the week. This thing doesn't start to go until it is blowing some hard but she will go then, and lug sail to beat hell".

In August, 1942, the *Lucy Evelyn* was sold, changing hands for $22,000. Her new owners, the Lucy Evelyn Shipping Company of New York, planned to use her in trade with the West Indies. Writing in "The American Neptune" — October, 1942, issue — R.H.I. Goddard, Jr., said: "This transfer closes a long chapter in the history of the *Lucy Evelyn* and it seems unlikely that she can long survive the vicissitudes of nature and war which she will encounter in her new occupation". However, the tern was not done yet.

After a round trip to the Indies, returning north with a cargo of molasses, she was chartered to the U. S. Government. With Captain S. W. Barnes in command, she left New York in ballast, bound for Nova Scotia where she was to load lumber for Iceland. On October 26th, 1943, the schooner anchored by Handkerchief Shoal in Nantucket Sound to await a shift in the wind. After nightfall a gale swept down on the little vessel in her exposed position, and before too long her two anchor chains had parted, leaving her to drift to leeward towards shallow reefs. Her crew fought to get canvas on her, and somehow they got her under control, heading westward. As he had no anchors now, Captain Barnes decided to beach his craft on the sands at Vineyard Haven where she would be safe as the storm howled outside. However, owing to the wind and the tide in the darkness, the tern fouled the stone breakwater at the entrance to the harbor. Before long the rocks had pounded a hole in her bottom on the starboard side. That was the end of her voyage to Iceland.

Some months later Dr. Glenn of Oak Bluffs bought the schooner at a U. S. Marshal's sale for $3550; he sold her to a group headed by August Teixeira of New Bedford for use in the Cape Verde packet trade. The schooner was refitted. A deckhouse was built amidships for further passenger accomodations. She was put in first class condition. In March and April, 1946, she took aboard cargo which included lumber, cement, furniture, kerosene, bundles of clothing, three automobiles, and packages of food for the islanders who were said to be very short of supplies of all kinds. In early May the vessel was ready to sail with a crew of twelve and two passengers. There were two women aboard, one a passenger, and the other a stewardess.

After many delays, the tern was towed down New Bedford harbor on May 9th bound for the open sea. Captain John Costa who was in command was the only man who had ever been in sail; not one of his crew had ever had any experience although one man had done a trip or two in steam. Captain Costa could not set his topsails as there was no one aboard who could go aloft, and he could not go up as he had lost his right arm some years before on the *John Manta*. However, what the men lacked, Costa made up for it as he had spent much of his younger life under canvas. His last vessels had been the *Corona* and the *Capitana*.

The tow boat let the *Evelyn* free off Hen and Chickens Lightship. As her sails picked up the afternoon breeze, the mate set her log out astern; it was the same log that had been aboard the New Bedford whaling bark *Wanderer* when she was lost off Cuttyhunk in 1924. Thirty-five days later the schooner dropped anchor in the Cape Verde Islands. John Britto, the mate, wrote: "About my voyage our arrival at St. Vincent on June 13th, 1946. We are all safe and sound at present, Thank God. No illness or accident. We came through a severe storm last five days then fast sailing followed by a calm for two weeks, but here we are."

The schooner's return to the States was a hard one. Leaving the islands, she had stopped at Dakar, West Africa, before setting out for New Bedford on September 20th with 21 passengers, ten of them women and five children, and a crew of 28. She had 250 tons of salt in her hold. When she was in mid-Atlantic, a heavy gale smashed the steering gear, and from then on the crew had to steer with an improvised apparatus of wires manipulated by four men. She was only 280 miles off Block Island, not far from her destination, on November 5th when a second storm struck. The men could not hold their vessel to her couse, and before the gale blew itself out, the tern was 250 miles east of Currituck, North Carolina. There the Coast Guard picked her up and towed her into Norfolk on November 22nd, 63 days out from Dakar.

After the passengers had gone ashore, the tern was repaired. On February 15th, 1947, she set out from Norfolk for New Bedford. After a quick run up the coast, she was in sight of the Vineyard Sound Lightship on February 21st. Captain Costa, who had been on deck much of the time, turned in for a nap, but when he was called not long after, a blinding blizzard had blotted out all signs and buoys. A gathering gale carried away her jibs which had all been new in Norfolk. Then the mainsail ripped, first a few small rents before shredding before the icy blasts. The crew, used to the warmth of the Cape Verdes, were numbed by the cold, so much so they could hardly work the schooner. The mizzen boom cracked, forcing them to furl still more sail. As the driving blizzard reached its height, Captain Costa ran for deep water under forestaysail alone; he would at least not have a lee shore out there, and he knew the tern was a good sea boat.

Before the storm had cleared the *Evelyn* was out on the Georges

[243]

Banks where the fishing dragger *William J. O'Brien* sighted her, sending a call to the Coast Guard for aid. On February 27th the cutter *Legare* appeared on the scene as the tern was slowly working her way in towards land. The small cutter gave her a towline for the 200-mile hike to New Bedford. Heavy seas made slow going, and caused the line to part several times. On March 2nd the Coast Guard cutter *Algonquin,* a much larger vessel than the *Legare,* took over the towing duties, making much better time. However, as the two craft approached Gay Head, a second storm reaching full gale proportions struck.

In the early morning hours of March 3rd, when 4½ miles west of Cuttyhunk, the tow line parted again. The *Algonquin* was unable to sight the tern after that in the driving scud. The schooner drifted off on her own in the raging seas before the 60-mile an hour winds. About 8 o'clock in the morning Captain Costa found that he was getting into shoal waters. He ordered the anchor dropped, but the chain promptly parted. A second anchor was dropped. It held. The *Evelyn* was about a half mile from the beach near Mattapoisett. Later in the day a tug took her safely into New Bedford, 16 days from Norfolk.

Her next outward passage was a leisurely one with 10 passengers and a general cargo; she left New Bedford in late June, 1947. During the next few months she ran between the Cape Verde islands. It was not until March 3rd, 1948, that she departed from Fogo for New Bedford with seven passengers and 20 crew. A stop was planned at Dakar to drop two of her passengers, but winds held her off, so she gave up the attempt. During her stay in the island trade, the *Evelyn* had made three other attempts to get to Dakar, once with 84 passengers, but she failed each time.

The passage home was a hard one. A storm opened up a seam in her stem so water poured in. As there was no gas for the pump, the crew had to pump by hand the entire way across the Atlantic. They moved fifty tons of rock ballast aft to lift the bows, and that helped somewhat. In mid-Atlantic the tern stopped a steamer to see if she could get a little gasoline, but without success. Although the tern had sailed with food supplies for three months, they did not last. A week before port was made the flour was gone, and by the time she got in, so had most of the other supplies.

The *Lucy Evelyn* anchored in the lower harbor of New Bedford on April 12th, 40 days out.

Until now the schooner's troubles had been at sea; the next

ones came from shore. Her crew sued for wages, and as her owners were unable to pay, the schooner was put up for auction. On June 2nd the top offer was $500; the bid was rejected. A week later she was sold to N. T. Ewer of Beach Haven, New Jersey, for $1550.

On August 3rd, 1948, it was announced that the schooner would be turned into a store on the beach near Beach Haven; It appeared that her sailing days were over.

Below are a few of her passages made during her last days in the local trade:

1936—arrived Hampton Roads, September 26th; 12 days from Perth Amboy.
1938—arrived New York September 18th; 5 days from Norfolk.
1941—arrived Machiasport January 23rd; 23 days from New York.
　　arrived Machiasport April 19th; 4 days from Port Reading, N.J.
　　arrived Port Reading June 11th; 80 hours from Bass Harbor.
1942—arrived Machias January 26th; 8 days from Port Reading.

Effie M. Morrissey

Some yacht designers have criticized the Gloucester fishing schooner type as poorly built and unable to stand up to hard usage over a long period, but the *Effie M. Morrissey* is a direct contradiction to their statements. Built in 1896 by J. F. James & Son in their yards at Essex, she was a typical Grand Banker of the period with her clipper bow and fine lines. Not quite a 100 feet long, she was well put together with locust treenails and Swedish iron fastenings, white oak knees and stanchions, and pine decks. Her masts were 74 and 76 feet in height while her main boom was 68 feet long, jutting out a considerable distance beyond her stern.

Named after the daughter of Captain William E. Morrissey, she was an active fishing schooner for a quarter of a century. In 1925, after she had completed a season of fishing out of Newfoundland off the Labrador coast, she was purchased by the late Captain "Bob" Bartlett for $6000. During the following winter she was given a complete overhaul in New York, an engine was added, and her holds turned into living quarters. Prepared to face ice in far northern waters, she was sheaved along her waterline, and otherwise strengthened.

For the next twenty years the *Morrissey* annually voyaged from New York to arctic waters, never sailing less than 6000 miles in a year, and one cruise covered all of 20,000 miles. These many expeditions were backed by different groups, the American Museum of

Natural History, the American Geographical Society, the Museum of the American Indian, the Smithsonian Institution, the Heye Foundation, the Chicago Zoological Society, and others. With the exception of the 1928 run, when Captain Bartlett took his schooner into Siberian waters, all his voyages were north of Labrador, to the icy waters of Greenland and Baffin Island. In later years, "Captain Bob", as he was affectionately called, crewed the *Morrissey* with college students who paid $1000 each for a summer of adventure and thrills.

When the war came, the aging schooner worked in conjunction with the United States Navy. In 1940 on the northwest coast of Greenland, she reached her most northern point, 80 degrees 33', less than 600 miles from the North Pole. Odd weather conditions had cleared the ice from her path, making it possible for Captain Bartlett to reach this usually inaccessible area. During the summer of 1941, she worked for the Government along the Greenland coast, and the following year did survey work for the Hydrographic Department of the U.S. Navy around the Hudson Strait and Frobisher Bay. The next three years found her laying out, and then supplying, military and weather stations in the northern waters. The Captain brought his schooner back to the States for the last time in 1945; on April 28th, 1946, the famous explorer passed away in a New York City Hospital.

The *Effie Morrissey* had carried explorers, scientists, Eskimos, policemen, schoolboys, soldiers, Navy men, as well as dogs, walrus, polar bears, musk oxen, and even Aleut mummies. But now, following her owner's death, she lay almost neglected at a wharf in Gloucester harbor, gathering the city soot on her decks and rigging. However, in 1946 she was sold, as Captain Bartlett had wished, by the executor of the estate, the money passing to his sisters. Two brothers in New York bought her, painted her white, and planned to sail for the South Seas, but she never started.

In November, 1947, a fire of undetermined origin swept the Morrissey's interior, doing considerable damage before she sank in Flushing Boat Basin, New York. Later she was raised and sold to the Pequot Marine Corporation of New London who, in turn, sold her to Mrs. Louise Mendes of Egypt, Massachusetts.

In the spring of 1948 the *Morrissey* was at New Bedford where she was converted into a Cape Verde packet schooner. Her engine was removed, making her a true windship once more. Still in good condition, she was ready to start a third period in her already long life, indeed a credit to her Essex shipbuilders of half a century ago.

On August 18th, 1948, she sailed for the Cape Verdes with 50 tons of food and clothing for cargo, and one passenger. She is still in service, her most recent trip to Providence being in the fall of 1964. Before returning to the islands she was overhauled at Fairhaven. The name she carries today as a packet is *Ernestina*.

Madalan

The steel brigantine-yacht *Illyria* was built in 1928 at Lussin-piccolo, Italy, by Marco Martinolich to specifications drawn by Henry J. Gielow of New York. Of 357 gross tons and 133 feet long, she carried above her foreyard, double topsails and a single topgallant which gave her a very sea-going appearance when under sail. Her first owner, Cornelius Crane of Ipswich, Massachusetts, took her out of Boston in November 1928, on an expedition to the South Seas for the Field Museum of Natural History in Chicago in search of land and marine specimens. When she returned to Gloucester in October, 1929, she had covered some 36,000 miles, most of which was in the Pacific.

In later years the brigantine was known as *Malaina*, then owned by George M. Moffett of New York. When the war broke out, the windship went into the service, but her rig was considerably cut down, and she was not the handsome vessel of her yachting days. In 1946, when the Government was through with her, she was offered for sale. John B. Pontes, a naturalized American citizen from the Cape Verdes, bought her for $35,000 to place her in the packet trade to the islands.

Now called the *Madalan*, she was rerigged with her yards and square sails. As a yacht she had had four double cabins, three bath rooms with shower and tub, a library and sitting room, plus space for the captain and the crew. Her deckhouse held the galley and dining saloon. Much of these accommodations were left as they were, but changes were made below deck forward to make room for cargo space. Although she had an engine, the propeller was removed as union engineers were too expensive to hire to run the motor.

In June, 1947, the *Madalan* took aboard her passengers at Providence; she sailed on the 8th for St. Vincent. It was a slow, summer passage with light winds, and it was 74 days before she arrived at her destination. Her return to the States in October was a good deal faster, taking only 39 days from Dakar to Providence, with 20 passengers and five barrels of rope tobacco for snuff as her only cargo. After staying in port for Christmas and New Year, she put out to sea in January, 1948. This was a winter crossing. Five days from land she ran into the start of a week of gales that gave her a beating. Under bare poles, all sail furled, she did 130 miles a day. Apart from having three kerosene drums and a hogshead of beef washed overboard, she came through without damage.

She returned to the States on July 27th, 48 days from Dakar. For seventeen days she had been becalmed 600 miles east of Bermuda taking away any chance of a fast passage. This time she carried 42 passengers. In order to have fresh meat during the voyage, a stock pen was built under the forecastle for four hogs, four cows, and 37 sheep.

In 1951, when the brigantine was about to depart from Providence in November, the word went around the waterfront that this was to be her last voyage as a packet ship, and that she was to become a schoolship, working out of New York, with Count Felix von Luckner, the famous "Sea Devil" of World War I, as her captain. However, the plans fell through, and she carried on in the island trade.

During her 21-day run to Providence in 1953, two men on board, a passenger and a supercargo died; they were buried at sea. On the trip back to the islands in January, 1954, the mate, John Brites, was washed overboard by a wave. The following wave washed him back aboard, unhurt.

In 1957 the *Madalan* was laid up in the islands; she was for sale. Sometime later, when unattended, she developed a leak, sinking into deep water.

CHAPTER XII

Hulks And Barges

∿∿∿∿∿∿∿∿∿∿∿∿∿∿∿∿∿∿∿∿

IN THE Half-dozen years before the United States entered World War II there were a number of aging schooners which were ending their days as hulks or on the end of tow lines as barges in New England waters. Even today a few remain, but the majority of them have been broken up or burned, and they are hardly even a memory now. As they passed, so passed an era of great ships and wonderful seamen; their like will never be seen again.

The following are some of these hulks and barges:

Alice L. Pendleton

In 1918 a large four-mast auxiliary schooner named the *Hauppague* was launched at Wilmington, North Carolina, from the yards of the Naul Shipbuilding Company. She was 1394 gross tons and some 228 feet long. Under Captain John C. Sweeney, she made a maiden trip to Portland in the spring of the year. Late in May she was heading back south for Norfolk. On the 25th, when 25 miles off Barnegat Lightship, and in company with the schooner *Hattie Dunn* which was about four or five miles from her, she was stopped by a German submarine. Sinking the *Dunn,* the Huns turned to the *Hauppague.* After Captain Sweeney had put over his boats, he was forced by the Germans to place bombs in his own vessel after giving the enemy his food and supplies. As the large schooner started to sink, the American captain offered her to the Germans for $1500; they turned him down! Filling with water the *Hauppague* rolled over on her side, then turned turtle. Captain Sweeney and his men were held prisoner aboard the submarine for several days before being set ashore.

On June 15th, the *S.S. Ameland* sighted the schooner bottom up, her propeller visible, in Latitude 37 degrees 33″ North, Longitude 75 degrees, 25″ West, off the Delaware coast. Later in the month, the floating hulk was picked up, and towed into port. By the end of September she had been repaired, and was ready for sea again.

Renamed *Alice L. Pendleton,* the four-master entered the coasting trade as a pure sailing ship, her engines removed. For many years she was actively employed out of New York in the southern lumber trade. She was finally laid up there in the fall of 1928.

Some months after, plans were made to turn her into a cruise ship. In April, 1929, she was taken to Noank, Connecticut, to refit for her new adventures. However, she never put to sea again, and her remains were still to be seen in 1965.

For most of her active years she had been owned by the Pendleton Brothers of New York. For some reason, perhaps a mistake, she was listed in the "Merchant Vessels of the United States" as a former 'sch.ywl'.

Annie B. Mitchell

For many years a fine three-mast schooner was laid up at Rockland, Maine. She was the *Annie B. Mitchell,* built at Madison, Connecticut, back in 1889. A good sized vessel of 463 gross tons and 145 feet long, she was employed in the coasting trade between New England ports and New York, somehow managing to outlast the majority of her contemporaries.

Her long life was not one of continued good luck. In October, 1919, when bound with coal from South Amboy to Maine, she went hard ashore on Steele's Ledge in Penobscot Bay near Bangor. A wrecking lighter had to free her. Ten years later she was again aground. This time it was in June with a stone load from Long Cove to New York when she struck Mussel Ridge near Rockland. The Coast Guard cutter *Kickapoo* pulled her clear. Although still leaking after temporary repairs, she crept down the coast, taking things easily on her way to her destination.

During her last years under sail, the *Mitchell* was busy in the granite trade from Maine ports to New York City, frequently returning with coal. A typical year might be 1930. She arrived at New York on January 11th with stone from Long Cove. After discharging, she took aboard coal at South Amboy for Lubec. Clearing City Island on April 20th, she was at Rockland ten days later; the next hop took her to Lubec. Early in May she again loaded at Long Cove, and was back in New York on June 9th. She sailed on her return June 27th, but was back in New York less than a month later with another load of stone. August found her once more in Maine loading, and on October 2nd she sailed into New York from Vinalhaven. She went north with coal from Hoboken for Eastport, departing on October 18th. Some anxiety was felt for her safety when she was not sighted for two weeks, but she finally made Salem on November 7th. Captain Arthur Anderson reported all well although he said that the tern had been through frightful weather on her way up from New York. Then she pushed on for the north of Maine. After discharging, she was laid up for the winter at Rockland.

The *Mitchell's* last active year was in 1931. She made at least a half dozen runs to Portland from Somes Sound, each trip with 500 tons of granite. In the fall she took a load to New York, returning to Camden with coal. On November 30th she arrived in tow at Rockland; she never went to sea again after that, and her hull gradually fell apart at an old wharf in a corner of the harbor.

Some of her passages may be of interest:
1928—arrived New York April 22nd; 11 days from Portland.
     arrived Rockland October 8th; 11 days from New York.
     arrived New York November 2nd; 6 days from Vinalhaven.
1929—arrived New York July 15th; 14 days from Boston.
1930—arrived Rockland April 30th; 10 days from New York.
1931—arrived New York September 24th; 6 days from Portland.
     arrived Rockland November 5th; 13 days from New York.

Augusta W. Snow

One of the small fleet of schooners that were broken up at their wharf in East Boston in the late 1930's was the old four-mast schooner *Augusta W. Snow* which had been built by E. & I. K. Stetson at Brewer, Maine, in 1905. She was not a large vessel of her class, being only 830 tons and 183 feet long. Her entire life was spent in the coasting trade.

For her first ten years, the *Snow* was handled by her builders, but early in the first World War she was bought by the Smith Shipping Company of Bangor. In 1917 Crowell & Thurlow added her to their fleet in time to pick up some of the war profits. Not a bad sailer, she seems to have kept clear of trouble. In February, 1921, when a severe winter storm struck the coast, the *Snow* was lucky enough to keep just ahead of the gale during her run north from Jacksonville with 475,000 feet of lumber, slipping into Boston ten days out — a good passage.

Owing to her age, the *Snow* was one of the first schooners to be laid up when the depression hit, and in 1927 she was moored at

Boothbay Harbor to await better times. Two years later, when she was towed to New Bedford, it was rumored that she was to enter the Cape Verde trade, but nothing came of the move. In February, 1930, she was brought to Boston to lay up; she never sailed again.

By 1939 she was just a hulk, her masts gone, lying in the mud, swept by the tides. Her remains were removed not long after.

Bright

The *Bright* was a 2176 gross tons five-mast West Coast schooner which had been built by the National Shipbuilding Company at Seattle in 1918. Like so many of the Pacific coast windships, she was not handsome, but she was able to lift a big load. For her first year or two she was owned by the Minehaha Motorship Corporation of New York, and then by the Bright Navigation Corporation, also of New York. Her entire life was spent on the East Coast.

After the war profit's bubble had burst, the *Bright* found times most difficult. She required a large crew, and as this ran up her expenses, she was laid up early in 1924. Late in the fall she was libelled. At the ensuing auction, she brought only $3500 although six years before she had cost $200,000 to build. She returned to sea in 1925, one of her first trips being to Boston with coal from Norfolk. At the end of the year she had a hard time with storms. Sailing from Boston on December 7th for Norfolk, she was blown off-shore by winter gales. When it was feared that she had gone "missing", the Coast Guard cutter *Seneca* picked her up in a helpless condition at sea with her sails in tatters.

In 1926 the five-master lost her headgear in a crash with a steamer; that ended her sailing days. For a time she lay in Portland Harbor. In March, 1928, she was sold to a Portland junk firm. A year later she dragged ashore on The Brothers in Portland. She looked a forlorn sight with her bowsprit gone, and only topmasts on her jigger and spanker masts. Her remaining years were spent as a barge on the end of a tow line. In May, 1937, the *Bright* completed an extensive overhaul to her hull in Boston. At the time it was said that she had the longest timbers in her hull of any sailing ship afloat. When she towed out, she was bound for Charleston, South Carolina, to load 3000 tons of fertilizer for Baltimore. Later tows brought her back into New England waters with coal.

Her end came in September, 1940. She was hit by the *S.S. Hawaiian* in Chesapeake Bay, foundering shortly afterwards.

Brina P. Pendleton

Pendleton Brothers, Incorporated, of Bath launched the large four-mast schooner *Brina P. Pendleton* in 1918. Of 1522 gross tons and 220 feet long, she was part of the Pendleton fleet for a number of years, working chiefly out of New York in the coastwise trade. Although a good carrier, she was not a particularly fine sailer, and as such, she lasted less than ten years; in 1928 she was cut down to a towing barge with her bowsprit, spanker mast and topmasts removed.

A year later she arrived in Boston behind a tug; she had brought 26,000 railroad ties from Jacksonville. During the next decade she was in and out of various New England ports. Few who saw her ever realized that she had once carried a full set of sails as her lines were heavy and full, almost as if she had been built as a barge.

The *Pendleton* lasted until April, 1946. On the 15th she was anchored off City Island in Boston harbor with a load of coal when she caught fire. Her crew of two were saved while fireboats poured water on the blazing hulk all night. There was not much left of her by dawn.

Cora F. Cressy

The *Cora F. Cressy* was a mammoth five-mast schooner of 2499 gross tons and 273 feet long. Built by Percy & Small of Bath in 1902, she was designed for the coal trade, and could lift about 4,000 tons of cargo. One of the most outstanding vessels of her day, she was a good sailer when deep although hard to handle when light, being on the cranky side. However, she had a good turn of speed, and it is said that she once took four cargoes of coal from Norfolk inside of 48 days.

The *Cressy* had a very high bow, probably the highest bows of any schooner on the coast, and these no doubt aided her in riding out a howling gale off Pollock Rip in 1924 when two other schooners went down in the storm with all hands; from then on she was known as the "Queen of the Atlantic Seaboard". In spite of her heavy lines, she was a magnificent looking vessel under sail, a picture of strength.

After she had been laid up for a spell following World War I, the five-master was sold out for $3610 in 1925. Reconditioned in Portland, she was put in dry dock in Boston for scraping. Her owners considered a charter to carry lumber from Savannah to

Fort Lauderdale at a rate to net $18,000, but they decided to send her to Norfolk to load coal for Key West, and to return to New York with railroad ties. Later, on her way south from Boston to Norfolk, she was blown off her course in a gale, and finally limped into Mayport, Florida, for supplies.

In 1926 the *Cressy* was 'lost' at sea when her commanding officer was killed by a fall through one of the hatches. As no one else on board knew how to navigate, the Coast Guard had to bring her into port. When the shipping slump hit in the late 1920's, the large vessel was laid up as she needed eleven men to sail her, and that was too expensive. She was last under sail in August, 1928, when she lost much of her canvas in a blow, crawling into port as best she could.

In 1929 the *Cressy* was converted into a night club at Gloucester at a great expense. With her main deck housed over, she was very luxurious inside, and it was hard to realize that she had once been a coal carrier, or even a windjammer. Her masts still stood, and her bowsprit and jibboom remained in place, but that was all that she showed of her former glory.

In April, 1935, she was towed to Providence where she acted as a night club for the season, but a year later she went back to Boston. Business fell off as the vogue waned, and the *Creesy* just lay at her wharf. Finally, in 1938, she was sold to become a lobster storage hulk at Medomak in Maine. Her spars were hoisted out, and the housing removed. In March she was towed down east for the last time to end her days not so very far from where she was built. She was still there in 1965.

Courtney C. Houck

The 1627 ton, five-mast schooner *Courtney C. Houck* was built in Bath in 1913 by the G. G. Deering Company who operated a dozen large four-and five-mast schooners in the coasting trade. After running the *Houck* for many years, the Deering Company sold her to Crowell & Thurlow in 1926. She continued to sail for another four years, but on account of her size, being too large to handle economically in days when competition had become so severe, she was layed up at Boothbay Harbor about 1930.

A flush-decked vessel, she had been well built, and despite her age, she had remained in comparatively good shape through the later years. If conditions had improved she would have gone back to sea again, but as the call never came, she slowly rotted away. By 1937 she was in very poor form with the muddy tide waters pouring in and out of her hold. In October of that year she was bought at auction by Bernstein and Jacobson of Portland for $255. They stripped her down, and by 1940 her sticks were out of her, only the worn, bare hull remaining with thick weeds clinging below the high water line, but her name was still clearly visible, and her home port, Boston, still painted across her stern.

Edna M. McKnight

Amongst the large schooners laid up at Boothbay Harbor during the late 1930's was one particularly battered old hulk, mastless and broken; she was the *Edna M. McKnight,* once of the Crowell & Thurlow fleet of Boston. Built by R. L. Bean of Camden in 1918, she was a good sized four-mast schooner of 1326 gross tons and 209 feet long.

During the first few years of her life she was kept busy in the coasting trade, operating from the Maritime Provinces to the West Indies. As a rule her passages were on the slow side; for instance, 23 days from Turks Island to Boston with salt in October and November, 1925. However, on occasion she showed she could step along if given the right conditions, and on March 7th, 1926, the *McKnight* raced into Boston harbor only 19 days from New Orleans with molasses. This was considered good sailing for this type of vessel, and it is not likely that very many of the windships ever did much better between the two ports.

The big schooner's sailing days came to an end the following year. Deeply laden with 863,000 feet of lumber, she had cleared from Gulfport, Mississippi, in late November bound for Boston. She was off Cape Henry, Virginia, when she was struck by a gale of hurricane force. In a short time her canvas had gone to shreds. Huge seas smashed at her hull, opening up her seams. Slowly she settled until only her cargo kept her afloat. She appeared to be gradually breaking up under the pounding. Captain Alvin Loesche with his bride of less than a year and his nine-man crew were in a desperate plight when the British steamer *Radnor* came on the scene. With some fine seamanship by the "Limey", all hands were rescued, leaving the *McKnight* on her own. That was on December 7th; on the 28th she was sighted in Latitude 33 degrees 50' North, Longitude 63 degrees 30' West. A few days later an ocean going tug picked up the wreck, towing her into Bermuda where she remained until she was taken on to Boston. In September,

1927, she was towed to Boothbay Harbor for repairs, but she was too far gone. Her rotting hulk has been there ever since.

Freeman

The *Freeman* was a hefty four-mast schooner which came from the famous Cobb yards at Rockland in 1919. An average sized vessel of her type, she was 1070 gross tons and 192 feet long. Her active life was spent along the Atlantic seaboard freighting coal, lumber, and such cargoes.

The *Freeman* had her first serious accident in mid-January, 1922, when she crashed with the *S.S. Munalbro* in a thick fog off Gay Head. The four-poster had 1627 tons of coal aboard which she had lifted at Norfolk. With her headgear carried away, and some $3000 worth of damage done, she was towed into Boston for repairs. A month later she was bound outward, this time heading for Brunswick, Georgia, to load railroad ties for Portland.

The *Freeman* made the newspapers again in October. Loaded with coal, she was bound for Bangor when she met a rum-runner some miles off the entrance to New York. The captain, feeling the need for a drink, traded some of the schooner's provisions for a number of bottles of liquor. Reeling drunkenly before long, he came on deck and chased the helmsman away from the wheel. He next brought the vessel's head around so that she was heading straight for the Long Island shore. The crew realized that if they held their course the schooner would pile up shortly, so they "mutinied" by seizing their captain and putting him in irons. The mate took charge, and after anchoring the schooner, he went ashore to notify the owners who sent out a new captain to replace the drunken one.

In November, 1925, the *Freeman* arrived at Baltimore with a cargo of woodpulp from Port Medway, Nova Scotia. A few days before, she had been caught in a severe gale 60 miles from the Virginia Capes, and before the storm letup, she had lost much of her canvas. An accident of this sort could easily take all profits from the voyage, and more than one good schooner was laid up simply because her owners could not afford a new suit of sails.

The *Freeman*'s windjamming days ended in 1929; she was laid up at Boothbay Harbor, remaining there until the second World War. In 1940 she was sold, and not long after that she went under the Canadian flag. However, she did not return to the seas as a windship, but became a barge out of Halifax.

She was still afloat in 1947, but was sunk outside of Halifax some time later to get rid of her hulk.

Guilford Pendleton

At Noank, Connecticut, today there is a crushed hulk lying on her side on the beach by the high water mark. Although she has square ports cut in her hull, it is obvious that she was once one of the many windships that worked on the high seas. The only name visible is *Annex*.

She was originally launched in 1918 from the Baxter Shipyard at Jacksonville as the auxiliary four-mast schooner *George H. Barnes*. E. G. Potter of New York owned her for the first year or two of her life, but by 1921 she had become part of the Pendleton fleet, renamed *Guilford Pendleton,* and with her engines removed.

She had a comparatively short sailing life for less than seven years later she had retired to become a barracks, an annex of the New York State Merchant Marine Academy. Eventually she was towed to Noank to rot out her days.

Harry G. Deering

The G. G. Deering Company of Bath turned out some fine fore-and-afters during the first two decades of the present century. The last example of their work to have been active was the *Harry G. Deering*, a fairly large four-mast schooner of 1342 gross tons and 211 feet long, launched in 1918. The Deering Company operated her for a good many years, but in 1926 she joined the Crowell & Thurlow fleet.

Like her sisters, the *Deering* was employed in the coasting runs. For a considerable period she worked in the phosphate trade between Tampa and Norfolk and Baltimore. She also loaded lumber, coal, and granite on occasions; she was probably the last four-master to take granite away from the quarries at Rockport on Cape Ann. It was in November, 1925, when deep with Rockport stone, that she was nearly lost on a voyage to Galveston, Texas. By the time she was off the southern Floridian coast, she had developed such a bad leak that it was all the pumps could do to keep the water down. With that heavy cargo, she would not have stood a chance if she had filled. However, she got a tow into Key West where repairs were made.

The *Deering* was in trouble again in October, 1931. Hit by

a bad gale 25 miles east of Cape Cod, she lost part of her headgear and after sails as they were ripped by the winds. She was out of control when the Coast Guard cutter *Mojave,* sighting her signals of distress, towed her into port. After she got new canvas, a tug took her on to her destination at Calais with her Norfolk coal. Not long after this, she was laid up at Boothbay Harbor.

In 1938 she was towed down to the Cape Cod Canal to be used in an attempt to raise a sunken tug. She and the *Helen Barnet Gring* were to act as pontoons. However, the venture failed, and the four-master went back to her moorings. She spent most of 1939 at anchor in Portland harbor. With her masts removed, she was now a barge but it was not until 1941 that she found much work. However, she did not last long for while loading scrap metal in a Cuban port, the cargo fell through her aged bottom.

Herbert

A short distance above the road bridge across the Annisquam River at Gloucester an ancient hulk is lying in the marshes. She is not much to look at now with her masts gone and her timbers rotting, and there are few who pause to look at the last of the Rockport stone schooners.

Named the *Herbert,* she was launched at East Boston in 1883. Strongly put together to stand up to the heavy strains of the stone trade, she was 114 gross tons and 91 feet long. Although she had a typical coaster hull, she had, like all stone schooners of her day, her masts very far apart by stepping the mainmast well aft. This gave room for a derrick boom to swing.

For many years she was owned by the Rockport Granite Company, working out of the small Cape Ann port. She did not remain a sailer long, becoming a towing barge before 1910. With her mainmast removed, she henceforth moved at the end of a towline. In the early 1930's she became an art school in Gloucester. The class room was built on her main deck with its roof supported by her boom. Later she sank to the harbor bottom at East Gloucester, staying there for several years.

Shortly before World War II, she was sold for $25 (she had cost $10,000 to build), and her new owner had her pumped out before moving her to her present site where her bones formed part of a small boat yard in the marsh.

Hesper

The handsome four-mast schooner *Hesper* was to have been launched on July 4th, 1918, from the yards of the Crowninshild Shipbuilding Company at South Somerset, Massachusetts. The large crowd, which had gathered for the ceremony, were greatly amazed when the *Hesper*, after moving some forty feet down the ways, stopped. The ways had buckled under her weight. Following several attempts to move her, it was decided to jack her up so that new ways could be built under her. She finally took to the water on August 23rd after several more problems.

Designed by the yard foreman, E. J. Blinn, she was a fine vessel, more than 210 feet long and some 1348 gross tons. Built of oak and pine, she was strongly put together. Her first owners were Rogers & Webb of Boston.

In time to catch some of the war-boom trade, the *Hesper* made several offshore runs, at least twice crossing to Lisbon with coal before running down to Venezuela to load guano back to the States. In later times she was kept busy in the coastal coal and lumber trades. Like most other sailing ships, she had her mishaps and woes with the years.

In 1920 she left Norfolk on February 27th with 2000 tons of coal for Boston. She had made Vineyard Haven on March 4th, but it was on the last lap that she met bad weather which jumped from southeast storms to northwest gales, driving her far off course. She lost her spanker and other canvas before she crawled into Portland on March 9th. She had to wait there until new sails could be sent up to her from Boston before proceeding on her way.

In February, 1925, she had an odd accident when getting under way in Boston harbor for Jacksonville. Her forward steam capstan was heaving in her chain when it suddenly refused to break the anchor clear; the anchor had fouled something on the bottom. A lighter had to be called before the *Hesper*'s hook could be freed from a seven ton anchor which it had fouled in the depths of the harbor mud. A month later when the four-master returned to Boston with a cargo of lumber, she grounded, and it took nine tugs to pull her free. She was somewhat strained on this occasion which was not surprising considering the forces which were put against her.

By 1928 the *Hesper* was laid up at Rockport, Maine. In January of that year a terrific wind storm forced her clean through her wharf, scattering piling and planks in all directions, and wrecking the structure, but the schooner, pushed up on the beach, was little damaged. Later she was moved to Portland. In June, 1932, she was auctioned off to settle claims against the vessel. She was bought by Frank W. Winter for only $600.00; sail was now at a low ebb.

On September 1st, 1932, the *Hesper* arrived at Wiscasset, Maine, in tow. She has remained there until this day. As the years passed, so she aged. Her masts stood until about 1940 when they were cut down. Lack of business brought about her end. With the four-mast *Luther Little* alongside of her, she has been a popular subject for camera fans touring the coast of Maine.

Horace A. Stone

The *Horace A. Stone* was a fine four-mast schooner that came from the ways of E. & I. K. Stetson af Brewer, Maine, in 1903. She was 1376 tons and 208 feet long. During her first years she was operated by her builders, but in 1907 Crowell & Thurlow took her over. She was by no means a flyer, and had several over-long passages on her record. On July 25th, 1919, she sailed from Mobile with 860,000 feet of lumber for Buenos Aires. An average passage would have been from 60 to 75 days. August went by, then September and October. There was no sign of the schooner. Her owners were beginning to get worried when she eventually came in from the open sea on November 17th, 115 days out. Her run north was not much better, taking 90 days to Boston with 1500 tons of cattle bones for cargo. When south of the equator, she had met a series of storms which had smashed her rudder head, causing plenty of trouble.

She was bothered with rudder problems again in January, 1923. Loaded deep with 18,000 railroad ties for the Boston & Maine from Jacksonville, she had to have the Coast Guard tow her into Charleston, South Carolina, for repairs before she could carry on.

When the slump came to shipping, she was laid up at Boothbay Harbor. However, in December, 1925, her owners felt that they could put the *Stone* back into service, and she was towed to Boston for hauling and painting. Less than a year later she was found in distress off Cape Cod during a wintery gale. Both her anchors had been lost, her sails were in tatters, and she wallowed with water in her hold. The Coast Guard, always ready, saved her again. She carried her last cargo in 1928, and was then laid up.

In 1930, after changing hands, some $60,000 was spent converting her into a floating dance hall and restaurant. After serving as a women's club in Bangor, she was towed to Provincetown and later through the canal to Providence in August. A month later she was back in Boston, and in October she was sold for $2500.

The *Stone* was back in the newspapers in December when she very nearly capsized at Long Wharf on account of a faulty seacock flooding her hold. In February, 1931, new owners considered restoring her to a commercial carrier, but nothing came of it. In August she was towed down to New York with the hopes of selling her there, but there were no buyers; she was brought back to Boston to lay up with the other schooners that were dying at a wharf at the head of the harbor on the East Boston side.

She sank at her moorings in February, 1933, resting on the bottom in the mud, but fully visible at all tides. Her remains were not removed until late in 1939.

Jennie Flood Kreger

The *Jennie Flood Kreger* was a huge five-mast schooner which was built for Crowell & Thurlow by Mathews Brothers of Belfast, Maine. Not only was she the largest vessel of their fleet, but also the largest windship ever built in that port. She was 243 feet long, 42 feet beam, 19 feet depth, and 1838 gross tons. Launched early in March, 1919, she was christened with flowers instead of champagne; she was named in honor of the wife of Captain W. R. Kreger who became her commander. The entire town turned out to witness the ceremony.

During her first year or two, the *Kreger* was quite successful as there was still a demand for ships, and she was kept busy. She was not a fast sailer, but could lift a good load which was most important. In March, 1921, she was bound from Newport News to Portland with coal when the *S. S. Eugene V. R. Thayer* crashed with her in a thick fog off Cape Henlopen. The five-master lost all her headgear as well as much of her bow, leaving her in a crippled state. Later she was towed into Lewes, Delaware, where she got temporary repairs before towing on to Portland. When her coal was discharged, she was taken on to Boothbay for a refit. In August she was sold by auction at a U.S. Marshal's sale to satisfy claims brought against her by the steamship owners. However, she remained with the Crowell fleet.

The *Kreger* continued in service a few more years but by the late 1920's she was laid up in New York; there was no business for her. On October 17th, 1930, she arrived at Boston from Perth Amboy to lay up at Chelsea. She never put to sea again. For a few years she remained in good condition although she was damaged by a fire in December, 1932. A year later she was on fire again when her watchman's galley stove overheated, setting the cabin alight. As her hull rotted, her masts were removed. Her remains were still visible in 1939, but after a young boy drowned while swimming in her water-filled hold, she was broken up to supply firewood for the needy.

Luther Little

The *Luther Little* was a four-mast schooner which ended her sailing days when still in her prime owing to lack of cargoes and shortages of crews. She had been built in 1917 at Somerset, Massachusetts, by Read Brothers Company. More than 204 feet long, she was 1234 gross tons. The first World War was on when she entered trade, and her owners were able to pick up some of the lush profits that were going to any craft that could carry a cargo. For a time she was not only in the coasting trade, but traveled deep water as well.

In July, 1920, she was very nearly lost when she went aground at the mouth of Fort Liberte Harbor, Haiti. At the time she was deeply loaded with logwood for Chester, Pennsylvania. She remained hard and fast for two weeks, and at one time it was felt locally that she could not be salvaged, but she eventually was pulled clear. Her bottom was badly chewed up, but there was not much other damage.

The *Little* continued to sail until the middle 1920's when she was laid up. In June, 1932, she was auctioned to satisfy claims, but she did not go back to sea. Instead, she was laid up at Wiscasset. Although she was still in good condition, there was no call for her nor her type. She aged with the years, and today she is but a hulk as she lies alongside the *Hesper* not far from the main auto road where it spans the river.

Marie De Ronde

The *Marie De Ronde* was built as an auxiliary five-mast schooner by the Grays Harbor Motorship Corporation of Aberdeen, Washington, reputedly at a cost of $480,000. A large vessel, she grossed 2376 tons, and was more than 266 feet in length. Launched in 1918, she did not remain a power vessel long as her engines were soon removed. For a period she was owned by the Oriental Navigation Company of New York, but after they had had her laid up for some time, they sold her in 1922 to Boston parties who ran her between Boston and southern ports.

In October, 1922, bound from Norfolk to Searsport with 3500 tons of coal, she lost her headsails in a blow. Limping into Vineyard Haven in a leaking condition, she was later towed to her destination. In the fall of 1923 she made a lengthy trip to Tampa, taking all of two months. Before she made port, her owners had feared that she had foundered with all hands. Returning north in November, she was heavy with 30,000 railroad ties when she met a storm in the Gulf of Mexico. Badly leaking and in distress, the schooner was picked up by the Coast Guard off Tortuga. After repairs at Key West, she was towed the remaining 1500 miles to Boston to save time.

The five-master was auctioned for $6200 in October, 1924, after she had been laid up in Boston for a number of months. She swung to her anchor chain in Rockland harbor for several more years after that, and was finally cut down to a towing barge in 1933. For a short time she brought coal north to New England ports, but in December, 1935, loaded with 3300 tons of coal for Boston, she caught fire ten miles off Fire Island, New York. The blaze attracted much attention as it was visible for many miles. A Coast Guard cutter sank her with gunfire to prevent her from becoming a menace to navigation.

Mary H. Diebold

The *Mary H. Diebold* was a handy, fast five-mast schooner of 1516 gross tons and 223 feet long. Built by the Newcastle Shipbuilding Company in Maine in 1920, she became part of the Crowell & Thurlow fleet, spending her active days in the coastwise trade from the West Indies to the Maritime Provinces.

In July, 1927, after taking coal from Norfolk to Rockland, she was laid up at Boothbay Harbor to await a charter. She did not get back to sea until June, 1928, when she returned to Boston to be overhauled. She then loaded a heavy cargo of Cape Ann granite at Rockport for Miami. Some weeks later she was reported ashore on Great Isaacs in the Bahamas. For a short time there was doubt if the schooner would stand up to the strain of being grounded with such a dead weight load. However, after 50 tons of rock had been jettisoned over the side, she was floated free.

The *Diebold* was kept busy through 1931. In March of that year she was 11 days from Wilmington, North Carolina, to Boston with 27,500 ties for the New Haven Railroad. Captain W. H. Davis amazed the waterfront spectators by spurning the assistance of a tug until he was opposite the Fish Pier, having sailed all the way in under canvas through the narrow, tricky channel. Her next charter was coal from Newport News to Rockland.

The five-master was laid up at Eastport in 1932, and in 1936 was sold to be a store ship there. A couple of years later she was broken up.

Maude M. Morey

The *Maude M. Morey* was another of the large four-mast schooners which were launched in time to catch the profits of the first World War. Built by the G. G. Deering Company of Bath in 1917, she was 1364 gross tons and 207 feet long. Her builders managed her for the first years of her career, but in 1926 she became part of the Crowell & Thurlow fleet. However, not long after, she was laid up as the demand for sailing ships had ceased.

The *Morey,* although not much of a sailer compared with some of the other windships of her day, seems to have kept clear of trouble, never making the headlines. One slow voyage was noted, though. On October 20th, 1923, she sailed from Jacksonville bound for Boston with 22,000 railroad ties for the "B. & M". Three days before this, on the 17th, the four-mast schooner *Jessie G. Noyes* had sailed from Boston for Jacksonville. Arriving in the Floridian port, the *Noyes* took aboard 24,000 ties, and set sail for Boston on November 8th. On the 22nd she arrived in Boston, having done the round trip while the *Morey* sailed north. In fact, the *Morey* did not put in an appearance until December 9th; much of her time had been spent behind the Delaware Breakwater waiting fair winds.

The four-master's last active years were nearly exclusively in the coal trade, from southern ports to Maine. In April, 1928, she made a smart run from Norfolk to Eastport, taking only six days. A year later, when bound south to Norfolk from Rockland, she was in a collision with the *S. S. Westport,* getting badly shaken up, and having to undergo temporary repairs before loading. She was going to have the patched hole repaired at Boothbay Harbor in 1930, but instead she just continued to lie at her wharf there.

After sitting through the years in the mud, gradually deteriorating, the *Morey* was towed away to Portland with the *Zebedee E. Cliff* in the fall of 1941. There was talk of refitting her for sea, but while her owners were considering the move, the Government stepped in, purchased the two vessels, and turned them into a breakwater in the outer harbor. Shortly after the end of the war, it is said, they were set afire as a July 4th celebration.

And so passed the era of the sailing ship in New England waters; the days of the wooden ships and iron men are but a memory.

Appendix

Rig	Name when-where built	Gross-net	Length - Beam - Depth
2-m. W sch.	*Adventure* 1926-Essex, Mass.	130- 62	107.0 x 24.5 x 11.1
2-m. S bgn.	*Albatross* ex-Alk 1921-Amsterdam		92 x 21 x 11
4-m. W sch.	*Albert F. Paul* 1917-Milford, Del.	735- 661	174.5 x 37.0 x 14.4
3-m. W sch.	*Albert H. Willis* 1914-Phippsburg, Me.	567- 487	157.7 x 34.1 x 14.2
3-m. W sch.	*Alfred & Emily* ex-*Venture* 1937-Meteghan, N.S.	200- 85	111.0 x 27.3 x 13.5
3-m W sch.	*Alhambia* ex-*Bertha L. Waters* 1919-Bridgeswater, N.S.	147- 81	115.2 x 27.3 x 10.6
4-m. W. sch.	*Alice L. Pendleton* ex-*Hauppauge* 1918-Wilmington, N.C.	1394-1295	228.0 x 40.0 x 19.0
2-m. W. sch.	*Alice S. Wentworth* 1905-Wells, Me.	68- 65	73.2 x 23.7 x 6.1
3-m S bk.	*Aloha*.... 1910-Quincy, Mass.	659- 329	180.1 x 35.6 x 17.0
3-m W sch.	*Alta C.* 1927-Bear River, N.S.	62- 48	86.5 x 19.5 x 7.5
4-m W sch.	*Alvena* 1901-Eureka, Cal.	772- 687	186.4 x 37.9 x 14.3
2-m W sch.	m/v. *Amendra* ex-*Anna Sophia* 1923-Dennysville, Me.	200- 146	102.0 x 30.6 x 8.5
4-m. W sch.	*Anna R. Heidritter* ex-*Cohasset* 1903-Bath, Me.	694- 610	185.0 x 37.1 x 13.5
4-m. W sch.	*Annex* ex-*Guilford Pendleton* ex-*George H. Barnes* 1918-Jacksonville, Fla.	1611-1456	200.0 x 41.6 x 24.5

Rig	Name when-where built	Gross-net	Length - Beam - Depth
2-m. W sch. *Annie & Ruben* 1891-Bath, Me.		129- 122	87.1 x 26.4 x 6.8
3-m W sch. *Annie B. Mitchell* 1889-Madison, Conn.		463- 397	145.3 x 34.1 x 11.9
4-m. W sch. *Annie C. Ross* 1917-Bath, Me.		791- 686	175.5 x 38.2 x 14.0
2-m W sch. *Annie F. Kimball* 1886-Boothbay, Me.		41- 38	59.3 x 19.5 x 5.7
2-m. W sch. *Arbella* ex-*Lavolta* 1870-Ellsworth, Me.		204- 173	104.0 x 28.0 x 11.4
3-m. S. sch. *Atlantic* 1903-Shooters Is., N.Y.		303- 206	144.5 x 29.5 x 13.1
4-m. W sch. *Augusta W. Snow* 1905-Brewer, Me.		830- 671	183.3 x 36.5 x 17.1
2-m. W sch. *Australia* ex-*Alma* ex-*Ella Alida* 1862-Patchogue, N.Y.		35- 29	67.0 x 18.9 x 4.8
4-m. W sch. *Avon Queen* ex-*Jessie Louise Fauquier* 1918-Hantsport, N.S.		1035- 953	201.8 x 39.2 x 18.5
3-m. W sch. *A. W. Chisholm* 1920-Dayspring, N.S.		175- 146	116.4 x 26.3 x 11.4
3-m. W bkn. *Bear* 1873-Greenock, Scotland		1675-	198.6 x 29.9 x 18.8
3-m W shp. *Benjamin F. Packard* 1883-Bath Me.		2156-2014	244.2 x 43.3 x 26.7
3-m W sch. *Bessie Marie* 1929-Burlington, Nfld.		181- 152	108.6 x 26.4 x 10.5
3-m. S sch. *Betoine* ex-*Grete Kure* ex-*Betoine* ex-*Henford* ex-*Ballycorus* ex-*Horizon* 1918-Groningen, Holland.		223- 168	115.0 x 22.1 x 10.3
2-m. W sch. *Bloomer* 1855-Eden, Me.		51- 48	64.3 x 21.8 x 6.2
2-m. W sch. *Bluenose* 1921-Lunenburg ,N.S.		154- 79	112.0 x 27.0 x 15.8
2-m. W sch. *Bowdoin* 1921-East Boothbay, Me.		66- 15	75.7 x 20.2 x 9.4

[267]

Rig	Name when-where built	Gross-net	Length - Beam - Depth
5-m. W sch.	*Bright* 1918-Seattle, Wash.	2176-2011	258.3 x 48.6 x 24.2
4-m W sch.	*Brina P. Pendleton* 1918-Bath, Me.	1513-1404	220.1 x 41.5 x 21.9
3-m. S bkn.	*Capitana* ex-*Georgette* ex-*L'Oiseau* ex-*Radiant*	190- 277	142.0 x 28.1 x 15.1
2-m. S sch.	ex-*Xarifa* 1927-East Cowes, England		
	m/v. *Caroline*	252- 226	115.5 x 30.7 x 10.2
3-m. W sch.	ex-*Stewart T. Salter* 1919-Parrsboro, N.S.		
3-m. W sch.	*Charles & Vernon* 1919-Bridgewater, N.S.	347- 296	136.2 x 32.0 x 11.8
3-m. W sch.	*Charles H. Klinck* 1901-Noank, Conn.	522- 444	150.3 x 35.0 x 12.6
3-m. W shp.	*Charles W. Morgan* 1841-New Bedford, Mass.	314- 298	105.5 x 27.6 x 17.5
3-m. W sch.	*Citnalta* ex-*Esther Adelaide* 1917-Fox River, N.S.	470- 425	148.0 x 36.0 x 12.4
3m. W sch.	*City of New York*	502- 238	147.9 x 31.1 x 17.1
3-m. W bk.	ex-*City of New York*		
3-m. W bkn.	ex-*Samson* 1885-Arendal, Norway.		
2-m. W. sch.	*Clinton* 1886-Millbridge, Me.	31- 23	52.2 x 17.4 x 6.1
4-m. W. sch.	*Constellation* ex-*Sally Persis Noyes* 1918-Harrington, Me.	1034- 912	187.0 x 38.3 x 19.4
3-m. W fgt.	*Constellation* 1797-Baltimore, Md.	1278-	176.0 x 41.0 x 21.0
3-m. W fgt.	*Constitution* 1797-Boston, Mass.	1444-	175.0 x 44.5 x 23.5
5-m. W sch.	*Cora F. Cressey* 1902-Bath, Me.	2499-2089	273.0 x 45.4 x 27.9
3-m I bk.	*Coriolanus* ex-*Lina* ex-*Eugenia Emilia* ex-*Tiburon*	1053- 957	217.4 x 35.2 x 20.1
3-m. I shp.	ex-*Coriolanus* 1876-Dumbarton, Scotland		

Rig	Name when-where built	Gross-net	Length - Beam - Depth
2-m. S sch.	*Corona*	136- 129	104.3 x 24.0 x 16.4
1-m. S slp.	ex-*Colonia* 1893-Bristol, R.I.		
5-m. W sch.	*Courtney C. Houck* 1913-Bath, Me.	1627-1357	218.9 x 42.7 x 24.6
	brg. *Daniel M. Munroe*	1216- 888	220.7 x 35.0 x 21.0
3-m S bk.	ex-*Olivia* 1892-Dumbarton, Scotland		
3-m. S shp.	*Danmark* 1933-Nakskov, Denmark	777- 555	188.6 x 33.0 x 17.0
3-m. S sch.	*Dauntless* ex-*Undaunted* ex*Karina* 1911-Port Richmond, N.Y.	513- 412	168.2 x 33.5 x 18.5
3-m. W sch.	*Director II* ex-*Adventure* ex-*Sachem* ex-*D. D. Mackenzie* 1920-Chester Basin, N.S.	168- 119	119.9 x 25.0 x 11.0
2-m. W. sch.	*Dorothy G. Snow* 1911-Shelburne, N.S.	98- 91	98.0 x 23.0 x 9.8
3-m. S bk.	*Eagle* ex-*Horst Wessil* 1936-Hamburg, Germany.	1634-	194.0 x 39.0 x 16.5
5-m. W sch.	*Edna Hoyt* 1920-Thomaston, Me.	1512-1384	224.0 x 41.1 x 20.8
4-m W sch.	*Edna M. MacKnight* 1918-Camden, Me.	1326-1203	209.4 x 41.2 x 20.3
4-m. W sch.	*Edward L. Swan* ex-*M. Vivian Peirce* 1919-Thomaston, Me.	1511-1380	224.0 x 43.2 x 20.8
3-m. W. sch.	*Edward R. Smith* 1911-Phippsburgh, Me.	565- 492	158.2 x 34.5 x 14.1
2-m. W sch.	*Edward Trevoy* 1883-Boothbay, Me.	93- 88	81.4 x 22.8 x 7.8
3-m. W sch.	*Edwin G. Farrar* 1912-Phippsburgh, Me.	573- 498	158.8 x 34.6 x 14.3
2-m. W sch.	*Effie M. Morrissy* 1894-Essex, Mass.	119- 51	93.6 x 23.8 x 10.2
3-m. I bk.	*Emery Rice* ex-*Bay State*	1261- 450	244.0 x 32.0 x 15.0
3-m. I bk.	ex-*Nantucket* ex-*Rockport*		

Rig	Name when-where built	Gross-net	Length - Beam - Depth
3-m. I bkn.	ex-*Nantucket*		
3m. I bk.	ex-*Ranger No. 4* 1876-Wilmington, Del		
2-m W sch.	*Emma* 1871-Stockton, Me.	54- 46	63.5 x 23.7 x 5.4
2-m. W sch.	*Endeavor* 1938-Stonington, Me.	55- 43	70.8 x 21.3 x 5.8
2-m. W sch.	*Enterprise* 1909-Deer Isle, Me.	57- 42	70.5 x 21.8 x 6.8
3-m. W sch.	*Esthonia* ex-*Vincent A. White* 1918-Alma, N.B.	495- 452	163.4 x 35.5 x 12.8
2-m. W sch.	*Eva S. Cullison* 1888-Baltimore, Md.	48- 35	70.5 x 21.0 x 6.2
3-m. W sch.	*Eveline Wilkie* 1918-Margaretville, N.S.	405- 323	138.5 x 32.6 x 12.1
2-m. W sch.	*Fahe* ex-*Gaultois* 19-- Head Bay, D'Espoir, Nfld.	92-	
3-m. W sch.	*Fieldwood* 1920-Canning, N.S	483- 398	154.6 x 33.8 x 13.0
2-m. W bgn.	*Florence C. Robinson* ex-*Annapooranvamm* 1929-Jaffna, Ceylon.		89.0 x 19.0 x 8.0
4-m.S bk. m/v	*Foz Do Duro* ex-*Abraham Rydberg* ex-*Star of Greenland* ex-*Hawaiian Isles* 1892-Glasgow, Scotland	2345-1944	270.0 x 43.0 x 23.5
3-m. W sch.	*Francis Parsons* 1919-Cheverie, N.S.	270- 237	112.8 x 31.0 x 11.1
3-m. W sch.	*Frank Brainerd* 1908-Rockland, Me.	244- 244	123.4 x 30.9 x 8.7
3-m. W sch.	*Frederick P. Elkin* ex-*Seaman A. O.* 1919-Cape d'Or, N.S.	470- 435	152.0 x 35.5 x 12.7
4-m. W sch.	*Freeman* 1919-Rockland, Me.	1070- 959	192.4 x 39.0 x 19.4
3-m. W sch.	*General A. W. Greely* ex-*Donald II* 1919-Shelburne, N.S.	215- 200	109.6 x 27.0 x 11.2
2-m. W sch.	*George B. Cluett* ex-*Giant King* 1920-LaHave, N.S.	199- 72	127.4 x 27.6 x 11.0

APPENDIX

Rig	Name when-where built	Gross-net	Length - Beam - Depth
3-m. W sch.	*George E. Klinck* 1904-Mystic, Conn.	560- 460	152.6 x 36.4 x 12.6
2-m. W sch.	*George Gress* 1885-Athens, N.Y.	67- 64	79.5 x 25.5 x 6.0
2-m. W sch.	*Gertrude L. Thebaud* 1930-Essex, Mass.	137- 93	115.8 x 25.2 x 12.2
2-m. W sch.	*Grace & Alice* 1910-Calais, Me.	31- 19	52.6 x 17.5 x 5.9
3-m. S sch.	*Guinevere* 1921-Neponset, Mass.	508- 345	171.2 x 32.5 x 18.7
4-m. W sch.	*Harry G. Deering* 1918-Bath, Me.	1342-1163	211.4 x 41.0 x 21.1
3-m. W sch.	*Hazel L. Myra* 1920-Bridgewater, N.S.	223- 191	109.6 x 27.6 x 11.4
4-m. W sch.	*Helen Barnet Gring* 1919-Camden, Me.	1226-1127	202.8 x 40.4 x 20.8
3-m. W. sch.	*Helvetia* 1905-Rockland, Me.	499- 424	157.4 x 362. x 12.8
3-m. W sch.	*Henry H. Chamberlain* 1891-Phippsburg, Me.	246- 205	122.3 x 30.6 x 8.4
2-m. W sch.	*Herbert* 1883-East Boston, Mass.	114- 108	91.6 x 26.1 x 6.5
4-m. W sch.	*Herbert L. Rawding* 1919-Stockton Springs, Me.	1219-1109	201.7 x 38.5 x 21.9
4-m. W sch.	*Hesper* 1918-South Somerset, Mass.	1348-1231	210.2 x 49.9 x 20.4
4-m. W sch.	*Horace A. Stone* 1903-Brewer, Me.	1376-1237	208.5 x 38.6 x 20.7
3-m. S bkn.	*Jadran* 1932-	720-	190.3 x 29.0 x 13.8
2-m. W sch.	*James A. Webster* 1890-South Brooksville, Me.	74- 70	86.0 x 27.0 x 6.6
4-m. W sch.	*James E. Newsome* 1919-Boothbay Harbor	671- 574	178.4 x 35.6 x 14.7
3-m. W sch.	*Jean F. Anderson* 1919-Port Wade, N.S.	499- 396	140.0 x 33.3 x 12.7
5-m. W sch.	*Jennie Flood Kreger* 1919-Belfast, Me.	1838-1614	243.0 x 42.2 x 19.5
3-m. W Sch.	*John Bracewell* 1878-Bath, Me.	188- 140	107.8 x 29.8 x 8.0
3-m. W sch.	*Jose Gaspar* ex-*William Bisbee* 1902-Rockland, Me.	309- 206	133.1 x 31.2 x 9.3

Rig	Name when-where built	Gross-net	Length - Beam - Depth
3-m. I shp.	*Joseph Conrad* ex-*Georg Stage* 1882-Copenhagen, Denmark.	212- 187	100.8 x 25.1 x 13.5
3-m. W sch.	*J. T. Wing* ex-*Oliver H. Perry* ex-*J. T. Wing* ex-*J. O. Webster* ex-*Charles F. Gordon* 1919-*Weymouth, N.S.*	431- 373	140.3 x 33.5 x 14.0
4-m. W sch.	*J. W. Clise* 1904-Ballard, Wash.	845- 715	188.7 x 40.3 x 14.2
2-m. W sch.	*Katie D. Seavy* ex-*Joanna Durgain* 1902-Brooksville, Me.	66- 55	65.3 x 21.6 x 7.1
2-m W sch.	*L. A. Dunton* 1921-Essex, Mass.	133- 112	104.3 x 25.0 x 11.6
4-m. W sch.	*Laura Annie Barnes* 1921-Phippsburg, Me.	642- 518	181.2 x 36.0 x 15.3
3-m. W sch.	*Leona & Marion* 1920-Machias, Me.	313- 263	134.0 x 28.0 x 9.4
2-m. W sch.	*Liberty* 1896-Gloucester, Mass.	118- 96	93.6 x 24.0 x 12.6
2-m. W sch.	*Lillian* 1876-Boothbay, Me.	43- 43	56.0 x 18.0 x 6.6
4-m. W sch. 3-m. W sch.	*Lillian E. Kerr* ex*Lillian E. Kerr* 1920-Pocomoke City, Md.	548- 475	160.2 x 35.5 x 12.7
2-m. W sch.	*Lois M. Candage* 1912-Bluehill, Me.	44- 35	59.0 x 19.6 x 6.8
3-m. W sch.	*Lucy Evelyn* 1917-Harrington, Me.	374- 307	139.9 x 32.4 x 11.1
4-m. W sch.	*Luther Little* 1917-Somerset, Mass.	1234-1119	204.5 x 40.9 x19.6
2-m. W sch.	*Lydia M. Webster* 1882-Castine, Me.	47- 45	58.5 x 21.2 x 6.1
2-m. W sch.	*Mabel* 1881-Millbridge, Me.	40- 37	54.0 x 18.7 x 6.8
4-m. W sch.	*Mabel A. Frye* 1920-Harrington, Me.	1151-1036	193.8 x 37.4 x 20.4
2-m. S bgn.	*Madalan* ex-*Malaina* ex-*Illyria* 1928-Lussinpiccolo, Italy.	357- 243	133.2 x 30.0 x 14.6

APPENDIX

Rig	Name when-where built	Gross-net	Length - Beam - Depth
2-m. W sch. *Maggie* 1871-Dorchester County, Md.		72- 69	87.0 x 23.9 x 5.9
5-m. W sch. *Marie De Ronde* 1918-Aberdeen, Wash.		2376-2181	266.7 x 48.0 x 24.0
3-m. W sch. *Marine* 1919-Weymouth, N.S.		390- 340	147.0 x 34.8 x 13.0
3-m. W sch. *Mary B. Brooks* 1926-Digby County, N.S.		243- 214	99.0 x 30.1 x 10.1
5-m. W sch. *Mary H. Diebold* 1920-Newcastle, Me.		1516-1397	222.5 x 42.8 x 22.6
2-m. W sch. *Mary Day* 1962-South Bristol, Maine			83 x 23.5
2-m. W sch. *Mattie* ex-*Grace Baily* 1882-Patchogue, N.Y.		58- 50	72.0 x 23.5 x 5.8
4-m. W sch. *Maude M. Morey* 1917-Bath, Me.		1364-1245	207.7 x 40.1 x 22.1
3-m. W sch. *McLean Clan* ex-*U.S.S. Irene Forsyte* ex-*Irene & Myrtle* ex-*McLean Clan* 1920-Mahone Bay, N.S.		285- 140	125.2 x 27.6 x 11.4
2-m. W sch. *Mercantile* 1916-Deer Isle, Me.		41- 38	71.1 x 21.4 x 5.3
3-m. S . sch.*Migrant* 1929-Boston, Mass.		661- 319	200.3 x 34.2 x 18.5
3-m. W sch. *Minas King* 1918-Bass River, N.S.		550- 470	154.2 x 36.0 x 12.8
3-m. W sch. *Minas Prince* 1919-Spencer, Is., N.S.		511- 405	148.0 x 35.8 x 12.8
3-m. W sch. *Ofecia Gancedo* ex-*E. P. Theriault* 1919-Belliveau's Cove, N.S.		326- 254	136.0 x 31.6 x 9.7
3-m. W sch. *Peaceland* 1919-Annapolis Royal, N.S.		228- 203	112.6 x 29.2 x 10.5
3-m. W sch. *Rebecca R. Douglas* 1894-Bath, Me.		475- 299	138.8 x 33.9 x 9.5
2-m W sch. *Regina* 1891-Machias, Me.		116- 105	87.8 x 25.5 x 7.6
4-m. W sch. *Reine Marie Stewart* 4-m. W bkn. ex-*Reine Marie Stewart* 1919-Thomaston, Me.		1307-1186	218.0 x 41.4 x 19.4

Rig	Name when-where built	Gross-net	Length - Beam - Depth
2-m. W sch.	*Robertmax* ex-*Clara B. Creaser* 1920-Shelburne, N.S .	172- 114	127.1 x 26.6 x 10.4
3-m. W sch.	*Ronald C. Longmire* 1920-Meteghan, N.S.	183- 149	102.5 x 27.1 x 10.1
3-m. S bk.	*Sagres* ex-*Flores* ex-*Max*	1980-1829	263.6 x 40.0 x 24.6
3-m. S shp.	ex-*Rickmer Rickmers* 1896-Bremerhaven, Germany.		
3-m. W sch.	*St. Clair Theriault* 1919-Belliveau's Cove, N.S.	331- 274	135.5 x 31.6 x 11.0
4-m. S bk.	*Sea Cloud* ex-*Hussar* 1931-Kiel, Germany	2323-1187	254.0 x 49.1 x 19.0
3-m. S shp.	*Seven Seas* ex-*Abraham Rydberg* 1912-Stockholm, Sweden	327- 262	168.0 x 27.5 x 13.5
2-m. W sch.	*Shenandoah* 1964-South Bristol, Me.		108.0 x 23 x 10.5
4m. W sch.	*Snetind* 1919-Seattle, Wash.	1470-1305	234.5 x 45.1 x 18.3
2-m. W sch.	*Stephen Tabor* 1871-Glenwood, N.Y.	50- 41	63.2 x 22.1 x 5.1
3-m. S bkn.	m/v *U.S.S. Sylph* ex-*Intrepid* 1930-Boston, Mass.	596- 272	167.0 x 33.8 x 17.4
4-m. W sch.	*Theoline* 1917-Rockland, Me.	594- 509	172.0 x 34.8 x 13.0
3-m W sch.	*Thomas H. Lawrence* 1891-East Boston	374- 323	134.7 x 33.3 x 11.0
2-m. W sch.	*Thomas S. Gorton* 1905-Essex, Mass.	140- 92	106.6 x 25.4 x 11.5
3-m. W sch.	*T. K. Bentley* 1920-Advocate Harbor,, N.S.	509- 466	160.0 x 35.5 x 13.1
3-m. I shp.	*Tusitala* ex-*Sophie* ex-*Sierra Lucena* ex-*Inveruglas* 1883—Greenock, Scotland	1748-1624	261.0 x 39.0 x 23.4
3-m. S sch.	*Vema* ex-*Hussar* 1923-Copenhagen, Denmark.	533- 234	182.0 x 33.0 x 15.1

Rig	Name when-where built	Gross-net	Length - Beam - Depth
3-m. W sch.	*Victory Chimes* 1918-Cardigan, P.E.I.	297- 294	129.7 x 30.2 x 11.5
3-m. W sch.	*Victory Chimes* ex-*Edwin & Maud* 1900-Bethel, Delaware	208- 178	126.5 x 23.8 x 8.6
4m. W sch.	*Viktor* ex-*Josephine A. McQuesten* 1920-Rockland, Me.	1608-1462	230.0 x 41.9 x 22.8
3-m. W sch.	*Village Queen* 1923-Dayspring, N.S.	184- 123	90.0 x 28.5 x 11.0
3-m. W sch.	*Wanderthirst* ex-*Daniel Getson* 1917-Bridgewater, N.S.	361- 295	132.6 x 32.0 x 11.6
3-m. S sch.	*Wawaloam* 1918-Holland	500-	142.0 x 25.0 x 12.0
2-m. W sch.	*William C. Pendleton* 1857-Westerly, R.I.	33- 31	57.5 x 18.8 x 4.8
2-m. W sch.	*William H. Jewall* 1853-Nyack, N.Y.	46- 44	62.2 x 21.6 x 5.5
2-m. W sch.	*William Keene* 1866-Damariscotta, Me.	63- 60	68.2 x 20.2 x 7.5
5-m. W bkn.	brg. *Yag* 17 ex-*Marsala* ex-*City of Vicksburg* 1919-Pascagoula, Miss.	2423-2173	284.3 x 45.4 x 22.4
2-m. W sch.	*Yankee* ex-*Texel* ex-*Loosschoener* 4 1897-Holland	102- 81	92.0 x 21.0 x 12.0
2-m. S sch.	*Yankee (II)* ex-*Duhnan* 1912-Emden, Germany	114- 94	81.0 x 21.5 x 11.0
4-m. W sch.	*Zebedee E. Cliff* 1920-East Boothbay, Me.	1361-1254	206.0 x 40.7 x 22.6

Index

Abbott, Capt. Clifford, 175
Abbott, Capt. James, 168
Abraham Rydberg
  (a) 178-184, 270
  (b) 226, 227, 274
Abundance, 6
Acker, Capt. F., 97
Adams, 6. 7. 60
Adventure
  (a) 77, 269
  (b) 146-153, 266
Adventure II, 146
Albatross, 157, 158, 266
Albert F. Paul, 13-15, 266
Albert H. Willis, 2, 60-62, 117, 128, 129, 266
Albert Leo Schlageter, 213
Alfred & Emily, 62, 266
Alhambia, 62, 63, 266
Alice L. Pendleton, 248, 249, 266
Alice S. Wentworth, 147, 148, 154, 266
Alk, 157, 266
Alma, 137, 267
Aloha, 184, 185, 266
Alta C., 63, 64, 266
Alvena, 15-18, 266
Amendra, 136, 266
Amundsen, Capt. Roald, 71
Anderson, Capt. Arthur, 251
Annapooranvamm, 216, 270
Anna R. Heidritter, 18-20, 36, 266
Anna Sophia, 134-136, 266
Annex, 257, 266
Annie & Ruben, 136, 137, 267
Annie B. Mitchell, 250, 251, 267
Annie C. Ross, 21, 22, 267
Annie F. Kimball, 148, 149, 267
Antle, Capt. Thomas, 99-101
Arbella, 142, 267
Arthur D. Story, 172, 173
Athanas, Anthony, 148
Atlantic, 64-66, 76, 96, 267
Augusta W. Snow, 251, 267
Australia, 137, 267
Avon Queen, 22, 23, 267
A. W. Chisholm, 66, 67, 267

Baird, Capt. E. Marshall, 78
Bang-Melchior, Capt. Henrik, 67
Barnes, Capt. S. W., 242
Barr, Capt. Charles, 65
Bartlett, Capt. "Bob", 245, 246
Bay State, 215, 269
Bear, 185-193, 267
Ben Hur, 8
Benjamin F. Packard, 193-196, 267
Bertha L. Waters, 62, 266
Berry, Capt. Leonard, 128
Bessie Marie, 159, 267
Betoine, 67, 267
Blenhorn, Capt. Medley, 90
Blinn, E. J., 259
Blomidon, 70
Bloomer, 138, 267
Bluenose, 160-163, 167-170, 177, 267
Bohld, Capt. Oliver C., 223
Boggs, E. P., 126
Bowdoin, 138, 139, 267
Bowker, Capt. Francis E., 26, 33
Bram, Capt. Thomas, 16, 17
Bremen, 156
Bright, 252, 268
Brina P. Pendleton, 253, 268
Britto, John, 243
Brooks, Capt. William, 109
Burgers, George, 6
Burns, Capt. William, 121
Bushway, Jay, 93
Byrd, Admiral Richard E., 71, 72, 74, 189

Cape Forchu, 18
Capitana, 238, 239, 243, 268
Caroline, 125, 268
Catherine G. Scott, 11
Chaney, Capt. Almand B., 47, 64
Charles & Vernon, 68, 268
Charles D. Stanford, 48
Charles F. Gordon, 105, 272
Charles H. Klinck, 68-70, 93, 268
Charles W. Morgan, 198-202, 222, 268
Charlevoix, 112
Christensen, Theodore, 47

Citnalta, 70, 71, 268
City of New York, 6, 7, 71-74, 268
City of Vicksburg, 222, 275
Clara B. Creaser, 170, 274
Cleopatra's Barge, 167
Clinton, 149, 268
Cohasset, 18, 266
Colemen, Capt. Bennett D., 18-20
Colford, Capt. Lawrence, 175
Colonia, 238, 269
Columbia, 161, 168, 170
Constellation
  (a) 51, 268
  (b) 203-205, 268
Constitution, 205-209, 268
Coombs, Capt. J. L., 58
Cora F. Cressey, 253, 268
Coriolanus, 232-237, 268
Corkum, Capt. George H., 66, 82,
  83
Corona, 238, 243, 269
Costa, Capt. John, 242, 243
Courtney C. Houck, 254, 269
Cox & Green, 8
Crane, Cornelius, 247
Croft, Capt. E. L., 88
Crynor, Capt., 55

Daniel Getson, 74, 75, 275
Daniel M. Munroe, 209, 269
Danmark, 209-213, 226, 269
Dauntless, 76, 269
Davis, Capt. W. H., 264
D. D. Mackenzie, 76, 269
Decker, Capt. Milton C., 36
Delawanna, 160
Director II, 76, 77, 269
Donald II, 91, 92, 270
Doris F. Hamlin, 8, 27
Dorothy G. Snow, 237, 238, 269
Douglas, Capt. Robert S., 155
Duhnan, 157, 275
Duke, Capt. John E., 136
Dunham Wheeler, 8
Dunphy, Capt. S., 68

Eagle, 213, 214, 269
Earle, Capt. Arthur, 175
E. C. Adams, 85, 86
Edna Hoyt, 8, 10-13, 269
Edna M. MacKnight, 255, 269
Edward B. Winslow, 40
Edward L. Swan, 8, 48, 269
Edward R. Smith, 78, 79, 269

Edward Trevoy, 163-165, 269
Edwin & Maud, 156, 275
Edwin G. Farrar, 79-81, 269
Effie M. Morrissy, 245-247, 269
Elena, 65, 96
Elfreda E. Publicover, 5
Elizabeth Howard, 177
Ella Alida, 137, 267
Elliot, Capt. Frank, 145, 156
Elsie, 160, 161, 167, 172, 173, 176
Emery Rice, 214, 269
Emily F. Whitney, 196
Emma, 139, 270
Endeavor, 139, 140, 149, 270
Enterprise, 140, 149, 150, 270
E. P. Theriault, 81, 82, 84, 273
Ernestina, 247
Erskine M. Phelps, 197
Esperanto, 160, 161, 168, 171
Esther Adelaide, 70, 268
Esthonia, 82-84, 270
Eugenia Emilia, 235, 268
Eva S. Cullison, 150, 270
Eveline Wilkie, 84-86, 270
Ewer, N. T., 245

Fahe, 166, 270
Farrell, James B., 229, 230
Fieldwood, 87-89, 270
Florence C. Robinson, 216, 217, 270
Flores, 224, 274
Ford, Frank F., 106
Foss, Capt. Harold G., 8, 10, 35
Foz Do Duro, 184, 270
Francis, Capt. George, 165
Francis Parsons, 89-101, 270
Frank Brainerd, 236, 237, 270
Frederick P. Elkin, 90, 91, 111, 270
Freeman, 256, 270

Gancedo, B. P., 83
Gann, Ernest, 157
Gardner, William, 64
Gaultois, 165, 166, 270
Gavin, Martin, 114
Geldert, Capt. St. Clair, 104
General A. W. Greely, 91-93, 270
George B. Cluett, 140, 141, 270
George E. Klinck, 69, 70, 93-95, 271
George Gress, 141, 148, 271
George H. Barnes, 257, 266
George W. Elzey, 5
George W. Wells, 10
Georg Stage, 210, 218-219, 272

Gertrude L. Thebaud, 161-163, 166-170, 271
Getson, Capt. Byron D., 68
Giant King, 140, 270
Gilchrist, Capt. John, 52
Gleason, Capt. Charles, 37
Glennie, Capt. Donald R., 69
Glory of the Seas, 180
Gorch Fock, 213
Governor Ames, 10
Grace & Alice, 150, 271
Grace Baily, 154, 273
Grandee, 196
Gray, Capt., 53
Gray, Manton, 136
Great Republic, 180
Greenlaw, Capt. Elmer M., 139
Greenwood, Capt. L. A., 97
Griffin, Capt. Charles V., 237
Gubelmann, Walter, 227
Guild, Capt. Frederick B., 145, 148, 150, 155, 156
Guildford Pendleton, 257, 266
Guinevere, 65, 96, 271

Hall, Capt. Parker J., 141, 148
Hansen, Arthur, 217
Hansen, Capt. Knud L., 210, 211
Harold G. Foss, 8, 10, 11
Harry G. Deering, 25, 257, 271
Hartford, Huntington, 221
Hattie Dunn, 249
Haughn, Capt., 91
Hauppauge, 249, 266
Hawaiian Isles, 178, 179, 270
Hawkins, Capt. Havilah S., 145, 148, 153, 154
Hayden, Sterling, 217
Hazel L. Myra, 96, 97, 271
Healey, Capt. M. A., 186
Helen Barnet Gring, 8, 23-33, 258, 271
Helvetia, 97, 98, 271
Henry Ford, 161, 177
Henry H. Chamberlain, 98, 99, 119, 271
Henry R. Tilton, 4
Herbert, 258, 271
Herbert Fuller, 16
Herbert L. Rawding, 8, 19, 34-38, 271
Hesper, 259, 260, 262, 271
Higgins, Hiram, 241
Hogan, Capt. Felix, 177

Hopkins, Capt. George, 12, 13
Horace A. Stone, 260, 261, 271
Horst Wessil, 213, 269
Hurd, Capt. Donald P., 145, 146, 153
Hussar
   (a) 129, 274
   (b) 225, 274
Hynes, Capt. Leo, 146

Illyria, 247, 272
Intrepid, 217, 218, 274
Inveruglas, 228, 274
Irene & Myrtle, 99-103, 273
Irene Forsyte, 100, 101, 273
Irons, Capt. John T., 241

Jacob M. Haskell, 2
Jadran, 218, 271
James A. Webster, 150, 151, 271
James E. Newsom, 38-40, 85, 271
James L. Maloy, 142
James Slater, 4
James, Arthur Curtis, 185
Jaspar, Capt. J. H., 240
Jean F. Anderson, 5, 85, 103, 104, 271
Jennie Flood Kreger, 261, 262, 271
Jessie G. Noyes, 264
Jessie Louise Fauquier, 22, 267
Joan Kielberg, 5, 41
Joanna Durgain, 142, 272
Joe Lane, 155
John Bracewell, 104, 105, 271
John R. Manta, 232, 242
Johnson, Capt. Irving, 156, 157
Jose Gaspar, 133, 271
Joseph Conrad, 210, 218-222, 227, 272
Jones, Capt. Robert O., 13, 14
Josephine A. McQuesten, 8, 40, 275
Josiah Chase, 10
J. O. Webster, 7, 272
J. T. Wing, 105-107, 272
J. W. Clise, 40, 41, 272

Kaiulani, 197, 198
Karina, 76, 269
Katie D. Seavy, 142, 272
Kenedy, Capt. Louis, 6, 7, 74, 130-132
Kerr, Capt. Robert, 80
Knowlton, James T., 89
Kreger, Capt W. R., 261

L. A. Dunton, 176, 177, 272
Ladysmith, 4
Lambert, Gerald B., 65
Larkin, Capt. J. Henry, 177
Latty, Capt., 54
Laura Annie Barnes, 5, 41-43, 131, 272
Lavolta, 142, 143, 267
Leo, 4
Leona & Marion, 107, 108, 272
Liberty, 151, 272
Lillian, 152, 272
Lillian E. Kerr, 5, 43-46, 241, 272
Lina, 235, 268
Lincoln, 7
Lindsay, E. C., 239
Lipton, Sir Thomas, 161
Lizzie A. Tolles, 147
Loesche, Capt. Alvin, 255
Lois M. Candage, 152, 272
Long, Capt. Edward, 1, 7, 55, 105
Looschoener, 4, 156, 275
Lucy Evelyn, 9, 100, 239-245, 272
Luther Little, 260, 262, 272
Lydia M. Webster, 152, 153, 272

Mabel, 153, 272
Mabel A. Frye, 46, 47, 58, 272
MacLean, Capt. R. S., 48, 49
MacMillan, Adm, Donald B., 138
Madalan, 247, 248, 272
Maggie, 153, 273
Maid of France, 6
Maid of La Have, 5
Malaina, 247, 272
Malmberg, Capt. Oscar, 183
Margery Austin, 117
Maria Sony, 238
Marie De Ronde, 262, 273
Marine, 108, 109, 117, 273
Marsala, 222, 223, 275
Martin, Capt. D. J., 194
Martino, Capt., 15
Mary B. Brooks, 109, 110, 117, 273
Mary Day, 153, 154, 273
Mary H. Diebold, 49, 263, 273
Matheson, Capt. John T., 167
Mattie, 154, 273
Mattison, Capt. John, 106
Maude M. Morey, 59, 264, 273
Max, 224, 274
Mayflower, 170, 176, 177
McCuish, Capt. Donald, 173, 216
McFarland, Capt. Lewis, 94

McLean Clan, 99, 102, 273
McLean, Capt. Robert Alexander, 23
McManus, Thomas F., 176
McQuesten, F. B., 54
Melville, Capt. Frederick, 72, 73
Mercantile, 154, 273
Merriam, Capt. Burton E., 8, 130
Merriam, Capt. Calvin, 9
Merriam, Capt. George, 8, 111
Merriam, Capt. Joseph, 8
Migrant, 110, 273
Mihkel, 10
Mina Nadeau, 9, 117
Minas King, 91, 110-112, 273
Minas P rince, 9, 11, 112, 273
Mitchell, Capt. John, 240
Moffett, George M., 247
Monica R. Walters, 62
Moore, Capt. Arthur, 75, 121
Moran, Edmund Francis, 177
M. Vivian Peirce, 26, 47, 48, 269

Nancy, 78
Nantucket, 214, 215, 269
Nash, Capt. Charles I., 16
Nealley, B. F., 104
Nisbet, Capt. Jim, 154
Nova Queen, 8, 82

Oakley C. Curtis, 35
Ofecia Gancedo, 83, 273
Ogilvie, Capt. N. Hilton, 8, 116, 117
Ogilvie, Capt. Ralph M., 8, 61, 117
Ogilvie, Capt W., 8
Oliver H. Perry, 106, 107, 272
Olivia, 209, 269
Orozimbo, 99
Oxner, Capt. Harris, 87

Paine, Frank C., 161, 166
Palitana, 159
Palmer, Edger, 96
Parmenter, Lt. Richard, 100
Parshall, Capt. Dick, 145, 149
Parsons, Capt. Wallace, 172
Pasadena, 159
Peabody, Capt. John, 135, 150
Peaceland, 61, 100, 116-118, 121, 273
Pedersen, Capt. H. A., 88, 89
Peirce, Edward, 47
Peirce, Capt. Ernest J., 47
Pell, Theodore Roosevelt, 195
Perry, Capt. Antonio, 127

Peter Mehrhof, 141
Pettegrow, Edwin F., 97
Pettipas, Capt. Joseph N., 124, 125
Piggott, Grant H., 105
Pine, Capt. Ben, 168, 169
Plummer, Capt. William F., 8, 24, 25, 26
Pontes, John B., 247
Pope, Capt. George W., 43
Progress, 172, 173
Publicover, Capt. Archibald, 6
Publicover, Bruce, 5
Publicover, Charles, 5
Publicover, Elfreda, 5
Publicover, Capt. James L., 4, 5, 43, 44
Publicover, Virginia, 6
Publicover, Capt. William F., 5, 6, 24, 25, 41, 42, 103
Publicover, Capt. Wilson, 58

Rangdale, Capt. Frank C., 121
Ranger, No. 4, 214, 269
Rawding, Capt. Robert L., 58
Rebecca R. Douglas, 9, 118-121, 241, 273
Reeves, Capt. John W., Jr.   95
Regina, 143, 273
Reine Marie Stewart, 48-50, 237, 273
Richard B. Silver, 6
Richard, John P., 6, 46
Rickmer Rickmers, 224, 274
Rickson, Capt. Robert W., 8, 11, 35
Robert E. Dean, 21
Robertmax, 170, 274
Robinson, William, 216
Rockport, 214, 269
Rodway, Capt. Alexander, 46
Ronald C. Longmire, 121, 274
Ronberry, Capt. K. E., 80
Rosario, Capt. John, 22
Ross, Capt. Alex, 21
Roué, William J., 62
Rowe, L. A., 104
Royall, Robert L., 51

Sachem, 77, 269
Sagres, 224, 225, 274
St. Clair Theriault, 122, 274
St. Paul, 196
Sallie C. Marvil, 10
Sally Persis Noyes 50-52, 268
Salter, Capt. Charles, 123
Samson, 71, 268

Santa Clara
  (a) 102, 273
  (b) 197
Santo-Andre, 225
Sarah Eaton, 99
Sargent, Lennox, 93
Sea Cloud, 225, 226, 274
Sea Fox, 7
Seaman A. O., 90, 270
Seaman, A. O., 90
Sesame, 5
Seven Seas, 181, 221, 226, 227, 274
Sharp, Capt Jim, 155
Shaw, Capt. A. M., Jr., 62
Shaw, Frank M., 193
Sheldon, Capt. Christopher, 157, 158
Shenandoah, 155, 274
Shepard, Capt. Albert M., 140, 149
Sierra Lucena, 228, 274
Skinner, Capt., 108
Small, Capt. Fred B., 150
Small, Capt. John S., 122
Smith, Capt. Wallace H., 9, 112-114
Snetind, 52, 53, 274
Snyder, Capt. Donald B., 145
Somerville, J. W., 43, 46
Sophie, 228, 274
Souza, John L., 238
Spendrift, 240
Star of Finland, 197
Star of Greenland, 180, 270
Stephen Tabor, 154, 155, 274
Stevens, Capt., 236
Stewart T. Salter, 123-125, 268
Sutton, H. L., 75
Sweeney, Capt. John C., 249
Swift, Capt. Frank, 145, 148-150, 152-154, 156
Sylph, 218, 274

Tanton, Ray M., 164
Tarkington, Booth, 143
Taylor, Capt. Allan B., 124
Taylor, Capt. John J., 90, 128
Texel, 156, 275
Teixeira, August, 242
Thebaud, Louis A., 166
Theoline, 1, 2, 7, 53-57, 241, 274
Thomas H. Lawrence, 126, 127, 274
Thomas N. Barnsdale, 8
Thomas S. Gorton, 170-176, 274
Thomas, Capt. Jeff, 146
Thomas, Capt. William H., 171